NOVELS AND OTHER FICTION

The Water Wheel (1933)
The Old Man's Place (1935)
Seventy Times Seven (1939)
The People from Heaven (1943)
A Man Without Shoes (1951, 1982)
The Land That Touches Mine (1953)
Every Island Fled Away (1964)
The $300 Man (1967)
Adirondack Stories (1976)

INTERPRETATIONS OF AMERICAN HISTORY

A More Goodly Country (1975)
View From This Wilderness (1977)
To Feed Their Hopes (1980)
The Winters of That Country (1984)

LETTERS

William Carlos Williams/John Sanford:
  A Correspondence (1984)

AUTOBIOGRAPHY

The Color of the Air, Scenes from the Life of
  an American Jew, Volume 1 (1985)
The Waters of Darkness, Scenes from the Life of
  an American Jew, Volume 2 (Summer 1986)

JOHN SANFORD

THE COLOR OF THE AIR

SCENES FROM THE LIFE OF AN AMERICAN JEW

VOLUME 1

BLACK SPARROW PRESS ■ SANTA BARBARA ■ 1985

For permission to reprint herein certain material from *To Feed
Their Hopes,* the author is grateful to the University of Illinois
Press.

LIBRARY OF CONGRESS CATALOGING-IN-PUBLICATION DATA

Sanford, John B., 1904-
  The color of the air.

  1. Sanford, John B., 1904-   —Bibliography.
2. Novelists, American—20th century—Biography.
I. Title.
PS3537.A694Z464 1985   813'.52 (B)   85-13514
ISBN 0-87685-644-X (v. 1)
ISBN 0-87685-643-1 (pbk. : v. 1.)
ISBN 0-87685-645-8 (lim. ed. : v. 1)

In honor of my father and mother
Philip D. Shapiro
1878-1972
Harriet Nevins Shapiro
1881-1914
and with love

A very good land to fall with
and a pleasant land to see
— R. Juet: *Discovery of the Hudson River*

A NOTE ON THE TITLE

In his *History of the Plymouth Plantation,* William Bradford wrote of the early hardships of the *Mayflower*'s company:

The season it was winter, and they that know the winters of that country know them to be sharp and violent, and subject to cruell and feirce stormes. Neither could they go up to the top of Pisgah, as it were, to view from this willdernes a more goodly country to feed their hopes.

From that passage, titles were derived for a quartet of commentaries on American history: *A More Goodly Country* 1975, *View from This Wilderness* 1977, *To Feed Their Hopes* 1980, and *The Winters of That Country* 1984.

Interspersed with the scenes that follow are fifteen pieces from the quartet. Each deals with a phase or force in the history of the country. For the subject of this autobiography, they furnish "the color of the air," a fast color, for history does not fade.

J. S.

Contents

The Color of the Air:
Scenes from the Life of an American Jew
Volume 1

THE COLOR OF THE AIR, I

FRANCISCO DE CORONADO – 1540
DRAW ME NOT WITHOUT REASON

In the year of the incarnation of the Lord 1540, Francisco de Coronado, with 300 horse, marched northward from Culiacan to seek the Seven Cities of Cibola that had been vouched for by Fray Marcos de Niza. There, the friar had affirmed, the houses were of hewn stone jointed with lime, the least of them two stages in height and some, as God was his witness, three, four, and even five, and the doorsills and lintels were a daze of turquoises, gems so like the tint of Heaven as to seem chips of fallen sky, and as in Heaven, the way was paved with blocks of gold. But Coronado did not find these cities, nor, in some ruin, some pale blue pile of residue, did he find where they had been. Two years he wandered, but he did not find them.

Long later, in the year of the incarnation 1886, at a place known to the Sioux as Kaw, or Kansa, which meant *people of the south wind,* there would be taken from the ground, where it lay deep in the buffalo-grass, a Spanish sword. It would lack a hilt, and it would be so rusted over as to suggest of rusting through; still when polished with brick-dust, a fine-made blade would slowly appear. Transversely graved near the tongue would be the name *Gallego,* in token of Juan Gallego, Coronado's captain, and lengthwise of the fuller would be this inscription: *No me saques sin razon. No me embaines sin honor.*

It would speak. *Draw me not without reason,* it would say, and it would give the Sioux as a reason, and it would say, *Sheathe me not without honor,* but honor must have been lost, for no scabbard would be found. It would be found in no nearby stream, no other stand of grass, no flat of sand—gone when honor went, it would never be found.

SCENE 1

FATHER (1878-1972)

In 1883, at the age of five, he came from Russia to the American States. If he remembered his days and nights in steerage, he never spoke of the ways in which they were spent; he never made mention of the sights he'd seen, the sky's colors, the spray-savor, the games and cries of other children, and you never knew the name and size of the ship. Where had her voyage begun, you've wondered, at what port on the Baltic—Stettin, was it, or Konigsberg, or Memel on the Courland Gulf? Had birds pursued her through the Skaggerak, had winds favored her in the Pas de Calais, had rains fallen off Finistère? What smoke and sail had she raised, and had she spoken them in passing or merely curtsied with the swells?

With whom had he come from Kovno *guberniya,* who had fed him, put him to sleep, sent him to play, warned him away from the rail and rigging? And when he spied the towers of Navesink Light, had he been alone or in company, had he known where he was—*die neue Welt!*—and did he find it, as said, *a very good land to fall with, and a pleasant land to see?* Or were the grapes gone from the Richmond hills, the wild red currants, the yews and oaks and the sweet-wood laurel? Did laundry fly where leaves had flown, did the waters churn no more with bream and barbel, were the winds not now perfumed?

You never learned who met him at Castle Garden, who led him through the streets of Mannahatta among the stages, the drays, the coming and going crowds, who read him the signs and named the structures, who stunned him with sudden views and sudden sound—a bridge that seemed about to spring, a train that ran above the ground. You never knew who carried his string-tied parcels and may have carried him, who bought him lemon Spritz when they came to Chatham Square.

The gutters were lined with carts—two-wheeled trays of fruit, dry goods, tinware, shoes—and beside them stood beseeching Jews whose din of dunning filled the air. Try this bread, they cried to passersby, buy these brooms, these papers of pins and picayunes, buy, please God, these nails and notions, this snuff and wine. In the quivering heat, silver, glass, and children flashed, scrags staggered by on spavined feet, and over all, above the color, the motion, the shivaree, faces in open windows cursed Columbus—*a cholera on Columbus!*—

or conversed across the tumult in the streets, the Cheap Jacks' pleas, the harness bells, the ceaseless fundamental tone of speech. Washing swung from fire escapes, awnings rippled, rippling their stencilled legends, and from cores and crusts and other droppings, gusts of birds arose. Through dim doorways came the bad breath of tenements, the sharps and flats of collisions in their small and gloomful rooms.

To one such tenement and one such group of rooms, to their meager salvage of bridal veils and bedding and broken sets of spoons, there came a five-year-old boy from Kovno to be welcomed by a sister, a brother, a *Landsmann,* whom?

Your father was here, in the American States.

SCENE 2

MOTHER (1881-1914)

A little younger than your father, she was born on the lower East Side of New York to parents who, like his, had emigrated from one of the Russian provincial governments—Suwalki, a *guberniya* southwest of Kovno on the Niemen. With those facts, your knowledge of her beginning stops, and she drops from history for twenty years. Somewhere there may still be a window she was seen from, somewhere a doorway she entered, a shop, a school; she was in being once on certain streets, in certain rooms and minds; but no record remains of her presence, and few who knew her are now alive. She seems to have begun when you did, to have lived thereafter for three thousand days, and to have ended by the time you reached ten, taking with her most of her words and ways, all her hopes and fancies, and even the sound of her voice. A handful of letters, a page or two of photographs, and she goes from life one night in July.

SCENE 3

ABRAHAM NEVINS (c.1857-1926)

He was your mother's father, but he enters your awareness late, at or near the time of her death. Until then, if he appeared to you at all, it was only at the edge of sight as something blurred, a color, a light, a solid in motion. And yet he must've been present within hours of your birth, he must've smiled upon you while you slept or nursed, and how, on the eighth day of your life, could he not have been the one who held you for the *mohel*'s knife? He would've been there when they named you *Yonkel Layv*, there for birthdays, for sunnings in the park, there when you were ill and he brought you a cup of silver. And still, the face you know so well now is missing, as if it never had a place among the pictures of your mind.

In Suwalki, the family name was Novinsky, and what you learned of his early days in America is what he told you when he was old. He peddled from a pack, he said, sold matches, tinware, needles, notions, spread his back-door wonders for the eyes of back-door wives. He spoke in signs, in broken English, in lines he drew in the dirt, and once, when sent on an errand (*I'll watch your pack, Ikey*), he lost the gains of a month on the roads of Missouri. Thereafter, the pack became a part of his body, and day and night he wore it as a kyphotic wears a hump, wherefore later trips had brighter endings. In no long time, he was able to quit his trade in gimcracks and forsake the turnpike: he had money now, and he sent it forth to do his work. He knew of usances (was he not a Jew!), and that was where his ducats delved, and well they did, for at forty he was rich.

He was a tall, rigid, handsome man, with eyes the blue of bluing and hair the color of ash. Long of leg and lean, he could walk forever, and you can see his stride yet, a yard in span at the least, unchanging and endless, and few could match it unless they ran. Watching him swing along a street, a beach, a path in the park, you'd call to mind the pack he used to carry, the rail-fenced roads, the farms afloat on grain—and as he never merely strolled, so he never merely sat. In no recall does he seem to be idle, to be passing the time or letting time pass him: he played no games, he had no visions, and when he spoke, it was to the point only, and what he said was final, especially if addressed to his wife.

He was her ruler, absolute and unappealable, and his throne was an arm-chair at the diningroom table, where she served him first while standing up. Not once in your memory did he call her by name, not once the lovely Leah, and for all that strangers knew, she was either *she* or nameless. Still, she bore him six children, three sons and three daughters, and of these your mother was the favorite — *Chai Esther,* she was called, and *Chai* became Harriet, but she was known to all as Ettie. When dead, she was not allowed to lie — *Ettie,* someone would say, or *When Ettie was alive,* and Ettie would revive and die another time.

SCENE 4

LEAH NEVINS, née Jacobson (c.1859-1934)

Love of God won her highest praise. *Eine fromme Frau,* she'd say of someone, or *Er ist zehr fromm,* and you'd gaze upon the man or woman, expecting to see a being in a blaze of light. She never seemed to know that it was she whose ways were pleasing, she who dwelt in grace. She'd've been distressed if told that she saw in others what she herself possessed, that they reflected her, that, being her glass, they glowed. But no one could've spoken so: she was too *fromme* to have heard.

Her eyes were a pale shade of blue that pales still further in her photographs, where she nearly shows no shade at all, merely gray space in place of eyes. Forty-five when you were born, she was ten more years becoming a presence you were aware of, and what you saw then was an old woman who seemed to have been old all her life. You couldn't imagine her young — always, you thought, she'd had those lines in her face, a deep criss-cross, as if her skin were something woven. Heavily built, she was massive in motion, but when she reached where she was going, deftly she did what she'd meant to do there.

In the streets, her pale blue vision did not fail her: she could always see the needy, and she'd point out *an olderly man,* a seedy woman, and give you coins for the cups of their hands. How often she was wrung by rags, a limp, a hungry face, a fit of falling! how her mouth would twist, as when she thought of daughter Ettie! Her mouth was her manifest of pain, but through all she had to bear, it never spoke a hurtful word. No one knew that better than you: when you'd tried her beyond endurance, the worst you ever heard was *The Devil shouldn't take you!*

Abe, she called your grandpa (she walked a pace behind instead of at his side, accepted all his ways, said nothing when he shamed her, often knew bad days), Abe she called him, but never in your hearing did he call your grandma Leah.

SCENE 5

SINAI SHAPIRO (c.1845-1911)

He was your father's father, and you remember him mainly as a beard that seemed to speak. It was full and white, save for a citron-yellow slit through which came words that were made of smoke. Whenever you were taken to see him, he'd give you a sack of rock candy, but your mind was on the beard that spoke, not on the sugar crystals, which you little liked and soon would throw away. He died when you were seven, and all that comes up with the bucket is a memory of white hair that called you *Yonkel Layv* though it must've known you were *Julian.*

You saw him for the last time at Hunter, in the Catskills, where he'd been sent to avoid the city's heat, but his heart, which was failing, failed the faster at two thousand feet, and soon his children were summoned for the final hours, and your father took you along. The first stage of the journey was made on the *Clermont,* a side-wheeler of the Hudson River Line, and the second over the Mountain division of the Ulster & Delaware. At Hunter, a carriage was hired, and you were driven to a farmhouse higher in the hills; there, in one of the bedrooms, the old man lay propped against a pile of pillows. Or was it only his beard that you saw, white fur that stirred with his breathing, and did you wonder why it said nothing now, not even *Yonkel Layv* instead of *Julian?*

That day or night, the breathing ceased, and your grandpa was dead, your father told you, and you watched a grownup cry. But to you at seven, *dead* was simply a sound, and it summoned up no picture, filled no empty space in the album of your mind. There were other sounds that you could see quite clearly—*water, fire, white,* and *lion*—but when you were seven, *dead* meant nothing you could even guess at, much less understand.

On the way back to New York, your father showed you a gold watch in a snap case, thick through the middle and heavily chased: it had belonged to your Grandpa Shapiro, he said, and now it belonged to you. Rock candy, a gold watch, a talking beard—were these what had made your father cry? On returning home, he put the watch away, but he must've wound it daily, because it was running when a year or so later you found it in a drawer. You sprang the lid and followed the slender second-hand as it stepped and stopped around the dial, you wondered what IV meant and XII, and then, without knowing why, you took the watch to school. Often during the morning, you drew it from your pocket, tripped the catch, and pretended to read the time. On the last occasion, you were careless, and it slipped from your fingers and fell to the floor. Picking it up, you listened to it, shook it, and listened some more, but within the case, alas, all was silent.

Dead, you thought—and now the word came with a picture, and you saw your Grandpa Shapiro, not the beard alone. He's dead, you thought; he stopped running.

SCENE 6

RACHEL SHAPIRO, née Lieberman (c.1845-1934)

Among the elders of the family, some held that her butchershop had been on Division Street, under the tracks of the elevated railway. Others, equally certain, placed it on Forsyth Street, on Eldridge, on Allen near Broome. The truth is that the Devil alone remembers where it was. Only he can say which walkup housed it, who may have passed and read the sign that spanned the glass: *Shapiro's Meat & Poultry,* it said, and below it were the *caph, shin, resh* of *Kosher,* which, as all the world knew, meant clean. Let the Devil find that window; no one else ever will.

Between those black and gold-leaf letters, though, surely a counter could've been seen, and a cutting-block, and, on hooks affixed to the wall, braces of fowl in their feathers, shanks of veal and mutton, and sausage-link festoons. And surely too all that *Fleischerei* would've been slaughtered as prescribed, with a single stroke of the knife by a reverential Jew. Even more would've been certain to patrons of the store. As its meats were unprofaned, so the hands of her who purveyed them, your Grandma Ruch'l, a wife among wives, mother of two daughters and five sons, and so faultless in her piety that she always wore a wig. Who, in the light of her little brown eyes, would've denied her *Frömmigkeit?*

Shameful to say, however, the same could not have been claimed for her husband Sinai. Though far from being a sinful man, it must be owned that he was further still from unearthly. It was known in many quarters that he was a smoker of Turkish cigarettes, a taker of snuff, and, let the truth be admitted, an occasional toss of Schnapps; but worst of his peccadilloes was his slavery to the *Schachfiguren,* those little pieces of wood that were used in the game of chess. Was he *Kosher* enough, his wife must've asked of God, to handle *Kosher* meat? —and God must've answered Nay!

In the family, it was bandied about that God had gone further in regard to Sinai, indeed, that He'd been mandatory in commending the backslider to a life among the *yeshiva bocher,* which is to say a life of Talmudic study. If the words were not quite spoken, they were the ones that Ruch'l heard, and acting on such hearsay, she sent her husband off to *schul,* there to sit in prayer-shawl and phylacteries while he pondered the wonders and wisdom of the Torah.

How shall it be conveyed that in the holy place, he slid still further? How, save by saying what must be said, that there too he fell in with low company — or did it fall in with him? Others there were in skullcaps, in vestments of mohair, in shoes of vici kid, and there too were smokers of cigarettes, gummers of snuff, and quaffers of brandy—and there too, in a basement room, men played a game with little pieces of wood. Alas and alack, they prayed seldom, those bearded and beautiful Jews, but alack and alas, how they sneered at certain moves, how they slapped their knees, how they crowed in victory and minimized defeat!

Your Grandma Ruch'l was never really in the dark about your Grandpa Sinai. She knew of the doings in the basement, but all she ever said was addressed to no one in particular, to a leg of lamb, perhaps, or a slab of *Kalbfleisch,* and it was this: *Eighty-eight black years on the Holzlach, acht und achtzich schwarz Yahr on the little pieces of wood!*

SCENE 7

HARRY W. PERLMAN (1902)

In his early days as a lawyer, your father told you, a man named Perlman came to his office in connection with a legal matter—the purchase of some building lots, it might've been, or the settlement of a claim. He'd never seen the man before, and he knew no more about him than his striped silk shirt bespoke and his diamond solitaire. His flair for flash was accompanied by a bent for making small of others, as though almost all were what he called them—chumps. To your father, he suggested the kind who'd play cards triumphantly, who'd make an ace slap as it struck the table, rather as if the table were an opposing player's face. Still, he seemed civil enough at the time, balking only a little at this term or that condition, and in an air of lukewarm good will, the commerce at hand was disposed of: documents were signed and sums of money paid.

A few weeks later, the man returned to the office, saying, as your father recalled

"I was passing by, Mr. Shapiro, and I decided to drop in,"
saying, as he used a gold clipper on the tip of a cigar,

"How long have you been practicing law, counselor?"
saying, when the banded weed was burning evenly,

"I presume, Mr. Shapiro, that you're a family man,"
saying through smoke and glowing ash,

"I'm surprised. I thought sure a man like you would be married. A professional man,"
and then, your father said, he rose to go, as if he'd come only to pass the time of day. At the door, though, he paused to inquire whether your father would take supper at his home a week or so thence.

The man was little to your father's liking, brash, shrewd, desirous of more, more—not the sort he admired, he said, and, as well you came to know, not the sort he was. He could hardly have failed to gather what his caller had in mind, but neither then nor later could he account for his curiosity about the sister, the cousin, the in-law he was plainly meant to meet. He was far from requiring the services of a matchmaker. Women liked him at once, and always the liking lasted. Still, though unable to explain his acceptance of the invitation, accept he did.

On appearing at the appointed place, he was presented to Perlman's wife— Rae by name, a small woman, dark-haired and beautifully-made—after which, for *der Appetit,* he was offered a measure of spirits. He was in the act of raising it to the health of the household—*L'chayim!* he was about to say—when a young woman entered from another room. She was dressed in white, he said, and, after half a century, he seemed still to see the sight. He saw too, he must've seen, the expression she wears in so many of her pictures, a look as at something approaching and not then far away. She was introduced as Miss Harriet Nevins, a sister to Rae, and in scarcely above a twelvemonth's time, she became your mother.

SCENE 8

PHILIP AND HARRIET SHAPIRO, née Nevins (1903)

Among your mother's possessions was a small wicker basket, and when it came to your hands in later days, you found it to contain a furl of telegrams, their yellow gone brown with age. They had been sent to her and your father on the occasion of their wedding at Vienna Hall — *Best wishes,* they said, and *A long life,* they said, and *May you always be as happy as you are today,* and today was the 15th of June, and the year was 1903. There must've been a photograph of the bride, and once at least you must've seen it. Long since lost as an object, a positive mounted on a sheet of cardboard, still it dimly appears when you summon it, and you strain at your mother's lace and train and the expression on her face, as at something less than the long life wished for, as at an end she knew was eleven years away.

For their wedding journey, they went to Atlantic City, where, according to your mother's inscription on a snapshot, they stopped at the Hotel Rudolph (*frequented by Hebrews,* a guidebook says, *from $3*). They're pictured in a wheel chair against a background glare that might be light on the sea or sunstruck sand, and they gaze at you as if they knew even then that you'd gaze at them and wonder how they spent those nights and days of June. And you do wonder, knowing that you'll never know whether they were at ease before others, at table, on the beach and boardwalk, and at ease when alone. Unknown now forever what she wore, what she said, what thoughts wound through her head, and wonder though you may, never to be found her frame of mind — was she grave or gay, did she please with what she gave him, did she think her husband kind?

They were not at all the same. (*After school,* your father told you, *I delivered meat to customers of the store. The basket weighed fifty pounds; on Fridays, it weighed more.*) Your mother had no armor: she went about without protection, unindured against the insult of the world. He was his own armor (*fifty pounds,* he said; *on Fridays, even more*). She prized the fanciful, and it was from her that you heard of Loki, of the Speaking Oak of Dodona, of moly, the herb that unspelled the spells of Circe; he, at one hundred and eighty pounds, could wrestle with the best. He was substance, she something light and variable, hardly to be measured, smoke.

None can answer now, but was she grave or gay, did she please with what she gave him, did she think his conduct kind . . . ?

SCENE 9

MAY 31, 1904

Eighty years gone, the date divides the darkness and the light: in one of the rooms of a Harlem flat, the Spirit of God worked a wonder, and it was the evening and the morning of your original day. They're all dead now, those who may have been there for the event, and lost with them the look of the place, the disposition of the furniture, the pattern of the paper on the wall. They know who waited at a window, who spoke and who was silent, who stood about in the hall, they heard the sounds of generation through a transom, they saw who glanced at watches that told them only the time—and they're dead now all. You try to turn your mind back to the moment of your beginning, hoping to find what must've been entered in some fosse, some sulcus—there, under the sediment of eighty years, you think, you'll come upon the things you long to see and hear of that last day of May in 1904.

There'd be a final fetal instant, and from an amniotic cavity, you'd emerge to join the world. Your first sight of it would be the little blue hand of a gas-jet, and then there'd be great frightening faces, there'd be warmth and cold and laughter and the wind of thankful words, and all these you'd store away—for another day the names, the remarks about your size, your conformation, and the color of your eyes.

What thought your mother and father of the few convulsive pounds that egg and sperm had wrought? Were you required, like their painting of cows at pasture, like their walnut suite and Shakespeare set, were you their hearts' desire? You try to force your memory, but long before it reaches your beginning, it ends in swirling sleaves of steam.

SCENE 10

2 WEST 120th STREET

In Harlem, the course of Fifth Avenue was blocked by a ten-acre square of trees and lawns and railed-in walks called Mount Morris Park. Walled on all sides by private brownstones, the area was also confronted here and there by a block of flats, and one of these, known as the Gainsboro, was your place of birth. In one of its rooms, on the 31st of May, 1904, there was a sudden rush of membranes, cords, and serous fluids, and on that tide you became one of the lesser wonders of the world, a white male begotten of Harriet Esther, 23, occupation none, by Philip, 26, attorney, on some night or day then nine months gone.

On your certificate, filled in and signed by one S. A. Agatston, M.D., you were identified as Julian Lawrence Shapiro. The paper is still on file with the Registrar of Records of the state of New York, but apart from you, nothing else has survived of the event described. In the gears of time, your mother's labor has been lost, and if your father paced outside the door, his steps have gone to waste, and so have the generations that passed along the street. The offal that you came with was long ago ingested by a shark off the Jersey shore, the park has had a change of name, the Gainsboro stands no more, your mother and father are dead and Agatston, M.D., too. Only that sheet of paper remains, foxed with age like you.

SCENE 11

AND THEN ZIPPORAH TOOK A SHARP STONE (1904)

The cards were engraved in script. *You are cordially invited,* they read, *to attend the Brith Milah of our son on Tuesday June 7th,* and many came to hear the benedictions and pour the ruby wine. On your eighth day, even as the Lord had ordered Abraham, many saw you brought into their presence, fretting a little, reaching for nothing dimensional, clenching your toes, pissing perhaps in the depths of your clothes. Many watched as you were placed on a cushion, many listened to a sing-sung series of ancient blessings, many tried the dark red wine. Instead of a flint, a knife of steel was used, and not by Zipporah, wife of Moses, but by some *saddik,* a pious old man with a long white beard and a long black coat. Many lifted their eyes to the blade, held up for a moment to the light, upheld to the sight of the Lord, and many followed it down to the work at hand, the docking of your member to make you a man, and then there was blood on your dress, which would never be washed, and many drank their blood-red wine.

Then you were named, *Yonkel Layv* in Hebrew, or Jacob Louis, from which your mother somehow contrived Julian Lawrence. After certain further beseechments of the Lord, you were taken away for a change of clothing, leaving behind the felicitations of the assemblage, a few crumbs of sponge cake, and the syrup dregs of ceremony wine. Soon, lying in a nearby room, you would piss a little more, and then you would sleep, and it would be the morning and the evening of the eighth day.

SCENE 12

THE GAINSBORO YEARS (1904-09)

Photographs betoken a summer or two in the Catskills and others at the shore, but you can recall nothing of such excursions from the Gainsboro flat, your sparsely-peopled five-room world. You know now that there must've been family and neighbor invasions, but save for your father's and mother's, no faces come to mind, and even theirs are only dim souvenirs that rise and fall and churn like smoke. You remember his bay-rum aura and her singing (*Rings on her fingers, bells on her toes*), you remember a claustral fear of nightclothes, a running fall with a water-glass and a gash above your eye—those and other shreds, and that is all.

Where, you wonder, are the bright novelties that fascinated sight? where are the good and bad colors, the sexual textures? Where are the shades of aunts and cousins and tradesmen, of the seamstress, the corsetière, the woman who did the wash, and why, even after your sister was born, are there still only three in any room? You think of catch-as-catch-can wrestling (*fifty pounds, on Fridays more*) and then of Greco-Roman myths, and this is what you fix on: what did I see unseen in those days, what did I hear unheard?

SCENE 13

SUMMER AT TANNERSVILLE, a photo (1905)

On the lawn of a hotel in the Catskills, your father, with you on his arm, is standing before a treee, and seated on a chair close by, your mother is inclined toward him, so that her head appears to be resting against the arm that's holding you. The years have made the print fade from black and white to bisque and brown, and the sky has turned to beige. Lines once sharp have lost their edge and forms their definition, and in the distance a group who seem to be watching a game or a display may in truth be doing nothing, may merely have chanced to gather where they'd live beyond their lives in sun and umber shade.

You study yourself, a year-old boy in a sailor suit, with small dark-dot eyes staring at the camera, and you realize that he's gazing straight at you from the other end of the century. He's there on a mountain lawn that slopes toward Schoharie Creek, he's there between your father and your mother, he's breathing sachet powder and clear Havana smoke, he's hearing the voices, the laughter, the birds of 1905 — he's doing what you're doing, peering through time at you.

You wonder what he saw in the recesses of the lens, the bellows, the picture-taker's hood, whether he was pleased with what you'd made of him, whether the frown he wears is for some failure of yours, a wrong road travelled or the right one missed. You peer back through the hood, the bellows, the lens, you try to find a little-boy mind, but he stops you with those constant eyes, and all you learn is how you looked in the summer of 1905.

THE COLOR OF THE AIR, II

VIRGINIA DARE — 1587
FIRST LADY

BORN: *At Roanoke Island, North Carolina, 18 August 1587, to Eleanor, wife of Ananias Dare, Esq., a daughter, Virginia.*

Nine days later, Governor John White, grandfather of the first English child delivered on American soil, sailed for home *for the present and speedy supply of certain known and apparent lacks and needs, most requisite and necessary.* It took him three years and three hundred and fifty-five days to return, and he found *the houses taken down and the place very strongly enclosed with a high palisade of trees, with curtains and flankers, very fortlike; and one of the chief trees or posts at the right side of the entrance had the bark taken off, and five feet from the ground, in fair capital letters were graven* CROTOAN, *without any sign or cross of distress.*

He searched for some time, that grandfather of Virginia Dare, but of the one hundred and sixteen souls he had left behind on the dunes, he found no wind-grayed bone, no salt-faded rag, no blurred or bottled word, no word at all save the word CROTOAN; he found no stiff scalp with stiffened hair, no coshed-in skull, no scaled pot, no rotten pone, no written word save the word CROTOAN; he found no telltale ash, no mildewed trash or unstrung beads, no wax tears from some sprung-for candle, no hound on a grave, no grave on stilts, nothing but the lone and graven word CROTOAN.

There were voices on the sand and in the air, but they spoke no tongue that White could understand. There were clouds of heron crying *as if an army of men had shouted together*; there were parrots, falcons, and merlinbaws; there were clam-birds, there were wrens in the cattail, there were plover and willet and clapper-rail — but their cries made no sense in English ears, and the search, begun at that right-hand gatepost, ended there. Gazing at the still strange word, White spelled it once aloud, as if charging it to make its own meaning known, but CROTOAN it was and only CROTOAN, and he reboarded ship and sailed away forever.

Had he stayed longer, would he have found the fact of the matter? Would he have found, in some Indian town, one hundred and sixteen mummied heads on poles? Would he have found their teeth slung on Indian necks, their skin drawn tight on drums? Would he have found the pots in use, the rusted wrecks of tools, the torn Bibles, the clothes again but wrongly worn. . . ?

DIED: On or near Roanoke Island, North Carolina, Virginia Dare, daughter of Ananias and Eleanor Dare, on an unknown day between 1587 and 1591.

SCENE 14

UNDESIRABLE CITIZENS (1907)

Moyer, Haywood, Pettibone—

A time would come when you'd sense that you'd caught the names before. Years hence, they'd seem to be familiar, and you'd deem them nothing new. At three, though, you thought them only sound: at three, you played on the floor of a furniture forest, where the flowers of the carpet looked real enough to pick. From above you, voices—those of your father, your Grandpa Nevins, your Uncle Dave—and words drifted down to you that you did not understand. But having been uttered in your presence, having caused vibrations at a rate greater than 15 per second, they were heard and recorded by your mind. And when the coming time came, you'd wonder who'd said *why* and *which,* and who'd said *what* in reply.

Late in December 1905, the former governor of Idaho, Frank Steunenberg, was killed by a bomb set to explode when he opened the gate to his garden. Rewards totaling $15,000 were offered for the arrest and conviction of the perpetrators.

Haywood, Moyer, Pettibone—

Down on the floor, you stacked lettered blocks of wood—L on Q, F on L—making houses that spelled nothing, or you rolled wheeled things through the botanical thicket of the rug, or you pretended to be in hiding (from what? from whom?).

Moyer, Pettibone, Haywood—

The names settled down upon you, and the names of places too—Denver, Boise City, Coeur d'Alene, Fort Sherman—and all of them, though you were unaware of doing so, you saved for later days.

When questioned, a man calling himself Tom Hogan stated that he was a buyer of wethers, that is to say rams, but he was unable to explain the disguises found in his satchel or the full set of cracksman's tools. On further interrogation, he broke down and confessed that he was Harry Orchard, or Albert Horsley, the last being his real name.

Sometimes it may have been your father's voice and sometimes your grandpa's or your Uncle Dave's. But whichever you may have heard, it bore spores of fact, places, dates, names, the course of the wars at the mines, and one day, still a few dozen years away. . . .

34

Haywood, Moyer, Pettibone —

On the statement of Harry Orchard, they were arrested, indicted, and placed on trial in Caldwell, Idaho, the scene of the Steunenberg murder. President Theodore Roosevelt issued the opinion in advance that they were guilty of incitement to bloodshed and violence and that they were undesirable citizens.

One day, you'd read that declaration, but then you were still on the floor, and the day was still afar.

In protest against the President, people all across the country wore buttons reading I AM AN UNDESIRABLE CITIZEN!

Above you, someone may have said *I wore one too.* Would it have been your temperate father? Would it have been your grandpa, back-road peddler, merchant with a pack? Or would it have been the hot one, your Uncle Dave? Some day you'd know, when time enough had passed.

Haywood, Pettibone, Moyer, Dave. . . .

SCENE 15

THE PANIC OF 1907

In salvaging those times, you rarely see your father's face. He's there, you know, but you seem not to have taken his full measure, as you might've done with a tree. Almost always, he enters your perception on the plane where you dwell, ground level, and you simply suppose the system that grows overhead. His hands, his voice, his smoke and lotion air, all come from that higher region, and it's only when he reaches down to raise you that you realize his size. But more often than not, you're at his feet, pushing some tin engine, some trolley along a pair of lines in the carpet: you're sheltered there, shaded from the sun, while you cause your wheels to run beneath the tree.

You see him entire one morning when you're three. He's shaving, and you're standing nearby, taking in the rasp of the razor and the perfume of the soap, and now and then he glances down at you, and once he smiles and winks. As he pats his face with witch hazel, he says *Do you think you're big enough to bring me a glass of water?* and you say *Yes,* and you hurry away to your mother, who pours it for you and sends you back. You trip on a ruck in the rug, and you fall, still holding the glass, and you smash it with your head. You hear a cry from your mother, but it's your father you try to see, though all you see is red.

35

It was only later that you learned of the other panic of the year, of how Morgan played at Solitaire and Teddy R. went hunting bear in the Cajun country (and shot one, by Jingo!) while banks and your father failed.

SCENE 16

SISTER RUTH, THE STARVED CUBAN (1908)

You were four years old at the time of her birth, but you seem not to have known she was coming despite all the signs of a change—the preparations, the quiet commotion, your mother's growing size—nor did you register your sister's presence even after she'd arrived. You must've seen her crib and perambulator, you must've watched her being bathed and suckled, noted her strange conformation, and even made her cry, but the sights and sounds come back as surmise only, those you suppose you saw and heard. Looking back, you fail to find her: your world at four would not allow her in.

Smaller than normal when born, she recalled photos taken of the war with Spain, of children in Las Guasimas, in Camaguey—the Starved Cuban, your Grandpa Nevins labeled her, and her dark complexion bore out the phrase. She was named Rachel Pearl, but to your mother and soon to all, it became transformed to Ruth. In a series of snapshots, she grows before your eyes, in parks and streets and doorways she grows, on steps and chairs and laps, she drinks from a milk bottle, she holds a bitten piece of bread, she carries a parasol, a doll, her clothes lengthen, her hair is worn in older ways, she grows. But only in the pictures; in your mind, she can't be found.

SCENE 17

THE PRECIOUS STONE (1908)*

In the winter, the stove would sometimes steam the kitchen window, and you'd clear it with your sleeve and stare out into the air shaft at flakes so slowly falling you could follow them down with your eye. Some were caught

---

* From *To Feed Their Hopes*, University of Illinois Press, 1980.

by the grating of the fire escape, where they made wales of white, a corduroy mat that reached the kitchen of the flat across the way. In the spring and summer, the window was often open, and while your mother talked with her neighbor, you'd climb out onto the fire escape and peer between the slits at lower landings, at flowerpots, a cat asleep on a sill, a boy with a bat and ball.

You can't recall what was spoken past you from one kitchen to another: you heard the voices, your mother's and the neighbor's, but for all you knew, there were no words, there was only a murmuring, as between two chipper birds. And yet you remember the stone, you can see and feel it still, you've never forgotten the stone! It was smooth, as though gnashed by the surf, ground among other stones, and, red in hue and nearly round, it looked not a little like a plum. You weren't told where the woman had found it or why she'd brought it home—it was simply a plum-like stone—but she thought it rare and prized it, and rare and prized it became to you. You couldn't say, you could never say, why that one stone was so enviable, but whenever it comes to mind, you hone, now as then, to own it, to hold it in your hand.

A day came when you did own it, a day when, unseen by your mother or the neighbor, you crawled across the fire escape, took the stone from a drawer, and bore it off to your room. There for a time you toyed with it, turned it in your fingers, palmed it, held it up to the light, tasted it, even— you owned it, you thought, the red stone plum belonged to you. And then other things drew you, a hook-and-ladder and its always galloping team, a box filled with bricks of colored clay, lead soldiers on one knee and firing, and the stone was put aside, allowed to roll away.

You must've fallen asleep on the floor—you're there, you think, when your mother awakens you, and all about you are tin and leaden presences, paper, wood, and plasticine. But it's stone that your mother inquires about, stone that the red stone face behind her demands without a sound. *Julian, did you take this lady's stone?* your mother says, but you're looking up at the anger just beyond her, and you say nothing. *Julian,* your mother says, *did you take the stone?* And now you bring it out from under a corner of the bed, hand it to your mother, relinquish it forever, and she gives it to the woman, saying something quietly and listening to something loud (*the little thief!* was it?), and then the woman goes away.

SCENE 18

THE CABONAK YEARS (1909-12)

The Cabonak was an apartment house on St. Nicholas Avenue and 120th Street, and before its doors the horse-cars ran. It was an older building than the Gainsboro, and its rooms seem to have been darker, or else the doings you remember there were done on grayer days. The rooms overlooked neither trees nor greensward. They faced row on row of windows, wide-open eyes, you thought them, a show of surprise at you for staring, perhaps, or at the droppings left below between the rails.

When you first saw the word *Cabonak*, in gilt and black on a transom above the entrance, you thought it a misspelling. Something else had been intended, you supposed, and letters had been omitted or printed out of place, but whatever the error, it had never been repaired. *Cabonak,* you pondered, *Cabonak,* but after many a rearrangement, it never revealed the mistake. In the end, you were forced to make what you could of the order as given, and you persuaded yourself that: *The Cabonaks were a tribe of Indians who lived on St. Nicholas Avenue.*

Your mother's reason for the move across Harlem to the Cabonak was the presence, just around the corner, of Public School 81, called the Model School. On its upper floors, student teachers were trained in the latest theories of education, and on the lower, where six grades of pupils were taught, the theories were put into practice. The standards of the school were the highest in the borough of Manhattan, and though it was your mother's desire to enroll you, only those children who resided in the district were permitted to attend. The Gainsboro lay outside it; the Cabonak lay within.

In your recalls of the time, you still see much in slides, in cards of captured action, and your mind moves from one to another as if they were postals in a rack. What they tell is an unsequential story, a series of episodes shuffled by time, and, like the name of the building, they suggest a meaning that you cannot decode

the Cabonak, you think, and the Model School, and you see teachers in your home drinking tea, and they come in summer for a stay at the shore. Miss Gibson, you think, and Miss Blauvelt, and Miss Morey from a place called Troy—the same or another Troy, you wonder, and you summon up Hector dead and nine times dragged 'round the city walls. The Model School, you think, and the Cabonak, and you see your mother at her rosewood upright, and you enjoy her voice and her somber face *rings fingers bells toes and she shall have music wherever she goes.* And, looking beyond her, you see the dining-room with its papering of maroon brocade, and slowly one of the slides in your mind begins to move

the family is at table, and your father is trying to cut some mass that lies on his plate, some God-knows-what, under- or overdone, solidified, elusive, willful, almost, and finally he takes up the knife-proof lump of matter, carries it to an open space near the sideboard, and bounces it off the wall. *What fun!* you think, and you laugh—*He's playing ball!* you think, *he's playing ball against the wall!*—and laughing all the harder, you glance about for other laughter. There is none. What you find instead is your mother in tears behind her hands, and at once your laughter goes. *Rings fingers bells toes,* you think, and the slide come to a stop

SCENE 19

A PLACE OF SPELLS (1909)

It was from your mother that you heard of enchantments, of wizards, of carpets that rode on the wind. She read to you of such things, of course, but you didn't know what reading was, and you thought that the sword in the stone, the potions, the incantations, were inventions of her own. On a certain day, though, as she walked you through the streets of Harlem, she told you that soon you'd see where those wonders came from. It was called a library, she said, and there, on shelves that rose from floor to ceiling, were objects known as books. At first, you'd take them to be little boxes with brightly colored lids—and in a way, they *were* boxes, she said, because while others contained shoes, or biscuits, or odds and ends, these were full of something called knowledge, in fact all that was known of the world. You'd hardly imagine that boxes so small could hold so much, she said, but like the charmed caskets of her stories, they held whatever the mind was able to suppose. Yes, she said, books were really magic boxes—and now she pointed out a building that you'd never seen before. As she led you toward the door, she said *Remember, this place is filled with spells.*

SCENE 20

THE PATERNAL RELATION (1909)

On a Saturday, if the weather was fine, your mother would tog you out in your best—she dressed you well; it was all the best—and your father would take you downtown to his office in Nassau Street. There he'd spend the morning with his associates, and they'd talk of hard money, of the standstill times, and after a while you'd hear your father say,

"Does anybody want to buy a nice quiet law practice?"
and there'd be Amens from all around the room.

You'd be outside among the files and the bookcases, amusing yourself at one of the typewriters, or tightening the wheel of the letter press, or wandering about between the stacks of law reports—*40 U.S.,* you'd read as you passed, and *114 New York.* Wherever you went, you'd be spied on by a swiveling fan from its bracket on the wall, watched while you played with the switch-board jacks or made bubbles burst in a bottle named Great Bear. Voices would come to you through sunbeams filled with dust, and you'd stare up at steel engravings, wondering who *William Maxwell Evarts* was, and *Salmon Portland Chase.* You'd glance at calendars and their scatter of red-letter days, you'd pick at briefs, seals, supplements, and when you came upon a copy of the *Law Journal,* you'd make up a joke about the yellow *Journal* of William Randolph Hearst. Taking the paper, you'd go into your father's room, and shaking the pages at him, you'd say,

"I thought you said you never read the *Journal,*"
and after a moment's silence, lawyers began to laugh.

And then your father would take you to lunch, and as you crossed City Hall Park, he'd say,

"That was a pretty good one, kid,"
and now you'd be at the Astor House (*much frequented by business-men*), where you'd sit on a stool at the great circular counter in the rotunda, and just like a man of business, you'd eat an inch-thick slice of rare roast beef. Afterward, you'd ride up Broadway on the open car, and your father would read you the names of the streets—Lispenard, Prince, Bleecker, Great Jones—and at Madison Square you'd start to walk, and hand-in-hand you'd go through the dead-air smell of theatres and the fresh-bread smell of Mouquin's, and you'd pass hotels and beer-breath bars and a building called The Met, and

finally you'd stop before an overhead sign that said *The Times.*

You'd say, "That's your paper!"

And your father would say, "Can you read the words below the name?"

And you'd say, "All the news that's fit to print,"
but the afternoon was well along by then, and you were too tired to ask about the news that wasn't, and your father would take you home.

And later still, when you went to bed, he'd drift down the hall with his smoke (he never smoked till the Sabbath was over), and leaning across the pillow, he'd muss your hair and say,

"That was a pretty good one, kiddo,"
and then the light would go out, and you'd fall asleep.

SCENE 21

DISSENT (1909)

> *To obey is better than sacrifice*
> — 1 Sam.15.22

One of your mother's pleasures was to dress you in the best, and one of yours, while so bedecked, was to go your willful way. For a particular occasion, a holiday, a shopping-tour, a birthday party, or for no come-off at all, she'd lay out some starched and glaring outfit, lisle socks, and a pair of buckskin shoes, and after you'd put them on, she'd brush your Buster Brown hair and crown you with a broad-brimmed sailor. Gotten up so, so you were expected to remain, almost as though you were needed only to bring the clothes along. Within them, then, you'd feel hindered, as by an outer skin, and when you were led toward the streetcar or the subway or someone's festive event, you'd begin, it seemed, to expand, and your white linen suit, scalloped and embroidered, would no longer fit you, and your chalked shoes would grow too tight. You'd hardly have gone a block before you tried to escape from what you were wearing, because if worn but a few steps further, it would cease to be external and become a part of you.

Wild, you were called for throwing yourself on the sidewalk, for rolling in the dust, the grime, the ash, all the offcast of the passing world. Wild, your Aunt Rae would say, a wild and wicked thing, while your mother merely stood there, gazing down at the ruin you'd made of her work, her love of arraying dolls. *To obey is better,* she may have thought, but she said nothing, simply looked down at you with the same sad face she shows in many pictures. But your Aunt Rae could speak, and she spoke, saying *If I were you, Ettie, I'd tell Phil,* and you still can hear the words.

Ettie did tell Phil once, but all he did was make you promise to be an obedient boy.

SCENE 22

THE MATERNAL RELATION (1909)

It was no great way from the Cabonak to the Model School, a hundred yards or less, and you could cover the distance, day-dreams and all, in scarcely a minute's time. Even so, on rainy days, you did not go home for lunch; at your mother's orders, you waited for her in your classroom, and she brought the meal to you. You grew to hope for rain, to enjoy its slant across the courtyard and the tufts of splash on the tiles, and when the noon bell rang and the room emptied, you'd stand at a window, watching classmates hasten from the building and disband along the street. For a while, then, there'd be only the quiet, the wet pavement, and, muffled by the panes, a horse and wagon passing below. And then you'd see an umbrella that seemed to be walking by itself, and you'd follow it through the doorway, and after a moment you'd hear footfalls, and your mother would enter the room. She'd set the umbrella down open, and it would drip drops from its ribs to the floor, and then a paper sack would lie before you—your rainy-day déjeuner.

You didn't wonder about the others, those who'd turned their collars up and fled away through the street. It was no concern of yours how far they had to go, how wet they'd be when they got there, and what they'd have to eat. Your lunch was in that paper sack (a white-meat chicken sandwich, peppered lightly and celery-salted, and a half-pint bottle of milk), and it didn't occur to you that only you had been so favored, that no mother but yours had saved her son the rain. Nor did you ask yourself what had imbued her, drawn her out-of-doors so that you might stay within. You knew only the primaries, pain, heat, thirst, envy, and it was beyond your power to expand your understanding to embrace your mother's act. And yet, how could you have missed her look when you opened that paper sack?

You gave no thought to others then, you were troubled not at all by what

42

others may have said: *Sugar-tit Julian! Ladyfinger Julian! Scared of melting in the rain!* No one had ever called you *Percy* to your face. . . . To your face, you think, and you recall a letter you wrote to your mother:

Dear Ma, you said, I had 4 out of five on one day and four out of 8 on another, the latter which was not good. I was playing marbels with a boy who was a good fighter and lost an imme, and would not play out. For a long time he was after me. On yesterday he saw me coming out of school and he saw me but insted of coming up to my face he waited till I was out of the yard and caught me by the shoulder, and as I saw him I dropped my books and swung around and hit him in the head and he turned red. Your affectionate son Julian Shapiro.

Those were the days when paper sacks, as though of themselves, came toward you through the rain. Who would've dared to call you *Percy* to your face?

SCENE 23

MORRIS AVENUE, LONG BRANCH, N.J. (1909)

Of that summer's mural, only three panels remain.

. . . a day of croquet colors, red, blue, black, white, and you hear the whack of wood on wood and watch a ball roll toward a wicket, a banded stake, another ball, and someone (Cousin Jasper?) cries *You missed.* . . .

. . . a day of humming heat, and a man comes in from the roadway carrying a suitcase so burdensome that it breaks him over to one side and makes him seem deformed. Setting it down at the top of the stoop, he smiles through sweat and speaks a strange language, or, since it has no meaning for you, it may be only an utterance and not a language at all. But your Grandma Nevins nods, as though familiar with the tongue, and at once the suitcase is opened, revealing fold on fold of embroidered linen, a pile that looks faintly blue, with scalloped edges, clusters of eyelets, and filigree. A tablecloth is flown for the family's inspection, and while they finger it, you breathe its outland perfume, a spice, an herb, some foreign mordant, a flavor that, like the language, you cannot understand. . . .

. . . a day of little play, of crawling under the porch and listening to rockers creaking and deadened talk, a luckless day for four-leaf clover, a day of picking up stones and shying them away, a day of . . . and as you pass a rain-barrel at a corner of the house, you hear a rustling in the downspout—a bird? — and then wonder fades in the sun, but that night the sound comes back to mind, and you imagine wings trying to fly inside the pipe, feet trying to climb, you think of the water below and dark sky above, and all at once you feel as though you're in there yourself, trying, trying, like the bird, and dying between the water and the dark, but the bird doesn't die that night, or the next, or the next—it's still alive and trying to fly!—and then one morning as you pass the barrel, you see a sparrow floating on old rain, and now, you think, you can put it out of your mind, but it never goes out, it stays, still rustling, still trying to fly, and you're the one that's going to die. . . .

SCENE 24

RUBEOLA (1910)

You were lying in a darkened room, floating, you thought, not on a stream, but on the gloom itself. There was neither bed beneath you nor cover above: there was only a sense of being borne by nothing you could feel toward nothing you could see. From time to time, words seemed to come alongside and accompany you, as if they too were free in the void, and though you didn't understand them, you heard such things as *diaphoretic* and *ipecacuanha* and *104 degrees*; they produced no pictures, though, they were simply sounds in the dream. But now and then, something else drew near, not a sight or a sound but a fragrance—and you'd breath deep, as if it might not come all the way.

Miss Bevan, your nurse was called, and for all you know, she had no given name. Miss Bevan, you thought, and there she was, the fragrance, not of flowers, fruit, or herbs, but linen, flannel, lisle, and you wondered where they touched her, her throat, her wrists, her arms, or places that were warm, soft, rounded, and hidden from the eye. *Fomentations of alcohol,* someone said, and soon, you knew, she'd move along your body with a cool and pungent hand, and then you'd feel her turn you, and you'd forget to breathe while you waited for the cold exciting entry of a little rod of glass.

She was always sent for when there was sickness in the family, and you remember her occasional presence until the summer of 1914, when you reached the age of ten. Thereafter, fifteen years went by before you saw her again, and it's still unclear why you did so then. You sought her out, but what did you hope to find, you wonder—that she'd stopped where you left her, stepped aside from time to give you time to arrive? Did you think she'd still be twenty-five, still suggest a transit of perfume across some room you had in mind? What drew you when you found her name among old papers, what did you intend as you went toward where she lived, as you stood before her door? What were you doing there at the age of twenty-five?

She didn't recognize you. When you mentioned your mother, she recalled the connection, but you were nothing, a visitor at best, more than a canvasser, perhaps, but less than a guest, a caller whose stay was expected to be short. Nor, had you seen her anywhere else, would you have known her—flown at once the fancy that time had marked time for her through all those fifteen years. You watched her place a cylinder on the spool of a gramophone, set the stylus, and grind the spring (who was singing, did she say—Sembrich, Farrar, Calvé?). You watched, and what you saw was a Miss Bevan who could never have made you listen for her coming, never have touched you, stirred your head with ethanol, never have done what she did with a little tube of glass.

Melba, Patti, Emma Eames? When the singing stopped, you went away.

SCENE 25

PHYLLIS G. (1910)

She lived in one of the Cabonak flats, on the floor above you or the floor below, and you'd see her—or, rather, pass her, because to you she was barely visible—in the entry hall or on the street outside the door. She had only the smallest effect on you, like a pastel color or a breath on glass. She was pale and thin, almost transparent, and she seemed to form a mere momentary film on the eye. You were aware of her, though, because you knew she was aware of you: she watched you coming, and you could sense that she watched you go. For some reason, her mother assumed that since you were her daughter's Jack, she must be your Jill, but all you can recall is speaking to her once.

Coming home from school one afternoon, she walked behind you all the way. You knew she was there, but you pretended to be unwitting until you reached the door. As you paused to let her precede you, she said *How does your hair get to be so white, Julian?* and Julian, soon to be the Boy King, said *I drink milk, and it goes to my head.*

SCENE 26

CHILDE JULIAN, BOY KING (1910)*

You were six years old, and on the morrow, at your birthday party, you'd
be crowned king of the kindergarten, and you'd rule your subjects, children
too, all through the long, the endless reign of a summer's afternoon. There'd
be a procession in the courtyard of the school, and robes of purple paper would
be worn and stoles of ermine crape, and there'd be a banquet royal of cake
and ice cream, and the loyal would come with tribute and lay it at your feet —
pencil boxes, tins of paint, tops, sacks of marbles, and (please!) an agate that
would never miss.

Now, on the eve of your coronation, one last rite remained to be performed:
your choosing a queen for the evergreen day. Making the choice, though,
would be ceremonial only: she who'd wear your diadem was all but named,
well-nigh known. She was the daughter of a neighbor who loved in the flat
above or below your own, and whenever she came to mind, you saw her
as something gray, a color in the rain, and for all you knew the rain was
real, for she always seemed to you quenched. There was no good will between you, and neither was there ill: there was no will at all. Even so, with
no word said, both she and her mother had managed to draw a pledge from
the absence of a denial, and because it was all one to you, you let the inference
lie.

When school ended for the day, the kindergarten girls were lined up and
put on display, as though some seigniorage were being arranged for you, a
first-night right at six!, and you were bidden to pass your vassals and single
out your bride. Only one of these could win your favor — indeed, it was already
won — wherefore the rest merely endured your eye and wished it would pry
somewhere else. It came to you, as you moved along the line, that you were
seeing many of the girls for the first time. You'd been in the same room with
them for a year, you'd passed them in the street, spoken to them, called them
by their names, even, but never until now had you gone beyond the faces,
voices, shades of hair. They were separate, you saw at last, they were single
and different things, and no two, like clouds, were quite the same — and all
at once one of them simply reined you in. Before, she'd been part of a mass,

*from *To Feed Their Hopes.*

a brick in a brick wall, a voice, a name, a forgotten shade of hair—but she was beautiful! beautiful!, and you were filled with wonder, ravished, as you took her by the hand and turned to the teacher: you'd found your queen.

From further along the line, there was a lone and anguished cry, and you forgot it never. It was in your mind all night—you dreamed it—and it was still there the next day, when you were crowned king and skipped about the courtyard with your queen, the unforeseen. Of the one you hadn't chosen, you told yourself *She wasn't pretty,* but her cry was there through your day-long reign and lifelong memory. *She wasn't pretty,* you told yourself, but what you'd done, and you knew it, was make her think the same.

SCENE 27

CHILDE JULIAN, etc., cont'd. (1910)

One day that fall, during your first year at grade school, you and your mother were walking along 120th Street on your way to the library that faced Mount Morris Park. From Seventh Avenue to Lenox, both sides of the block were lined with brownstones, private houses three stories high with matching windows, cornices, and semi-sunken areas between pairs of matching stoops. Only the numbers on the doors were different, the color of the curtains, the flavor of the basement air. As you passed, you sampled the emanations, breathing deep of cuisines, textiles, personal perfumes—of strange atmospheres, of strangers. And then, in a corner of one of the windows, you saw a nameplate of white glass, and you stopped, staring at the black-lettered oblong, and your mother stopped too, saying nothing and waiting for you to speak.

"What does M.D. mean?" you said.
"It means Doctor of Medicine."
"I didn't know her father was a doctor," you said, and you read the name aloud. "Karl Darmstadt, M.D."
"Do you think she knows your father is a lawyer?" your mother said, and she smoothed and smoothed your hair as if she could feel it through her glove
"I don't know," you said. "We don't talk any more."
"You never told me that."
"I talk to her, but she doesn't answer."
"When did she stop talking to you?"
"Right after being my queen."

"So soon?" your mother said, and then she looked up at the nameplate, and, just as you had done, she read the words aloud. "Karl Darmstadt, M.D."

"What does that mean — Darmstadt?"

"Darmstadt is a city in Germany."

"Maybe that's where he comes from."

"Maybe," your mother said. "Do you still think his daughter is pretty?"

"Oh, yes. She's pretty even when she's mad about something. She was mad when she came to my party, but she was still pretty."

"What was she mad about at the party?"

"I don't know, but I could see it on her face."

"I could see it on her father's face," your mother said. "He didn't want her to be your queen."

"But *she* wanted to be! She said she wore her best dress to be crowned in!"

"Julian," your mother said, and somehow your name seemed longer than it ever had before, "he didn't want his daughter to be the queen of a Jew."

You were well along the street now, and the house (*Karl Darmstadt, M.D.*) had merged with all its neighbors and become part of a brown wall three stories high. "I'm not going to try to talk to her any more," you said.

"Why not? Has she stopped being pretty?"

"No. She's still pretty."

"Does she look mad when you think of her?"

"No, just pretty."

THE COLOR OF THE AIR, III

THE JESUITS — 1632-49

THE FIRST KNEE ON CANADA

We caught fireflies in the darkening meadows,
And threading them into on-and-off festoons,
We hung them up before the altar and the Host,
And they made light for God, Ghost, and Jesus
While we, adoring, put the first knee on Canada.
Who's that nailed to the cross, Blackrobes?
If he's an enemy, let your chief eat his heart,
But if he's an Oke, you've killed yourselves
Unless you burn tobacco and invite him down.
Take our advice about such things, Blackrobes;

Listen to us, for we know the ways of the land,
And you, on your knees like women making food,
Have already offended us with your ignorance.
Fireflies must not bow down to graven images!
We said, "Unhappy infidels (meaning Dogges),
You that live in smoke only to die in flames,
Repent you and choose between Heaven and Hell!"
We said, "The sky is the palace of thunder,"
But it was clear that they did not understand.
"The sky," we said, "the blue wigwam overhead,
The sky is the home of thunder, comprenez?
And thunder is a turkey-cock, a cock but a man,
Yet in one thing he is neither man nor bird,
In one thing strange to all that walk or fly:
He comes forth only when the wigwam is gray.
Grumbling, he flies to earth to gather snakes,
Snakes and other objects that we call Okies,
And if you see flashes of fire as he descends,
That fire attends the beating of his wings,
And if the grumbling now and then is violent,
Be sure his children have been brought along.
"Which do you choose?" we said. "Heaven or hell?"
We said, "Heaven is a good place for Frenchmen."
"Which do you choose?" we said. "Heaven or hell?"
We said, "The French will not feed us in Heaven."
"Which do you choose?" we said. "Heaven or hell?"
We said, "Do they hunt in Heaven? do they dance?
Do they make war or hold festivals in Heaven?
If not, we will not go, for idleness is evil."
"Which do you choose?" we said. "Heaven or hell?"
We said, "If our dead are in hell, as you say,
If for want of a few sprinkled drops of water,
Our babies live in hell, we would go there too. . . ."

SCENE 28

UNCLE JEROME, "ROMIE" (1894-1946)

Up to the age of ten, you heard, he was a bright and handsome boy, blue-eyed and blond, and on growing taller, he promised to favor his father, though he was a ringer even when small. The family took much pride in him, and all of them vied to wheel him through the streets, to pause and show him off in the park. At school, he was said to be out-of-the-common. He dashed at the knowledge offered as though it were a door, and the more he acquired the wider it seemed to open, and he was still in the course of learning when he smashed against a wall. He was rising ten, they say, when on a certain day he was found at home in the sun-room, where sewing was done in the mornings and tea was sometimes served. In one hand he was holding a dying canary and in the other a hat-pin, a spit now for the canary's eyes. At his feet, the parquet was speckled with a few drops of blood, but he appeared to be unaware of the bird, the pin, the spotted floor: he was staring at what only he could know of, and what it may have been was a blank where once he'd seen a door. Only moments before, he may have thought the door was there, partly open and widening more, and soon, he may have supposed, he'd leave the world he was in and join the one outside. But there was no door, no other world; there was only a surround of wall that to the end of his life he'd remain within.

For killing the bird, your grandpa gave him a flogging with his belt, but it was all wasted; he taught the boy nothing. When Romie opened that birdcage, he knew as much as he'd ever know even though mashed with a mace. He was examined by doctors, who gravely uttered strange and hopeless findings, and medicines were prescribed, and diets and baths were recommended, and when no change was shown, he became known at military academies, boarding farms, and institutions for the amelioration of abnormal behavior. Instead, alas, it grew, and no one knew that the fires he set in cellars, the bric-a-brac he broke, the rages and refusals, all were only a ten-year-old boy trying to escape from a long-sealed mind. He was his own prisoner, and he seemed to sense that he'd never get away.

SCENE 29

GARFIELD AVENUE, LONG BRANCH, N.J. (1910)

It was one of those shingle-sided cottages — a General Grant, they called it — and it had round towers at two of the corners, looking down on a porte-cochère. Along the right angle of the porch, lilacs hid the balustered railing and part of the turned-wood supports, and many a day you'd play there behind the shrubbery, pretend to be lying in ambush or to be under siege in a fort—any sham would serve that promised to while away a morning or beguile an afternoon. There were several such houses that you remember, all of them rented for the summer season by your Grandpa Nevins, and the seasons too were much the same. They were termless: once begun, they seemed to run on before you with never an imaginable end. In their magnitude, there was room for all manner of adventure; for every inclination, there was time.

Blackberry thickets lined the railroad track, and you knew of marshes where reeds and cattail grew. The beach was an empty mile in either direction, and you could mar its flawless finish with your footprints, shallow if you walked, deeper if you ran. And you could watch an osprey plunge beyond the breakers, follow flights of petrels that looked like the whites of waves. And there were chestnut trees to be shaken down, trains to be seen with cars named *Indian River, Bantry Bay,* and *Agamemnon,* and always, when all else failed to stir you, you could quarrel with your cousin at croquet. How many things there were to do! you thought while lurking among the lilacs wondering what to do.

That summer, you remember, Uncle Romie came home. He'd run away from a work-farm in Wisconsin, your Grandpa Nevins said, and, poor misfortunate boy, he'd made his way back across six or seven states only to find that the family was not in New York. Even so, by some incomprehensible process of thought, or possibly with no thought at all, with only his mapless mind, he seemed to know where to go. Managing to beg a ferry-ride, he soon turned up, as though led there, at the summer house by the shore, and it may be that from your lilac covert, you were the first to see him staring in from the end of the driveway, a gaunt, soiled stranger with eyes like the sky and ash-blond hair—a stranger, you may have told yourself, never wondering why you thought next of your Grandpa Nevins.

You soon enough learned his name and the nature of your relationship, but it took you longer to know why you were told to avoid him when he so perfectly suited your age. You were six, and not much more, though taller, was he: he was the ideal companion, it seemed, a grown-up who thought like you. No vivid terms were used to describe him—no one said he was mad, imbecilic, touched by the moon. He simply wasn't "right in the head," and when you asked what was wrong, you were given the same answer: there was something the matter with his head.

You'd look and look, but his head was just a head to you, neither better nor worse than your own, a round sort of thing with a pair of eyes and a pair of ears, with a nose, a mouth, and hair, and all that a head could do, his did—eat, speak, see, and hear. You didn't know, nor were you told, that it wasn't right inside. When you were about, he was usually sent away, but there were times when he contrived to join you at play, running with a kite or launching paper planes, and if your elders had seen him, they might not have spoken of his head: kites always flew for him, his planes seldom crashed.

And so the summer lazed along — there were days when you were sure that water poured more slowly, when time sulked and refused to pass — and then one Sunday morning, it was announced by Grandpa Nevins that two automobiles had been hired for a family excursion to Point Pleasant on Manasquan Inlet, a trip of about fifteen miles each way. All rejoiced until the second part of the announcement: Uncle Romie was to stay at home. He made a great to-do over the exclusion, but your Grandpa was not to be moved, and in the end Uncle Romie stopped pleading and ran from the room.

Drawn up soon in the driveway were a white Lozier and a green Pope-Hartford, with chauffeurs in attendance in the shade. The family, the women veiled and swathed in dusters, were about to descend from the porch when one of the drivers cried out and pointed down at the tires: in the gravel before all eight, a sprinkle of tacks lay everywhichway. While they were being swept clear, your Grandpa led Uncle Romie indoors and whaled him with his belt — maybe even with the buckle-end — after which, wailing through a door-screen, he still was left behind.

You remember some of the ride. You remember Elberon (*There in that house, President Garfield died*), you remember Deal Lake and Asbury Park and the sign on the gate at Ocean Grove, but you know now that all day went with never a memory of Uncle Romie, weeping in a doorway for a door that wasn't there. *He's not quite right in the head,* they said.

SCENE 30

A BOOK CALLED *PATRIOTIC AMERICA* (1910)

Your name and the date are on the flyleaf — *Julian Shapiro 1910* — but from your way of writing, the inscription may have been made a little later, after the death of your mother. It was she who'd bought you the book, written by one R. S. Ewing and, as the title-page recites, *embellished with engravings and drawings illustrating all that is noblest in the history of our country,* and it was she who'd read it to you from the first word to the last. *Four hundred years ago,* it began, and as you scan the phrase now, you come to feel that you're hearing rather than seeing it, that it's being spoken to you in your mother's voice and that you're listening as a six-year-old and marvelling with his mind.

The text was rarely more for you than a space between two pictures, lowering and dreadful tableaux these, in which the time seems always night: the skies are nearly black, and so too the seas and the earth, and fire burns without apparent light. Or, where day is meant, the sun is shown about to set, and then deeper yet the gloom becomes, and Pokahontas marries in rays that look like rain, and Columbus lands at dusk. Why, you wonder, was the past made so somber by R. S. Ewing, why was *all that is noblest* presented in the shade? You dreamt often of those representations: once you'd seen *The Capture of a White Child,* it did no good to close the book. The picture was in your mind, and there'd follow while you slept the picture actuated, and you'd hear it cry and watch it bleed, as with *The Duel Between Hamilton and Burr,* you saw smoke pour from a pistol and a body on the Hudson shore.

There were other illustrations. Chromos, some of them in color, appeared here and there among the pen-and-inks, and without turning pages, you can think some back to view. *A Charge of Confederate Cavalry at Trevillian Station,* wherein there is no station, only death at a gallop between the edge of a wood and the foot of a hill; and in *The Battle of Churubusco,* voltigeurs are scaling a parapet to fire point-blank at Mexicans wearing pipe-clayed bandoliers; and in *The Assassination of President McKinley,* there is O-mouthed horror as bullets perforate a pancreas, a kidney, and the muscles of the back.

But in these and in all the rest, though blood is shown and shells explode and ships steam through cannonades, there is no sound or motion but such as you supply: it's you who must say where the shrapnel goes, you who must start the flows of blood; for you alone the *Oquendo* is beached, and you bring Custer down to die in a ring of thrashing horses and no longer thrashing men. You know now that history happened, *all that is noblest,* but what did you think then, at six, when you could make it null by waking up?

SCENE 31

PAGES AND PICTURES OF AMERICAN HISTORY

The Fountain of Youth

Every afternoon, when you come home from school, your mother reads to you from your own history-book. *Patriotic America,* it is called, and this will be the fourth time she has come to the part about how the Spanish was looking for an island that was floating around on the ocean. You hardly have to listen, because you know the words by heart: *There is an island far out at sea, with rich fruit and beautiful flowers and great purple mountains. . . .*

"It should be fruits," you say. "Not fruit."

"You're right," she says. "Fruits, it is."

"You never told me what kind."

"Oh, blue plums, I suppose, and yellow pears, and apples like your face."

Far out at sea, you think, and you say "An island is a place in a surroundment of water, and you have to go there by boat. There was a Spanish man, Ponce de Leon, and he got in a boat and sailed across the sea to find the island."

"All that way for fruit—fruits, I mean?"

"He wouldn't go there just for that," you say. "He was looking for something else."

"Flowers, do you think?"

"An Indian told him there was a magic spring on the island, and if you drunk the water, he said . . ."

"Drank," your mother says.

"Drank. If you drank the water, you would not be old any more."

"What if you were young when you drank it?"

"That was against the law. You had to be old, so your hair would grow again, and your wrinkles would go away."

"I wonder how old Ponce de Leon was."

"I don't know, but he was an avigator, so I guess he was pretty old."

"It was a good thing, then, that he found the spring."

"He didn't find it. He sailed and sailed, but he never found it."

"Maybe he didn't look in the right place," your mother says.

Or maybe it was dark, like the pictures in the book. Or maybe the island was guarded by dragons or monsters with one eye. Or maybe the sailors were afraid the boat would fall off the end of the ocean. Or maybe the winds blew it hither and yon till it was too late.

"Maybe he got too old," you say. "Maybe he got so old that he could sail no more, and he died."

"Maybe," your mother says.

SCENE 32

MEET ME AT THE FOUNTAIN (1910)

So they said in their ads: *Meet Me At The Fountain.* It was in a tea-room on the topmost floor of Macy's, and when you and your mother were in the store, sometimes she'd take you there for lunch, and you'd sit at a table near a window and look down at Herald Square. You'd hear the sound of water falling into water, of words drowned in a blend of voices, of china frictions, an all-around drone that tended you to drowse. And then a fragrance would envelop you, and from wherever you were, you'd return to the display being set before you, steaming pots, little cups and saucers, and a bonbonnière of cakes. There, amid water-pour and murmuring, you were introduced to tea.

There was one uncommon flavor that you favored above all others, and though you never learned its name, the very air that bore it seemed drinkable, and to breathe it was to taste. Was it hyson, you later wondered, was it singlo, souchong, congou, was it pan-fired from Japan, was it Darjeeling, gunpowder, or Assam? You never knew.

It was on one of those days at one of those windows that your mother said, "I want to ask you something, Julian," and you gathered that she'd been watching you wander in your mind.

"What?" you said.

"What are you going to be when you grow up?"

"I'm going to be a lawyer," you said.

And she said, "Why?"

"Because you got to be a lawyer to be a judge."

"Then is that what you're going to be—a judge?"

"A judge of the Sucream Court," you said.

"What would you do if you were a judge of the Sucream Court?"

"I would give out justice for all."

"Did you think of that yourself?" she said.

"I heard Pop say it," you said. "One nation undivisible, with liberty and justice for all."

"Sometimes he makes a joke of it. He says liberty and just us. Or just ice."

"I can tell when he's joking."

"Justice for all," she said, "a very high aim," and then she looked away, not down at the street, the elevated tracks, the trolleys, the people, but over the tops of buildings at the clouds in the sky.

"Why did you ask what I'm going to be?" you said.

"I wanted to know," she said. "In case I'm not here."

SCENE 33

LEATHER BUTTONS (1910)

When you were six, clothes had no meaning for you except as a screen between you and the seasons of the year. There were clean clothes, of course, and there were soiled clothes, and there were those that were thin-spun and those that wore, but clothes as decoration, as shows of style, of sensitivity to cut and color, were foreign to your mind. To this, you can remember but one exception: you delighted in certain white lisle socks that your mother had bought you: they were fine to the feel, sensuous, and sometimes, when they were on your feet, you'd look down to admire their bands of burgundy, black, pale blue, brown.

Save for those several pairs of socks, you were seldom aware of what you wore, and therefore, knowing next to nothing of the extent and condition of your wardrobe, you accepted your mother's finding that you needed a new suit. What had befallen the others you owned (had you outgrown them? were they out at the knee or elbow? were they, unknown to you, passé?) was neither inquired into nor announced. You were in need of a new suit, your mother said, and on a Saturday afternoon, you were taken downtown on the upper deck of a bus to a store called Franklin Simon's.

Through the years thereafter, there were many such rides along Fifth Avenue, and what you saw on that particular day can't be sifted from what you saw at other times. The route, at any rate, was always the same, and as the high green coach blustered southward from Harlem—a Kells, was it, a Métallurgique, a De Dion Bouton?—you must've passed the Mere, just inside the wall of the park, the two parts of the Croton Reservoir, the elms that lined the drives and walks, and, where the park ended, the long street of spires and towers with mansions cowering at their feet. Below the still-building Library, you reached the bon ton area of Gorham's, Tiffany's, and the Union League, and there, at the core of fashion, was the Franklin Simon store.

A floorwalker led you through his textile and fragrant defiles to the Boys' Clothing Department, where a chair was provided for your mother while a sales-clerk fetched you a jacket, that you might try it on for size. He brought more than one before a fit was found, and then, studying your three images in a winged mirror, you saw yourself in cheviot, and you saw yourself in tweed. There came for your pleasure four-button sacks and Norfolks with bellows pockets, and there came Etons of flannel and blazers of serge, but it was mainly yourself, the three Julians, that you read in the glass while, on a handy table, a pile of rejects grew. Nothing had moved you save the Julian at the left and the Julian at the right: they were quite the reverse of the Julian that you knew.

"Oh, I like that one," your mother said, and for a moment you thought she meant one of your faces. Which? you wondered, and as you turned to learn the answer, all three left their frames. "What a pretty little suit!" she said, and she smoothed a shoulder and rolled a lapel. "I think it's very becoming. Don't you, Julian?"

But Julian had turned back to his three images, all of them wearing the same suit of homespun, worsted, gabardine. Whatever the fabric, though, your eyes were fixed on the buttons. Little knots of leather, they were—not buttons of bone nor buttons of brass. They were buttons made of leather!

"Leather!" you said. "I wouldn't wear a suit that has leather buttons."

"They're all the rage," your mother said.

"I don't know what that means—the rage."

"It means the going style. If you have a suit with leather buttons, you'll be dressed in the height of style."

The sales-clerk said, "They wear buttons like that in England."

"I'm not going to wear the suit in England," you said. "And I'm not going to wear it here, either."

"What is your objection?" your mother said.

"I haven't got any objection."

"I thought I heard a fuss about leather buttons."

"That wasn't an objection," you said. "It was a reason."

Did you note your mother's quiet and unspoken exasperation, and if so, why didn't you care? Was it a matter of wills, yours against hers, or was it yours against no will at all? You saw no insistence, you heard no caution against your father's anger—there was only a soft suggestion, hardly more than a weakness for . . . what? Leather buttons?

Your mother looked up at the clerk. "Please show him something else," she said.

And in the end, something else was bought—you can't remember what, but it sported no leather buttons. And then back uptown on the bus you went, past the Library-to-be, past the Temple Emanu-El, Delmonico's, the Savoy Hotel. . . .

SCENE 34

MISS MOORHEAD (1910-11)

You remember her as old—not merely older, as your mother was, or your aunts, but old, an old woman with gray hair wound into a circlet that seemed to move whenever she moved her head. A coil of gray braids like gray snakes, you thought, and she wore them on her head! And you remember too the way she dressed, in shirtwaist and skirt and hidden high shoes of which all you ever saw were the timorous tips. And you remember a watch pinned face-down on her breast (nursing, you'd sometimes think), and you remember that when you looked at her, you thought of *spick-and-span*.

She taught the first and second grades, and her classroom was on the ground-floor of the school overlooking the courtyard kingdom where Childe Julian had lately reigned. A dado of slate banded three of the walls, and in Spencerian script behind Miss Moorhead's desk, the motto of the week was chalked: *To thine own self be true*, it might read, or *Do manly deeds; speak womanly words*. None of these legends had longer than a five-day life, and, come each and every Monday, a new one would appear, born of itself, it might've been, during the weekend lull, and there it would be when the class arrived, another maxim for another round of time: *It is only the first step that counts*.

Your year of Miss Moorhead lies drowned in one overwhelming, one diluvian recall. Lost now the blackboard saying of that fateful week (was it *Who gives quickly gives twice?* was it *Where honey is, there are bees?*), but whatever it may have been (*Things that injure teach?*), that tidal memory floods you yet:

The class was at some fiddling task—plaiting raffia, stringing beads, coloring skies brown and trees purple, and heads were down and tongues were helping hands, when slowly, none knew whence, a most melancholy air began to pervade the room. As it spread, a head was raised here and another there, and soon all heads but the teacher's were up, and every neck was craning. And now the stink reached the front of the room, and the nose of the teacher rose to name and place it. She scanned the two dozen desks arrayed before her—at which sat the backside that had so foully blundered?

"There is a bad smell in this room," she said. "I want the boy who made it to stand up and come forward."

No boy stood, none went forward.

"All right," she said, "I want the girl, then."

But no girl responded, either.

"Someone," Miss Moorhead said, "some boy or girl has done a disgraceful thing. Whoever it was must own up to the deed."

No one owned up, neither boy nor girl.

"Very well," said Miss Moorhead, and after a round-robin glare, she wound up on the pupil in the first seat in the first row. "You!" she said, and she pointed to a spot at her feet.

The boy or girl did as bidden, whereupon Miss Moorhead stooped and sniffed at the back of a skirt — or was it a pair of pants? Knickerbockers or bloomers, whichever it was she tried for a tell-tale smell; she came away with nothing, and, proudly blameless, the pupil went back to the first seat in the first row. And now it was the turn of him or her who sat in the second seat in the first row — and again it was stoop and sniff and swift dismissal.

And so it went, and as the suspects dwindled in number, suspense heightened — and at last, at last! the culprit was reached. Bold as brass till then, a sobbing wretch he or she became when found to be the font of the excremental stench.

"Shame! Shame!" the class cried. "Everybody knows your name!"

What was it? you wonder. Was it Muriel, Cornelia, Esther? Or was it Morton, Leonard, Ormond, Julian?

SCENE 35

A LETTER FROM YOUR MOTHER, NOV. 1, 1911

She wrote it from Monroe, a village in the Ramapo Hills about fifty miles from New York. What she was doing there at that time of year is not now known. You remember nothing of her going away or her coming home, and of the time only a single frame of film is left of the series shot by your mind.

My sweet little son, she wrote

How did you enjoy the battleships. Did Uncle Davey explain them all to you.

I hope you are a good boy and when I go to Lakewood I will take you along with me as I could not enjoy it without you.

There are loads of turkey, geese, ducks, chickens, cows, pigs and ponies out here and I am sorry that you and sister are not here to see them.

I was through the hot houses yesterday where they grow all kinds of vegetables and flowers and fruit and the man gave me a bunch of rare flowers and some fine pears and he also gave me the enclosed

leaf which he cut off of a lemon tree. If you smell it you will see
that it came from a lemon tree.

Be a good little boy and take good care of Ruthy and study your
home lessons.

With a million kisses to you and papa and baby

I am

Your loving Mother

You're on a sightseeing boat with your Uncle Dave and your Cousin Jassie,
and you're looking over the rail at a line of gray ships anchored in the middle
of the Hudson River. You can see guns and turrets, birdcage masts, sailors
on the decks and in wherries riding below. But it's all a great still: nothing
in it moves, ships, men, the current of the stream, and no wind stirs what
clouds may have been in the sky. You see that one exposure, that one slide
of arrested motion, and even that soon disappears.

You can't recall the lemon-tree leaf, and if it ever flavored the folded page,
all that remains is the smell of age.

SCENE 36

THE SEAL OF YALE COLLEGE (1911)

On a triangle of white felt, bright blue letters were disposed in a circle, and
as you lay in bed, they faced you from a wall. The pennant, the only one
in the room, had been placed there by your mother, and you were compelled,
because you knew it held a secret, to try to break the code. Every night you
read the arcane message, and every morning when you rose — *Sigill Coll Yalen,*
you'd say in your mind, *Sigill Coll Yalen,* as though charging the words to
disclose themselves, to make their meaning plain. Given time, they might've
done so, but when your mother died, the pennant somehow vanished, and
for all you knew, she took it along, and it was only on other quads under
other towers that her ciphered wish was known. *Sigill Coll Yalen,* she'd sig-
nalled, and you read her late, on other walks in the shade of other elms.

SCENE 37

AUNT IDA (c. 1890-1969)

You were always glad to see her come. She was your mother's younger sister, and you liked her looks, her high-flown laughter, and the way she whirled about a room, with her hair undone and her skirts abloom. *Juno!* she'd call you as she pinched your cheeks, *Juno!* and then she'd pick you up and press you against her, and you'd breathe her in with the powder she wore, Coreopsis (how can you remember?), and you'd always hate to see her go.

SCENE 38

COTTAGE PLACE, LONG BRANCH, N.J. (1912)

The house was only a block from Ocean Road, and on clouded mornings you'd hurry to the beach to see whether the white flag had been raised over Reynolds' pavilion. If not, there'd be no swimming that day, and its hours would be long. There'd be no strongholds to build of sand and no moats to eat them away; there'd be no clams to dig for, no shells to suck for salt; and, worst of deprivations, there'd be no deeds to dare while seeming unaware of girls. Barred from the shore, you'd be forced to devise an inland pastime, but as you traipsed homeward from the boardwalk, you'd think of certain girls and hope they were aware of you. You'd never spoken to any of them, never been caught staring at this pretty one or that older one with little round things on her chest, and for all you'd allowed to appear, you supposed you were alone at the edge of the sea. But if others were deceived, you knew full well for whom your derring-do was done. Your perilous climbs, your leaps from heights, your somersaults and balancing, your braving of the waves — all were meant to be seen, admired, remembered by the pretty one and the one with those things on her chest.

This was such a day: no flag flew from the pavilion, and the sand belonged to the surf and the gulls. You were on your slow way home along Cottage Place, knowing that soon you'd have to choose among amusements that had all begun to pall. There was that high brick wall behind the house: you could shin up a tree again and pry down into the Hearn Estate, maybe learn at last what Hearn Estate meant. Or you could go to the Long Branch station and watch for your favorite engine, the Atlantic camelback (in your mind, you could hear it breathe). Or you could . . . but as you passed a hedge, you heard something else, and peering in, you saw a nest and in it a gaping almost-naked bird. You were reaching for it when your mother came down from the porch and drew you away with a scolding, the only one you can remember: *Don't ever try to do that again! Once you touched that bird, the mother would never have come back, and it would've died! Do you hear me, Julian?*

You did, but you were thinking ahead to other things, past brick walls, stations, locomotives with seven-foot drivers, you were thinking through the morning and the afternoon and on into the night, thinking of being in bed with the light turned off, thinking of how you'd pretend to be asleep when your Aunt Ida's guest came in — Minnie, she was called, but you never knew whether Minnie was short for Minerva or Minnie was her name. The house was full that week, and a cot for you had been placed in her room. She'd undress in the dark, you thought, but if she left the door open, you'd be able to watch her by the glow from the hall. And you thought ahead to what you might see — what? what was there to see? — and from your cot that night, you saw through lash-lowered eyes as far as petticoats and a camisole. And then for no reason — you hadn't stirred in your sleep, you hadn't feigned a sigh — she crossed to the door and closed it, and you saw no more.

And soon you *were* asleep, and you may have dreamt of breath-taking feats for this pretty one or that one with those little rounds on her chest.

SCENE 39

UNCLE LULU (c.1885-1900)

His name was Louis, but no one ever called him that, and there were some who never spoke of him at all. His coming to mind was an invasion, like pain, and only your grandma seemed able to bear it. *Lulu,* she'd say, and she'd rock herself and see him, no longer seeing you, and you'd try to imagine your own appendix bursting (was it a bomb, you'd wonder, would you hear the explosion?) and your death in a matter of days. He died at fifteen, four years before you were born. There are no likenesses of him, only the look that came to other faces at the mention of his name.

SCENE 40

AUNT RAE (c.1879-1962)

In the ten years you knew of your mother's life, her elder sister appears as a companion so constant that you can hardly recall them as separate people. Where one was, there you'd find the other, just before or just behind, like offsets of the same image. Rae was the smaller of the two, with eyes less blue and darker hair, but even so they seemed to be a double view of a single object. Still, for all the identity they suggested, they were very far from being counterparts within; indeed, when known they were scarcely to be thought of as sisters at all. In their differences of nature, all resemblances were lost.

Your mother, like her own, had the defenceless heart: it was proof against nothing. No plea ever failed to reach it, no sight of anguish, no knowledge of a loss; it had no cortex that sheathed it from the world. It lay exposed to every cup and hat, every *olderly* hand, every merely heard-of scant, and always, in giving quickly, she gave twice, once to relieve another and once to assuage herself. Sister Rae had no such liability. She came from between the same pair of thighs, she held the same blood in equal measure, she breathed air no less rare than your mother did, and she too knew the trend of the time. One, though, was moved to spend; the other one sought to save.

Hers was a cold home, you thought, a flat of six rooms all of them opening off the same side of a hallway. From end to end, a bordered runner ran, rather like a railroad track, and you'd chug along the lines and pretend to be a train. Of the parlor, you can recall only a grand piano that no one knew how to play and that therefore none was allowed to touch, and in the diningroom you still can see mahogany and cut glass in a fall of light from a floral chandelier. Little else returns—a bedroom set of Circassian walnut, still vivid because of the name, and a small round safe embedded in a wall. A cold place, you thought, and you never felt welcome there. Even then, you knew your aunt to be a counter of things, a watcher of food: she knew how many chocolates had been left in the box, how many apples eaten, how many slices of bread, and to avoid the word *chasar,* you'd stop your gluttony at three or four grapes. At table, her portions were stinting, and in the kitchen, except for staples, her cupboards were nearly bare. Was nothing ever left, you'd wonder, were there never any extras for the unexpected guest—and as she numbered her food, did she dole her body's favors?

SCENE 41

UNCLE DAVE NEVINS (c.1884-1947)

In the beginning, he moved through your mind only as a name, one that came with an epithet — *Dov der Wanderer, Dov der wandern Jude* — and you'd hear stories of someone in Bolivia or Peru, and you'd be shown a stamp you'd never seen, a postcard with an outland view. He was younger than your mother, but very near her age, and they were near too in other ways, and it was through her that you grew to know him, to learn of places and things called Titicaca and Illimani and Cerro de Pasco, and you wandered with him as he went sixty-three days in a barkentine from Callao to Port Townsend *blown out beyond the Sandwich Islands ran out of water had to drink rain,* and he sent you coins along with letters written in that quartermaster hand of his, so readable that it almost taught you to read, and you were shown pictures of crocodiles shot in the Rio Ucayali *4/27/09 This is a scene of tropical Peru Love to your new sister and yourself Uncle Dave,* and your mother would hold before you a name and address *Julian Shapiro 2 West 120th St. New York City Estados Unidos del Norte A.,* and she'd say that was you and where you lived.

Sometimes there'd be photographs of him at the copper mines — he wore riding breeches, you remember, and leather leggings — and there'd be a note about the altitude — *14,000 feet,* he wrote — but you wouldn't know what he meant, and you simply stored the number away. And there were times when he came back to the *Estados Unidos,* and you'd see photographs of someone in the uniforms of the California National Guard and the Coast Artillery, and it would be the Wanderer wandering for a while no more. You'd hear then of the Presidio and Big Basin, and you'd stare at a picture called *Paulhan Flying Upside-down at Tanforan* (who was Paulhan, you'd wonder, and where was Tanforan?), and there'd be news from other places, cards with other views, of Siboney, of La Paz, of the Chilean Andes, and you'd store them away with other names and with other numbers — Aconcagua 23,000 feet, and Tupungato, and Mercedario — and all the time you were living in Harlem, in the *Estados Unidos del Norte A.*

He was absent often, but rarely for long, and it was years before you saw that his pattern was flight and return: he'd range far, light for a while, and drift back, and then he'd be gone again, as if he preferred a life on the wing. But in time you saw still further, that he was more driven than drawn from he was the least in his father's eyes. One was bucking away at a wall, and another, all unwitting, had found a door and was dead: the third (*ran out of water had to drink rain*) was thereafter not much fancied, and he became the Wandering Jew.

You remember the room that your grandma always kept for him, you remember the boxes that held his little store of possessions, photos, old lottery tickets, souvenirs, and you remember the books in his closet by Brann the Iconoclast, by Ingersoll, by Tom Paine. But all that came later, along with the letters Debs wrote him from prison to thank him for the Havana cigars and the Panama hat. All that came much later.

SCENE 42

MISS BLAUVELT, TEACHER (1913)*

You were nine years old then, and you didn't know that the name was Dutch and that it meant *field of blue*: to you, it was simply the word you used when you spoke to her or evoked her with your mind. *Miss Blauvelt*, you'd say or imagine, and she'd be there and real or there behind your eyes. Nor were you aware then that you loved her, not at nine. You knew only that in her presence you had to remember to breathe and that the air seemed rinsed, as by a summer rain.

Her hair was braided and worn in a crown, and her face seemed part of her jabot, lawn, it might've been, and in a skirt that reached the floor, she appeared to be something borne, something on the wind, and you could hear her coming toward you and hear her going away; leaves, she sounded like, she made the sound of leaves.

She was your teacher for only a month, but you thought at the time that she'd always taught you and that the term would never end. She'd sail those aisles forever, skim past you on feet you couldn't see, trail the scent of sandalwood through that classroom or the fancied one in your head: there'd be no change; at nine, there was no change.

A day came when she said she had something to tell you, and you stayed after the class had gone for the day. You stood before her desk, you remember, staring at the locket she wore on a velvet ribbon, and you heard her say that she'd not be there the next morning — *lavender velvet,* you thought — no, nor

---

*from *To Feed Their Hopes.*

any other morning: she was going to be married, she said. It was as if she'd spoken of a sickness — *going to be married, going to be dead* — and the room went gray at midafternoon. You'd never see her again, you thought, and you looked up from the locket and tried to draw her in, draw her in, her face, her wreath of braids, the sound she made walking, the smell of sandalwood — you couldn't get enough! — and then you went into a dark hall that led to dark stairs. Where were you going, you thought, it was all dark.

THE COLOR OF THE AIR, IV

DEERFIELD — 1703
LOVERS OF THE UPPERMOST SEATS

FEB. 29, 1703-4

THE UNFORTIFIED HOUSE OF BENONI STEBBINS

STANDING ON THIS LOT WAS HELD BY

7 MEN BESIDES WOMEN AND CHILDREN

FOR THREE HOURS

AGAINST THE ASSAULT OF 200 SOLDIERS

AND THE WILES OF 140 INDIANS

UNDER A FRENCH OFFICER OF THE LINE

STEBBINS WAS KILLED

MARY HOYT AND ONE MAN WOUNDED

WHEN FORCED TO DRAW OFF

THE FRENCH HAD LOST THEIR LIEUTENANT

AND THE INDIANS THEIR CHIEF

The march began in snow, on the south bank of the St. Lawrence, and it wrote itself in three hundred miles of forest along the Richelieu and the Winooski to a stand of pines at Petty's Plain, and there, at the door of Deerfield, in snow it ended. Night was coming on, but no fires were made, though out across the still unwritten fields, fires could be seen inside the palisade. The panes of candled windows shone, and they that lay in the lilac drifts (Abenakis, Caughnawagas, and the French) ate the blown smoke of spitted meat. Two hours before dawn, they defaced the last white mile with their pacs.

All in the village — that is to say, all but its three Negro slaves — had lately engaged in a dispute about who sat where in church. To one of low degree, it mattered little, for his ass partook of his class, and any seat or none would have served; but to the rectal Elect, with their highborn bums, it mattered much. Voices, therefore, rose, and glass houses fell before stones. In the end, it was decreed that seating was to be by age, estate, and station, and the Seaters (Capt Wells, Lieutt Hoyt, etc.) were bidden to follow the following rules:

> *the fore seat in the front Gallery shall be equall in dignity with the 2d seat in the Body of the meeting house*
> *the fore seats in the side Gallerys shall be equall in dignity with the 4th seats in the Body*
> *the 2d seat in the front Galery shall equall in dignity the 5th seat*
> *the 2d seat in the side Galerys shall equall the 6th*
> *the hinde seat in the side Galerys shall . . .*

How sat they when the French and Indians came? Were they shot in the proper order, were their scalps lifted with due regard for rank and riches, or did they die anywhichway, like ordinary sons-of-bitches? No one knows, but however they went, forty-nine were sent to hell that night, where too there were seats to fight for, nigh or far from the fire.

Marched back to Canada—or toward Canada, for not all lived— were some five score captives. One who made it was Eunice Williams, seven-year-old daughter of the Deerfield preacher. Himself taken, he was long later ransomed, but Eunice the Indians would never give up, and though offered as much as a hundred pieces of eight, they said *We would as soon part with our hearts.* Nor was she eager to quit them, and loving them all, she grew to love one, and she married him and lived and died a squaw. She had no use for seats.

SCENE 43

HARK, HEAR THE MERRY MANDOLIN (1913)

Vouched for by Miss Blauvelt, you were permitted to skip a grade, and in the fall of the year, you were advanced to a class presided over by a teacher named McCall. You'd seen her in the corridors and sometimes on the street, and if you thought of her at all, it was with the hope that she might never set eyes on you: by every account, she was a scold at best and at worst a witch. Whenever met, she seemed to be in a fury at something recalled or something on the way. There were no intermissions: she was always asmolder

67

and on occasion ablaze. It was widely believed that she wore a wig.

You remember only two occurrences from the months you spent confronting her desk. They were unrelated except in the sense that one brought on the other, and when memory begins with either, it ends with both.

Miss McCall sounds a key on a pitch-pipe and says, "Colm Conlon, you will now rise and sing the song I've chalked on the blackboard."

There is no response from Colm Conlon: he is slouched in his seat and fast asleep.

"Somebody wake that boy up!" says Miss McCall, but no one stirs. "I said wake that boy up!"

Colm Conlon's neighbor says, "He's tired, Miss McCall, please."

"Tired! What right has he got to be tired?"

"Please, he gets up at five o'clock to go out on the wagon with his father."

"What wagon?"

"The one where they buy old clothes. I CASH CLOTHES! they holler from the wagon."

"To whom do they holler?" says Miss McCall.

"People up in the windows. People with old clothes."

"And what does Colm do to make him tired?"

"Oh, he runs upstairs with the cash, and then he runs down with the clothes."

"From five o'clock in the morning?"

"Yes, ma'am. Till school starts."

Miss McCall glances at her ledger and chooses another name from her list. "Julian Shapiro," she says, "rise and sing," and she gives you the key on her pitch-pipe.

You stare at the chalked ditty, as if under scrutiny the words would do your work and sing themselves. When they fail to respond to your will, you say, "I can't sing."

"Try," says Miss McCall.

"I can't."

"I order you to sing!"

Instead, you begin to cry.

"Julian," says Miss McCall, "either you sing the song or back you go to the class you skipped! Do you hear me?"

You sing. You sing *"Hark, hear the merry mandolin / Its message bringing / Plink, plinka, plinkplinkplink / Silvery sweet."*

The noon bell rings, and when someone reaches out to rouse Colm Conlon, Miss McCall says, "Let him sleep."

§

At the end of the term, you were promoted to a class taught by a friend of your mother's, Miss Titus. She'd been in your home at a *Kaffeeklatsch,* and you'd liked her because of her watch; it was attached to a reel, and when she let it go, it would run up her chest and lie between her titties. Miss Titus, you thought—you liked Miss Titus.

During the term, she forced you to embroider a doily.

SCENE 44

THE FAILING YEARS (1912-14)

When you appeared, they'd break off talk or turn to things of no importance, and you'd go about your doings unaware. You'd play or read or color flags, you'd dispose your leaden armies over floral Persian fields, you'd be intent upon a world at the level of the floor. But always in those days, it would seem darker than the actual hour, as though the sun had lost touch with time, leaving you in the nether shade. In those days, your concern was seldom with other regions, and if you asked any questions, you may not have heard replies.

They told you little of your mother's illness, but you'd not have comprehended if they'd told you much. What would you have made of such terms as valvular affections, of stenosis and diminished circulation of the blood? *Julian,* they might've said, *your mother is suffering from an inflammation of the endo-cardium, which is to say the membrane that lines the cavities of the heart,* but what would you have learned, what would you have seen that was hidden from the eye?

No one had to point out her lack of color—it was as if her blood had been cut with water—and you as well as any knew how easily she tired. For her, no act was effortless—even breathing, for she lacked the power to draw down deep. Stairs were forbidden her, and if she walked too far or stood too long, her feet would fill with fluids that only a day of rest would carry off. And there were other guides, signs posted inside herself showing her destination and the distance she still had to go—the lesions that narrowed the mitral valve, the blowing sound of obstructed blood.

In those days, her mind seemed to be in another country, and as though she found no pleasure there, it was rare for her to smile: she was somber when you came and somber when you went. No one tried to tell you why. No one said *The name of her disease, Julian, is endocarditis, and that blueness you see in her skin is called cyanosis, which results from insufficient aeration of her blood.* No one said *As to the edemic condition of her feet, as to her shortness of breath.* No one said *As to her fatigue, her quietude, her little cough, her gaze at far-off things.* No one said *She's going to die.* But all the same, you knew.

SCENE 45

THE SEASIDE SUMMERS (1909-14)

You never asked, nor were you ever told, who paid for your yearly stays at the shore. At the time, you knew only dimly what money was for: it was pretty paper, you thought, rather like the wrapping on a gift. But it wasn't clear where it came from or ended up when spent, and to you, therefore, it suggested the possession of celestial powers: it could materialize from anywhere, as a deity did in a myth, and it could also disappear. If pressed, you might've ventured the opinion, only slightly more mature, that it issued from your father—it was he who "made money." But at the word "made," what you might've thought of was an actual *making*, a manufacture, and you'd've fancied him cutting the bills, drawing or stamping the faces, printing the green-gold designs.

In fact, the money was supplied by your Grandpa Nevins. Year after year, he was the one who engaged those summer cottages that were dressed in white like summering ladies; you owed all those lawns and driveways to him, the elms, the lilac thickets, the empty stables where oats still lay on the planking and lofts still spoke of hay. But these providences, however you may have regarded them, were primarily for the benefit of your mother: she was the one for whom those sun-struck rooms were rented and those porches in the shade. You were scarcely in mind at all.

Without those asylums on Chelsea, Garfield, Morris, your mother would've sat the summers at some courtyard window, and you'd've played your games in the street. None of the volumes of Hun's Reports would've abated the city's heat, none would've incensed the air against its smell of other cuisines. But for your Grandpa Nevins, your mother would've languished there, declined from low to lower while staring at other windows that gave on other lives. She'd've died the sooner without those women in white on Garfield, Franklin, Cottage Place.

SCENE 46

A NICE QUIET LAW PRACTICE (1909-14)

At the corner of Nassau and Beekman Streets, there stood in those days an old red-brick building named Temple Court. Your father's office was on the topmost story, the tenth, and from some of its windows the East River could be seen, and the piers and cables of Brooklyn Bridge. In the central room, the walls seemed made of sage-green books, all, save for their serial labels, looking much the same. Many a Saturday morning you spent there, immured in buckram and listening to sounds that came as from other cells—the scratching of a pen, paper being torn, the striking of a match.

It was a quiet practice, as your father had said, and the more so it grew through the years. Had your mind been able to range, you might've imagined a change in the framed forensic faces above the several doors: you might've fancied gloom where pride once reigned and tears to be dried on a toga's hem. But you could see only with the eye, and what you saw was things—files and furniture of oak, a fan that turned from side to side, a black safe, the brass fittings of a switchboard. You missed all but the mood that imbued the air, and that only because it must've struck you as harder to breathe. It must've grown heavier, become something less rare than gas, and wherever you were you felt its weight, in the rooms of Temple Court or on your toy estate at home.

A quiet practice, said your father, but he made no reference to his unpaid bills, to fewer and cheaper cigars, and your weekly allowance stayed where it was, at a princely twenty-five cents. Did he speak and joke less often, though, and did your mother leave her rosewood piano closed? And what of the silverware, did it disappear with her emerald brooch, her diamond lavalière? And were they deaf, you wonder, to your momentous concerns—the velocipede you longed to own, the circus at the Hippodrome, a picnic in the park?

Only a handful of their letters remain, some of them undated or lacking an address, some with mislaid pages and meanings incomplete, but even so they plainly tell of your mother's illness and of your father trying to buy her health

I just baked in the warm sun, she said,

and he said *My darling Harriet, I hasten to write, having heard that you intend*

71

coming home. Forget home entirely. Just think of yourself. There is nothing so good for you as rest and since you are away for a rest, you might as well take a good one, and when you come back you will be good and strong.

A thin packet of letters, five or six from each, but there must've been more once, long lost now or long since thrown away, and though you ponder the intermissions, they yield nothing, they never fill. How can you guess what may have passed between the two, what one of them chose to say or the other to withhold? Did she mention the blue at the base of her fingernails, the swelling of her feet, did he promise to join her at Simon's Farm only to beg off with a cold? How often did she apply for a remittance

I received the enclosure in your last letter, she wrote, *and it has already been passed to a third party. Money has a tendency to melt in this neighborhood,*

and what sum did he send in reply? Was it earned at the quiet practice (was a case settled? a fee paid?) or did he post-date a check and then borrow to make it good?

Hard times, as the scanty letters show, but you wish you knew what was said in those that were lost, thrown away, never written.

SCENE 47

OF BOATS AND TRAINS (1911)

During those summers at the shore, matters of business would sometimes take your father to the city on a Saturday, and to give you an outing, he'd invite you to go along. The trip would be made by train, and you'd see the Shrewsbury through the windows, and the Raritan, and then, beyond the Passaic, you'd cross the Hackensack Meadows, a great flat of reeds and cattail and sinuous creeks, and you'd stare out at pig-pens among the ash-heaps, at shanties that seemed to sprout from trash, trash themselves, and then suddenly you'd be in the Hudson tunnel, and the world would be erased.

You'd pass the morning at the office in Nassau Street. There'd be the letter-press to play with, the water-cooler, the switchboard jacks, and at last your father's door would open, and you'd be in a spill of talk about estoppel certificates, mechanics' liens, and quitclaim deeds, and there'd be pleasantries and handshakes, and

Your father would say, "Is it true what I heard about you, kid?"

72

And you'd say, "That depends what you heard."

"I heard you lost your appetite," he'd say,

and then he'd laugh and ruffle your hair and take you to the Astor House or Dewey's or Whyte's and fill you full of food.

And afterward, holding his hand, you'd drift with him along lower Broadway, and now and then, when you glanced upward, you'd feel there was something different about him, something missing, as if his mustache were gone or his Panama hat, but you'd not know what it was until you passed a man who was smoking a cigar: your father was *not* smoking!

"You're not smoking!" you'd say.

And he'd say, "You're very observant."

"After lunch, you're suppose to smoke a cigar."

"It's Saturday. The Sabbath."

"What does that mean—the Sabbath?"

"It's the day God rested. He'd finished making the world, and He rested."

"Maybe He smoked while He rested. That's not empossible."

"When I was younger," he'd say, "my father caught me smoking on the Sabbath, and he made me promise never to do it again."

"Did you keep the promise?" you'd say.

And he'd look at his watch and tell you it was time to start for the docks and the Jersey Central steamer, but there never was time, and before you reached the foot of Cedar Street, you'd be running, and your father would beat you to the end of the pier, where the *Sandy Hook* was waiting, or, your favorite, the *Monmouth,* and after you'd gone aboard, you'd watch the deckhands cast off, and then twin screws would make the river cream, and you'd be sliding downstream toward the Battery and the bay.

From camp-chairs on the wheelhouse deck, you and your father would take in the harbor at twenty-two knots—the tugs and lighters, the car-ferries, the tramps at anchor, riding high and rusting. Below St. George, you'd pass a vessel moored offshore and flying a yellow flag.

"What country is got a yellow flag?" you'd say.

And your father would say, "That isn't the flag of a country. It's the quarantine flag, and it shows there's a contagious disease on board."

"Like swollen glands?"

"Worse."

"What could be worse than swollen glands?"

And then, after dropping the Narrows, the steamer would thread a lane of buoys, and with open sea to the east, she'd begin to roll a little, just enough to make the horizon appear to rise and fall, and then, within the five-mile arm of the Hook, the water would never break at all, it would merely seem to breathe. Soon now the *Monmouth* (was it the *Monmouth*?) would dock between trains on trestles, high black cars with scowling open ends, and then again, from a seat at a window, you'd stare at what you passed, the rip-rap that diked the shore, the Sea Bright dories lounging on the beach, stations called Water Witch and Low Moor—and then you were slowing down for Long Branch.

There'd be a carriage or two at the depot, there'd be sashed summer dresses, parasols, children held by the hand, and amid all these your mother would stand with your sister Ruth. As passengers came down from the cars, there'd be a general coming together, as though all on the platform belonged to the same family, but then groups would slowly form and begin to flow away.

"Did you rest today, Hatty?" your father would say.
And she'd say, "Oh yes. All morning and most of the afternoon."

And then she'd take his arm, and you'd start for home, and with boats and trains you were done for the day.

SCENE 48

EMMA TRENTINI (1912)

On the east side of Broadway, confronting the Metropolitan, were the corner minaret and the Arabesque façade of the Casino, a theatre given over to presentations of light and comic opera. Walking with your father or riding on the cars, you 'd passed its entrance often, but you'd never gone inside. Now, though, this very afternoon, you were due to attend a Saturday matinee: *The Firefly* was playing, and your mother had taken you along.

She was at the box-office wicket, you remember, and you were watching people enter the lobby, filling it with talk, smoke, perfumes, and through the grayed and scented air, beyond the parade of furs and plumes, you could see the bills and photos that lined the walls. All of them, the black-and-whites and the lithographs, were of the same small dark-haired woman, and from one of these in particular, your eyes could not be drawn. In it, she wore a gown that followed her every round and hollow, that traced her bust, her waist, her hips, a satin skin, you thought, that would surely bleed if torn.

Her hands were raised to a lace mantilla, as if to adjust its trail, and she was smiling—at you—through all that smoke and scent, and you let yourself fancy that the very picture of Trentini was about to begin to sing.

You were still fixed there, still bespelled, when your mother spoke behind you, saying, "I'm so provoked I could cry. There are no seats left, only standing room."

With your gaze on the swells and swales on the facing wall, you said, "I would be willing to stand in the standing room."

"I've waited weeks to hear her," your mother said, "but I can't be on my feet for three hours, Julian. It would be too much for me."

She took you somewhere else—anywhere, you thought—and what you saw that Saturday afternoon was a musical comedy called *The Spring Maid.* All you remember of it now is a row of girls with parasols and a row of men in red and white blazers; none of the music comes back, none of the comedy, none of the faces and names. Afterward, you and your mother walked for a while in the Broadway dusk and into the coming-on lights of Longacre Square.

"She has a voice meant for the singing of songs," your mother said. "Lyric, it's called, and hers is small and perfect."

You realized that she was speaking of Trentini, and you thought *small and perfect,* and then you surprised yourself with another thought, *just like her waist.*

"Some day you'll hear her," your mother said, "and then you'll know what I mean."

You never heard Trentini, but you always knew what she meant.

SCENE 49

BY MOTOR-COACH TO MORRISTOWN (1912)

Your mother called it a charabanc, a word you'd never heard. It was French, she said, and it meant a carriage with benches—*char-à-banc*—and when you saw it, you understood. It wasn't a carriage, of course; it was an automobile with six or seven crosswise seats, and for the afternoon excursion, they'd be filled with a party of women and children, and one of the latter would be you. You'd been promised a place beside the chauffeur, and long before the departure, you were down off the hotel porch to inspect the great machine. You climbed the waist-high running board, you tried the buttoned cushions, you took the measure of the tires and lamps and mud guards, and then, drawn by the steering-wheel, you sat yourself behind it, and at once you became driver/rider/engineer/captain of the ship. Trying dangers lay before you, ambush/avalanche/flood/typhoon, and all your skill was called for, all your courage, all your tomswiftery, and fighting the hazards of man and Nature, coolly you worked the wheel/the brake/the shift/the horn—especially the horn! In some way, it seemed essential that in braving peril, you set up a clamor, and, accordingly, again and again you clenched the bulb, and again and again you produced a squawk, ever the same raucous note—and then suddenly, worse luck! the rubber split, and the horn went from a bray to a sigh. You forgot the Scyllas that lay ahead, the maelstrom/the floating mines/the isles of ice, and tried to restore the former sound, but all you could hear was a puff of air. You fled.

When you found your mother, you told her that you'd changed your mind about sitting next to the chauffeur. "I'm going to sit with you," you said.

"I'm glad," she said. "Now I'll be able to tell you about the points of interest. Washington's army was all over this country, and we'll pretend we're with him, we'll be back in the Revolution."

But you weren't thinking of the Revolution. All you could imagine was the motor-coach running the up-and-down road along the Whippany. At either hand and straight ahead, you could see the crossings, the narrow bridges, the errancy of other drivers, pinches requiring the use of the horm—and there *was* no horn!

"In Morristown," your mother said, "there's a place called Fort Nonsense. Isn't that peculiar name? And there's another called Jockey Hollow, where some Continentals mutinied because they were poorly fed and never paid. Won't it be fun to make believe we're there?"

But you were occupied with dreaming up collisions—crushed metal, broken glass, overturns like those of toys—and you had visions of strewn possessions, purses, parasols, gloves, shoes, a sunken fleet of dresses in the stream, and you heard screaming, and you saw blood, and for all such things, the blame would fall on you!

In one of the rearmost rows, you sat with your mother all the way to Morristown. Cars were passed and one-lane bridges crossed, and there were sudden appearances, hidden corners, stirred-up dust, and not once was the horn sounded for the trials of the road. But the moment would come, you thought, when the horn became vital, and just before a crash/an explosion/a roll down a hill, all that would be heard was a faint exhalation, a sigh—and you would be to blame!

At Morristown, you learned that before the coach had left Pine Brook, the split in the bulb had been discovered and repaired. Still, if anything *had* happened. . . .

"This is the Dickerson Tavern," your mother was saying. "Benedict Arnold was tried here for being too friendly with the Tories. He was let off with a reprimand and sent on to West Point. You know what happened there, don't you?"

it *would've* been your fault.

SCENE 50

THE BLACK BOX (1912)

Who broke the glass, you or Jassie? Who tore the curtain, stained the carpet, marred the table, the paper on the parlor wall? Who, Julian—you or Jassie? At the age of eight or nine, neither of you knew how to walk through a room: there was only one speed at which to reach where you were going—high. You must've supposed that whatever you were after was about to disappear. The rolling ball, you thought, would roll itself away, and therefore you pursued your aim in disregard of such baits and snares as waited in your way. In your wake, then, would lie the toppled tabouret, the scored veneer, the rug in disarray, the spilled milk of haste. *Who upset the lamp, who dented the door, the floor, the vase, who made the mirror fall? Was it you, Julian, or, Jassie, was it you?* In your Aunt Rae's household, when neither of you confessed, you were put to the test of The Box.

The box, the Black Box, was an invention of your aunt's. You'd never seen it, but as she described it to you and your Cousin Jassie, it was a container of no great size, plain in appearance and just large enough, she said, to fit over your arm as far as the elbow. Within the box, you were told, there was a magical mechanism possessed of two attributes: one of these was a knowledge of truth; the other was the ability to chop off a liar's hand. *Who cracked the windowpane? Jassie, Julian, who?* and if both of you denied the blame, your aunt would ask if you were willing to submit to the arbitrament of The Box. You were warned, though, that once your arm was inside it, nothing could stop its dreaded action: lie, and your hand was lost! Were you ready, then, your aunt would ask, and you'd say *Yes* and Jassie *No*.

You always said Yes, and always he said No, and you still wonder why your aunt persisted in her use of the Box. Did she hope for the day when (*Who chipped this dish? Who burned that hole?*) Jassie would say *Yes,* and you'd say *No?*

SCENE 51

THE CRIPPLE (1911)

The private house owned by your Grandpa Nevins stood on the south side of 119th Street. It was one in a line of a score or more extending from Seventh Avenue toward Lenox, each of them a face with a basement mouth and several square and staring eyes. After school, you and your Cousin Jassie would meet in front of the family brownstone and play throw-and-catch with a nickel rocket. At such times, not for long did you remain the Boy King in a sailor suit; quickly you became Big Six — Christy Mathewson! — and glaring at Honus Wagner, Edd Rousch, Frank Chance, you were about to pitch the fadeaway. From the numberless crowd ranged around you, a roar arose and stayed aloft — *Strike him out, Matty! Make him do a Casey!* — and winding up for Wagner, Rousch, Chance, Casey, even, you let the ball fly. *Hurrah for Matty!* you plainly heard, *Three cheers for Big Six!* and once more, if the mighty Casey swung, the mighty Casey missed.

There came a day when Jassie also missed and the ball bounced away along the sidewalk and into a neighbor's area, where it rolled through a doorway and disappeared. As Jassie ran to retrieve it, a strange set of sounds came from within the house — sounds that seemed to have been made by metal striking against metal, a clashing, a jingling, as from a shaken tambourine — and then a man, a crustacean! emerged, walking with the aid of canes and dragging his almost useless legs in a pair of heavy braces. You and Jassie stopped short and rubbered as he leaned against a wall and drew the baseball from his pocket, and, dandling it from hand to hand, he watched you watching him.

> For a moment, no one spoke, and then Jassie said, "That's our ball."
> "I don't know about that," the man said. "I found it in my house."
> "Before you can found a thing," Jassie said, "it's got to be lost."
> "You talk like a lawyer. Are you a lawyer?"
> "My father is a lawyer," you said.
> "We want that ball," Jassie said. "It belongs to us."
> The man said, "His father is a lawyer. Why don't you sue me?" and up

went the ball from one hand, and down it came into the other.

Jassie said, "You got no right to keep that ball just because it went in your house. That's stealing, and you could be arrested."

"You're starting to get snotty," the man said. "I don't like a snotty kid."

"And I don't like thiefs!" Jassie said.

"That'll cost you one baseball," the man said. "Get out of this airy-way!"

"I won't get out," Jassie said, "and you can't make me! You're only a cripple!"

Supported by the wall behind him, the man was able to kick, and his leg, caged in steel rods, struck Jassie on the hip and knocked him to the pavement. "Take that little bastard out of here!" the man said to you, "or you'll get some of the same!"

You helped Jassie to his feet and up the steps to the sidewalk level, and, crying as he went, he limped off toward your grandpa's house.

The man called after him. "Now who's the cripple?" he said.

That evening, you were told, a doctor was called to treat Jassie's bruise, a green and purple blotch that covered most of his lower back. From your father, who was also summoned by the Perlmans, you learned that there was concern about a possible curvature of the spine. *Cripple,* you thought, and the word still shocked you, even within your mind.

"Aunt Rae and Uncle Harry are talking about charging the man with assault and battery," your father said. "If they do, you'll be called on to tell what happened. What will you say?"

Cripple, you thought, and you said, "I'll tell what happened."

"What *did* happen?"

"Nothing," you said, "till Jassie called the man a cripple."

"If you say that, the police will let the man go."

"I would have to say it."

"Why?"

"Because if you was there, you would say it too."

SCENE 52

AN ILL WIND (1912)

Across the foot of the photo, a writing reads *Pine Brook, N.J.* In the frame above, seated on a boulder in a sloping field, are your mother and father, and you and your sister are leaning against their knees. Beyond the four of you, the field runs away toward a ridge of trees—runs, you think, and in your fancy it does run, as if stirred again by the wind of the day, and the images, though posed on paper forever, seem held for just the moment required by the lens. You feel, therefore, that you're living in two times and two places, those of the picture and those of the world outside: you peer in, as a camera once did, and you gaze out with an eight-year eye.

Pine Brook, you think, and plainly a stoned little stream appears, flowing slowly to join the Passaic a mile or so away. You see the sand square of a made beach, and out past a sagging guard-rope, you flounder in the current and hear your mother scream. . . .

Pine Brook, and while picking berries, you're stung by a bee, and from a spot on your palm, heat spreads in all directions, and you feel a throbbing in your fingers, as if your skin were too tight for your hand. . . .

Pine Brook, and you activate a hotel lawn — you people the shade of parasols, you wind up children and make them go, you watch your mother stop to rest as she climbs the verandah stairs. . . .

and you see yourself wandering in the area behind the kitchens — you pass the bakery, the ice-house, the laundry, the boiler-room, and then a KEEP OUT sign on the poultry-yard merely makes you go in. A man in a flat black hat and a long black coat takes a Leghorn from a crate and looks up at the sky (at what? at whom?), and as you follow his glance, he casts the bird away. You watch it land and begin to flee, and in a red and stunning flash, you see that it has no head. But it's running! you think, it's running! — and then with as little direction, you're running too. . . .

and at a depot down the road, you wait for trains, and when one of them finally comes, you stare at the engine, stopped just short of a tunnel, where it coughs softly and blows off steam. You ask where it's going, and the engineer nods at the tunnel and says *Livingston Manor,* and then the train begins to move. You read the lettering on the tender — *Lackawanna* — and you read it six times more on the cars, and now the train is gone. . . .

and a day in the hotel diningroom, and in the middle of a meal, you feel a sudden distention in the region of your navel, and hurrying out, you head for a door marked MEN a hundred feet away. Not yet at your goal, you mistake your symptom, you put your trust in Aeolus when in fact there was no wind, and, oh God, right there in the hall. . . !

Pine Brook, you think, and the year was 1912.

SCENE 53

THE MAN WHO KNEW GYP THE BLOOD (1912)

Your father had four brothers, three of them older than he and one younger. The last was named Jacob, but to you he was Uncle Jack. A favorite of your father's, he was often in your home, and even now, after seventy years, you can see him there smoking his cigarettes. Hassans, they were called, and Murads, and Turkish Trophies, and in some of their vivid boxes came a little square of leather embossed with a collegiate seal. Of several hues, those favors were, reds and greens and browns and blues, and they were twice fragrant, of themselves and of the fragrant weed. He'd save them for you, bringing many on every visit (Swarthmore, Bowdoin, Cornell, Purdue), and meaning one day to work them into a cushion-cover, your mother would put them away against the coming of the time. Now and then, you'd open the drawer they were kept in, and from the stacks of sorted colors, perfumes would make their flavors known, and you'd breathe deep, dreaming half-drugged of far-off things, but you never dreamt that your mother would die before the first of the leathers was sewn.

Later, when your father told you more than he'd chosen to tell you then, he used the word *shady* in speaking of Uncle Jack. "I don't mean dishonest," he'd say. "I mean he's drawn to the darker side of the street," and when you asked what drew him, he'd say, "Dark things."

In a certain brownstone on the darker side of Lenox Avenue, your Uncle Jack ran a faro-like gambling game called *stuss,* a Yiddish word from the Hebrew *shtuth.* Like any other card-game, it could be played for low stakes or high, as the players chose: at your uncle's baize, lights shone down on yellowbacks only, and piles of paper glowed. Being the proprietor, he took no part in the game: his earnings for maintaining the house and furnishing food and drink were derived from splits in the betting. One night, as he recounted to you himself, his share came to four thousand dollars, and as he walked home along the quiet avenue, a pistol was put against his back, and he was forced into a doorway (a dark one? you wondered, on the darker side of the street?).

"All your money," the gunman said, "and don't turn around."
"I don't have to turn around," your uncle said. "It's Gyp." And he did

turn around, saying, "Damn it, Gyp, this isn't much of a joke!"

"It's no joke, Jack. I want all that money. I saw you put it in your pocket."

"And six other people saw you watching! How long do you think the leader is going to let you keep it?"

"Nobody gives any orders to Gyp the Blood!"

"Gyp," your uncle said, "you don't need four thousand dollars for your nose candy. Here's a hundred. Buy a sniff and go home."

But Gyp insisted, and finally your uncle shrugged and handed over the money. The next day he spoke to the district leader, and within an hour he had the money back, along with a new wallet to replace the one that Gyp had thrown away. *Poor Gyp,* your uncle said, and he shook his head. When you reported the story to your father, you asked him about Gyp and why Uncle Jack had called him poor.

"He went to the Chair," your father said.

"For taking Uncle Jack's money?"

"For killing a man named Herman Rosenthal, a gambler. Gyp and Lefty Louie and Dago Frank, they shot him in front of the Hotel Metropole, and they all went to the Chair."

The shady side of the street, you thought.

SCENE 54

UNCLE DAVE (1913)

In the nine or ten years of your life, you'd never known anyone to match the Wandering Jew. Others were quite as real, of course, others had weight and mass and cast a shadow, but only he was a fiction too. When he told you of booby-birds and crocodiles, when you heard such words as Cerro de Pasco and Titicaca and Cochabamba, he seemed to be more than a teller of tales; somehow he became the tales as well. He was the magician, and he was the spell, and when he lifted the lid of his steamer trunk, you felt you were about to be shown his elixirs and potions, his store of wizard tricks, and indeed from his carefully folded clothes, the fragrance, the spirit of secret places arose, as if the air there were perfumed.

Late that fall, from wherever he may have been (Bolivia? Chile?), he returned to New York to attend the wedding of his sister Ida. He'd been absent for more than a year, ever since the dissolution of a partnership with his brother-in-law Harry. There'd been a dispute over nothing you knew of: your memory shows you only a shutter-instant of your Uncle Dave's anger, and then it comes to a close. But you do know that within a week of the quarrel, he was gone (to Ecuador? Peru?) and that now he was back from Bogota or Arequipa—your favorite uncle, the Wandering Jew, had wandered home.

In his affections, your mother stood next after his own, and your ranking with him was therefore high. He neither displayed nor spoke of it, but even so it was known to all: he had a preference for your mother and through her for you. Between his many migrations, he'd take you about with him wherever he went, but he spent no time in parks, and you were shown no nickelodeons or menageries (*They ought to put the people in the cages,* he said, *and let the animals go*). Instead, unable to endure a street that was straight, he'd find himself a winding one, and the two of you would end up at a boat-works along the *Rio* Harlem, or in the engine-room of a ferry, a *barca de pasaje,* or in the yards of the New York Central, which he called a *ferrocarril.* He'd stop anywhere to dig around in a bin of books, and if he came up with a prize, coverless, torn, soiled, he'd cry *A pamphlet by Terence Powderly!* or *Pinkerton's lies about the Molly Maguires!* And then he'd stomp off, swearing, scolding, carrying on about somebody named *Lackeys—the Lackeys of Wall Street—*till people turned to stare. He'd thumb his nose and say something funny, like *Running dogs of the ruling class!* and you'd both begin to laugh. *Running dogs,* you'd think, and at times you'd laugh when he wasn't there.

The wedding would take place on Christmas Eve, and as the event drew near, and with it the season, he spoke of a bridal gift for Ida and a Chanukah gift for you. But he had another nephew, your Uncle Harry's Jassie, and he lacked the heart to slight him for being his father's son. Accordingly, he took both of you to Macy's one day, and there, in the color and flash of its toy paradise, he told you what he had in mind. There were to be two presents of equal cost, he said: one was a large-size set of Meccano, the erector-set of wheels, rivets, and steel strips; the other was a three-day trip to Washington in his company. As your elder, Jassie was to have first pick, and he chose bang-off—the set of Meccano. Good, said your Uncle Dave, and when he added *Allagazam!* all paradise could hear the three of you laugh.

Great things were on the way—the wedding, the trip, the holidays—and you could see them coming, enjoy them before they came. But there was a leak in your cup of pleasure, a small one, true, but through it pleasure seeped, and the rapture-level fell. The diminution was caused by Jassie's relentless crowing: *I'll have that Meccano set long after your trip is over!* he said. *It's made out of iron or something! It's unbreakable! I'll still be playing with it when you forget*

83

where Washington is! You couldn't help wondering whether he was right. After all, that Meccano set was a thing, and you could see it and feel it. The pulleys and cranks, the cables, the perforated girders—you could weigh them, they were real. But a trip to Washington wasn't a thing at all: it was a ride on a train, and once you were there, what could you do but come back? You wouldn't even be sure you'd gone to Washington. For all you knew, you might've gone to Wilmington. So maybe Jassie was right; maybe he'd gotten the better present: *I'll be building stuff all my life—derricks, elevators, skyscrapers! And what'll you be doing? You'll be wishing I'd've picked Washington and left the Meccano for you!* Maybe, you thought, and another drop of pleasure drained away.

The wedding was celebrated in the banquet rooms of the Hotel Martinique, and what you remember of it is limited to a glimpse of white (a train? a veil?) and the color gray, worn by your aunt when, late in the evening, she tossed her bouquet on her way to the door. You can summon up no other sight: you can see no face or gown, and you hear no music or laughter or silver on china or the sound of your father's voice, if it was he who made the speech on the dais. Only a menu remains to fix the date and name the place. . . .

Sherry Amontillado was poured before the *Puree St. Germain,* and you wonder what your mother wore that night, whether she was well for once or weary, short of breath, blue beneath her rouge. And when the *Sea Bass Joinville* was served, did she let it lie untouched and sip her *Graves* instead? Could you see her from the children's table (whose children? and what were their names?), and when you saw the *Sorbet Prunelle,* did you know the yellow ice was made of yellow plums? And when the *Cassette of Sweetbreads* came, were you aware of where it came from—the pancreatic gland? And with the *Squab sur Canape,* were you allowed to try the *Grand Imperial Sec?* Was your father really called on, and as he raised a glass to Ida, what brotherly thing did he say? But only the menu remains, and all it tells you is *Bon Bons, Assorted Cakes, Ice Cream Souvenir.* . . .

The morning after Christmas, you were on the Congressional Limited as it slid down the tunnel under the Hudson and then climbed up to the Hackensack Meadows, a great marsh, your Uncle Dave told you, and along its tidal creeks, he said, bobolinks bred among the marigolds, and wrens and red wings too. And then there were miles of rivers, factories, leafless woods, farms that at a distance looked like little towns, and all the while your Uncle Dave ran on about the Jersey campaigns of the Revolution, about Monmouth over there on your left and Princeton on your right, and every so often he said one of his funny things, like *Lickspittles of the rich!* and then he led you to the dining-car, and you were eating turkey and biscuits as you crossed the Delaware (once, when they crossed the other way, he said, there were men who ate their belts), and afterward you sat on the observation platform, watching track flow out from under the train, watching trees and poles and the world run away—and then it was Washington. . . .

And then you were coming back.

With you came a headful of images, picture postcards, almost, a deck of disconnected views. They were piled in your mind as if for a magic-lantern showing on a sheet—now you saw the Monument, and soon you'd see the Dome. They were all there inside your skull, a pack of colored stills, but when you tried to give them order, they seemed to lose even their chance arrangement, and you were left with a confusion of sights, the Navy Yard merging with a mast of the *Maine,* the Mansion with the Mary Custis grave. The box at Ford's, the Petersen house across the street, the too-small bed you stood beside—all such particular things became a daze of blending exposures, and on the ride northward you tried to tell yourself that some day they'd be single again and fall into sequence, and you'd be able to say to Jassie that you weren't sorry, that you'd gotten the better present after all. But you couldn't, you couldn't.

For some reason, your Uncle Dave never gave Jassie the Meccano set, and you never found out why. Jassie might've made one of his fresh remarks, or he might've dropped the *Uncle* when saying *Uncle Dave,* but whatever it was, your cousin built himself no hoists with those little strips of steel, no lighthouses, no cathedrals. Alas, poor Jassie crowed no more, and in time he may have forgotten the large-size box of girders and bolts, just as, once they were over, you forgot your three days in Washington, forgot that room where a man died in a too-small bed with a ball in the back of his brain. . . .

THE COLOR OF THE AIR, V

THE DECLARATION—1776
REBELLION OF THE WELL-FED

> *. . . our lives, our fortunes, and our sacred honor.*
> —Declaration of Independence

There were fifty-six signers, all of them Gents: fourteen lawyers (among them a part-time moneylender), thirteen jurists (one a musician, *a writer of airy and dainty songs*), eleven merchants (i.e. smugglers), eight farmers (two being Tidewater rubes by the name of Lee), four physicians, a pair of soldiers, an ironmonger, a publisher, a politician, and the President of Princeton.

The Mob did not sign. The sailmakers, the cartwrights and the glassblowers, the grooms, the tapsters, the drovers and drayman—none such signed. The barbers, the fiddlers, the Wandering Jews, the horse-copers, the hatters and glovers, and those that stomped the high road with or without their scarlet letters—none of these signed, none made a mark. Only Gents wrote their John Hancocks, not cheap Jacks, not swabs or sweeps or keepers of an ordinary, not joiners or tinkers or catchers of rats at a penny a pound. That kind had lives, of course, but no fortunes, and therefore no sacred honor. The nobodies thus were missing—the mercer, the chandler, the hanger-on, the muff. To the City of Brotherly Love, no rough fellow, no greenhorn went, none but the Gent.

SCENE 55

THE CHARACTER COMMITTEE (1914)

There was a wind that day, and it blew at your backs as you and your father made your way up Park Row past the Tribune Tower and the abutment of Brooklyn Bridge. You could almost have stopped walking, you thought, and still you'd've been moved by the force behind you. The air was filled to visibility with curls and veers of dust, and scraps of paper flew and lurched, and once, between the trolley-tracks, a hat rolled as if someone had bowled it, but the sun shone all through that fall afternoon, and you felt you were breathing flakes of gold.

You noticed the man as soon as you turned the corner of the City Court building. He was still some way off, standing in the middle of the sidewalk, unaware that he was dividing the flow of passersby; nor was he aware of anything else, you thought, the wind, the glare, the time of day; he may not have known he was there. As you gazed ahead at his rose boutonnière, at the slant of his hat and his satin lapels, the word *dapper* came to your mind— *dapper,* you thought until you were almost abreast of him, and it was only then that you saw the wear and tear, the fray, the patch, the shine, the rose of the day before. You were taken by surprise when your father spoke to him.

"Glad to see you, Randy," he said, and he stopped to offer his hand.

The man came back slowly, as from another place or even another time. "Why, Philly Shapiro!" he said. "What a pleasant encounter!"

"This is my boy Julian. Julian, say hello to an old friend of mine, Mr. Randolph Samuels."

"A fine boy, Phil," the man said, though he hardly looked down to see. "How's Geschäft?"

"Quiet, Randy, quiet. And how goes it with you?"

And now the man did look down, but still, you felt, without remarking you. "Quieter," he said.

Then there was another handshake, and you and your father walked away along the railings of City Hall Park. *Seedy,* you thought, and you said, "Who was that man?"

Your father took a moment to answer, and by then you'd reached Broadway. "A lawyer," he said, and the wind ran off with the words. "He used to be a lawyer."

"I didn't know a lawyer could stop being a lawyer."

Ahead of you, the mile-long straightaway to Waverly Place was filled with glass-flash and whirling dust. "He didn't stop of his own accord," your father said. "He was disbarred."

"What's disbarred?"

"A lawyer is an officer of the Court, and that gives him the right to appear before the Bar. If he does bad things, though, the right can be taken away from him. That's called disbarment."

"What kind of bad things would he have to do?"

"Well, the Court would say it was a bad thing if he perjured himself— that means if he told lies under oath. Another bad thing would be if he used

87

money that belonged to a client. Lawyers can do many bad things."

"Which ones did Mr. Samuels do?"

"I really don't recall," your father said. "It happened years ago."

"He looked so good from far away," you said.

"And when you were near?"

Seedy, you thought, but you said, "Sad."

Leonard Street, Walker, Canal, Grand. "Sad," your father said. "That's a good word for him. That's what he is — sad."

Spring, Prince, Houston Street. "If Mr. Samuels done a bad thing," you said, "why did you talk to him, why did you shake hands?"

"What would you have done?"

"I would've been too proud to shake hands with a man that done a bad thing like lying or stealing."

"Suppose you'd known the man all your life," your father said. "Suppose you'd been boys together, gone to school with him. Suppose you'd been in his office and his home. Suppose you'd tried cases against him, played cards with him."

"I'm supposing," you said.

"Do you still think I should've passed him by as if he were a stranger?"

"Yes, I do! He done a bad thing!"

"You're right," your father said. "He done a bad thing. Instead of speaking to him, I should've kicked him. Instead of shaking hands with him, I should've spit in his face. That would've shown I was just as proud as you."

Bleecker, Bond, West 4th. *But the man done a bad thing,* you thought, and for a way you had nothing more to say.

"There's nothing wrong with being proud, kid," your father said. "But make sure you've got something to be proud of."

SCENE 56

EASTER IN ATLANTIC CITY (1914)

Your own holiday was celebrated in the same season: even as Christ rose from the dead and lived again, the children of Israel rose from the death of bondage. Take you, said the Lord in the age of the Pharaohs, take you a lamb without blemish, and on the fourteenth day in the month of Nisan, kill it and strike the blood thereof on your sideposts and lintels, that I may know your houses and harm them not as I pass over them to smite the first-born of Egypt, and His will was done, and the time came to be called the time of passing over.

Your mother had long been ill, and she was told to seek a change of air.

A change of air, the doctors said, as if in a place other than where she was, she'd breathe a new mixture of gases, one freer of dust and spores of yeast, one that contained more or less of xenon and less or more of water vapors. A change of air was required, they said, and in that season of bread without leaven and the risen Christ, she sought it by the sea.

She took you along with her. You were almost ten, heedless in the main, willful, hardly one she could talk to freely, and no help in case of need. Still, she must've wanted you to be with her, as if she feared to leave you, her first-born, behind. Of the journey from Manhattan, nothing has remained in your mind, neither the railroad (the West Jersey, was it, or the Reading?), the salt meadows, the barrens, the trees and towns and rivers passed. Pictures begin at the sideposts and under the lintels of a hotel, the Marlborough-Blenheim, and though faint at first, they clear as you near a man named *Reception*

do you see the actual face behind the desk, the stares of real guests, the exact bellboy, the one who was truly there, and do you hear the self-same page crying the self-same name — does memory bring back fact or fancy? Did someone verily say (the hotelier?) that the house was full, that he regretted, etc., that perhaps on another occasion, etc., and did he suggest the Shelburne, madame, or the Chalfonte, or the Royal Palace — or, with his gift of tongues, did he venture *Le Palais Royal. . . ?*

Hours later, when it was nearly dark, your hotel turned out to be the Islesworth *on the Boardwalk at Virginia, capacity 500, American plan, open all year, Wm Hyman, prop.,* and by the time a room was arranged for and your clothes were put away, your mother was weary, and she sent you down to dine alone

was she asleep when you returned, did you note her expression, her bluish beauty, did you sit at her side and watch her work at breathing?

Remembered or not, the room must've spoken of the sea. The carpet, the curtains, the walls and woodwork, the wicker chairs, all must've been as salt-seasoned as rigging. A change of air, the doctors said

when she woke, did she seem to see nothing for a moment, as if she were still in a dream, and did you wonder what the dream was about, or where it took her, or whether you were along, and when she finally saw you, did she say (or do you merely assume she said) *Did you have enough to eat?*

Yes, you told her if the scene took place — yes, you said, and then you read her a letter to your father that you may have written while below. It was on a sheet of Islesworth stationery, and under the date April 9, 1914, it read:

Dear Pa, I hope you are feeling well. We have changed hotels. I like this one better. How is baby. I am enjoying myself very much and wish you were with me. Please write to me as soon as you can. With love from all, I remain, your Loving son Julian. What did she say—that it was a good letter? And did you really think you were at a better hotel? Because it wasn't, she might've told you—it couldn't hold a candle to the Marlborough-Blenheim.

And now you again, Loving son Julian—did you ask why the Marlborough had refused you a room? And if so, did she say that they'd thought you were Jews? And then did you say, or do you wish it, *How did they know we were Jews?*

Was she slow to answer, did she go back down to her dream, leave you there in that mildewed room to wonder why you thought she was dying and soon would be dead. Dying, dead—but the words brought no meaning, and you let them fade. *How did they knew we were Jews?*

And what did she say to Loving Julian? That they knew without knowing your name, without hearing you speak, and that those who were facing away knew with the backs of their necks. *They know,* she may have said.

And did you say *What've they got against us? What did we do?*

And did she say *They claim we killed God's son, a man named Jesus.*

And did you say *How can you kill God's son? God wouldn't let you.*

And did she say *They believe he came back from the dead, and this is their holiday for his resurrection. They call it Easter.*

Three months more, and she was dead, and, behold, never has her stone rolled away and she risen.

SCENE 57

THE HOTEL AND BOARDINGHOUSE YEARS (1912-14)

In later times, your father seldom spoke of those last two years of your mother's life. It was as though they belonged to him, and even as an only son, you came to feel that they were a sovereign country, to be entered by permission, and then only within a given range. All the same, there was much you might've divined at a distance, known in your own country, and you marvel still that so little crossed your mind. A great change was in the making, but save for the laden air, it seemed not to have been perceived. What was taking place in that skinful of yourself, you wonder, what so concerned you that you hardly saw the doctors, their pince-nez, their pearl-gray spats? What games were you so deep in on the floor, what toys so absorbed you through those two years of gloom—or, on a San Juan Hill of carpet with your regiments of lead, could you almost be said to have left the room?

What you might've learned had you listened was that your father's funds were running out. His savings were dry and his earnings low and growing lower, flowing away in doctors' fees, in your mother's trips to the Pines and the seaside, in medicines, nursing, tonic wines. Had you heard above your gunfire at Bloody Angle, had you seen through your thought-up trees and smoke, you might've caught sight of your father's face when he said (did he say it?) that your home would be going next. There'd be no more of that oak and crystal world: the sideboard would be stored or sold, and the punch bowl and its set of cut-glass cups; and sold or stored the rosewood Knabe and the matching pivot seat; and to some other wall or none the Barbizon meadow and the pennant seal of Yale. All such things would be lost, and with them, in some chest of drawers, your hoard of card-size chromos that came with cigarettes—pictures of beacons (Ocracoke and Beachy Head), pictures of theatres (the Hippodrome and Drury Lane). Coming, he might've said, were the hotel years, the boardinghouse years. . . .

Hotel Cecil: You can see the entrance, but not even in your mind can you make yourself go in. For all you know, the plate-glass doors give on nothing; there's no lobby, no desk, no stairway to the upper floors; there's no inward, you think, no third dimension to the outer wall. Still, as though from nowhere, as a wind seems to rise, a boy emerges and hastens across the street (you're watching you!), and then, clutching a small bottle of cream (whose coffee was growing cold?), he hastens back. Alas, he trips on the curb and falls, and you fall with him, and lying side by side, the two of you stare at cream streaming over the pavement past islands of broken glass. And then you see the entrance again, and the rest of the memory dies down, as a wind does. . . .

Mrs. Behr's: You see the place in fractured glimpses, as through the pickets of a fence. Each is partial—you have no time for the full view, the act begun and ended, the completed speech. There are fragments only, and when put together, they make no more than a mass of fragments . . . two rooms (three?) that run the house from front to rear . . . you at a table copying the flag of Hesse-Cassel from a book called *Flags of the World* . . . a diamond you find on the floor (a million ice-cream combs!) that turns out to be a rhinestone . . . watching your mother dress for the theatre, a sight of white kid gloves that reach her elbows . . . asking her *How long do people live?* and as she starts to answer, *They live to be,* you hear and see no more. . . .

Mrs. Zimmerman's: You can't recall how long you stayed there, or even where it was, and all that's left of those weeks or months is a single image that comes back with sound and motion. The son of another boarder is showing you an apple-crate that he has made over into a stage. Kneeling behind it, he raises a curtain of shirt-cardboard, revealing a painted backdrop of columns and corridors, and then he moves some figures out from the wings, and he makes one of them say *Et tu, Brute!* just before he falls. . . .

Stein's Hotel: All the floors were tiled, you remember, as if the place were a six-story toilet. The lightest touch would roll a chair away, and a bed would move as you moved in your sleep . . . and in the halls, sometimes you saw a woman with black hair, and there was a glitter about her, a sequin air . . . and off a marble entry, there was a Biergarten where you sat with your mother once and watched dancers doing the *Turkey Trot*. She was sipping grenadine, you remember, but she didn't tell you it was merely a drink made of red currants; all you could think of was the word *drink*. . . .

Those were the hotel years, the boardinghouse years.

SCENE 58

THE DOWRY (1914)

Only once did your father make mention of the money your mother had brought to the marriage. It came to seventy-five hundred dollars, he told you, but he never regarded it as his, and he held it in trust for her until the hard times that followed the Panic of 1907. Then, with your mother's consent, perhaps even at her suggestion, he lent the entire fund to your Uncle Harry, who, hard-pressed, required it in order to complete the construction of a walk-up on Washington Heights. The property was soon lost to a mortgagee in foreclosure proceedings, and along with it went your mother's dowry. For several years, though in need himself, your father refrained from calling in the loan, but during the last few months of your mother's life, he was forced to appeal for a return of the money.

"I told him I was broke. I said your mother had been sick for a long time, and I had to have some money to pay the bills. I'd spent all I had, I said, and I'd borrowed where I could, and now there was nothing but the dowry."

"What did he say?" you said.

"He professed surprise. I hadn't lent him the money at all, he said—I'd invested it. I'd been his partner, and the money was gone."

"Did you stand for that?" you said.

You've never forgotten the look on his face. It was as though he were gazing at something distant, as indeed it was in time, and what he saw seemed to stir no memory of anger, only a mild sort of wonder that he hadn't been angry. "I said if that's how you say it was, Harry, then that's the way it was."

"I wouldn't've been so easy! I would've sued him!"

"It was his word against mine, Julian."

"But you're the one I believe!"

"You weren't there, kid," he said, and then, after a long time, "So you think your old man is honest."

SCENE 59

VARIABLE WINDS (1903-14)

Note: *These letters, along with two or three others given in full or quoted from elsewhere, are all that remain of the correspondence between your father and mother. That there once were many more is plain enough from a reading of those that survive. Your mother's indifferent health occasioned an unusual number of absences from home, and to these must be added her summers in the Catskills and along the Jersey shore. Being both of them proficient in the use of language, your father and mother must have written freely to each other at such times, and what was lost of such exchanges leaves runes that can never be unraveled.*

1. — An undated letter

Only page 3 is left of it, and what writing it holds is on the letterhead of Friedman & Feinberg, Real Estate, 329 East 116th St., New York, Tel. 255 Harlem. (Friedman was your father's brother-in-law Harris, husband of his elder sister Sarah). For some reason, your father gives his business address below his signature; from this, it would appear that the letter was written in 1903. It reads:

There is nothing to write at present besides to impress upon your mind the fact that you must enjoy yourself and get all the air you can.

I will close this little letter to my dear little wife, so good and so true, who is the sweetest on earth and no sweeter in heaven, with many kisses and fondest of thoughts

from your dear and bum husband
Philip Danl Shapiro
320 Bway N Y City

Give 2 kisses to mother   love to mother
Give 1 kiss to Ida
Give ½ kiss to Jerome   Regards to all

2. — An undated letter

Of this too, only page 3 is extant. The writing is on the stationery of Shapiro & Shapiro, Attorneys and Counselors at Law, 320 Broadway, New York. (The senior member of the firm was your father's eldest brother Aaron). The page reads:

> Miss Kayser rang me up on the telephone a few minutes ago and wanted to know what became of you as she has not seen you so long. I gave her your address and she said she would write you; you ought to drop her a line.
> There is nothing else that I can say just now except to state again that I *love* you and send you 100 kisses.
> Give my love to mother and children.
> Kiss mama for me when you are through reading this letter, and do not forget it; tell her this is from

Phil

3. — An undated letter

It is written on the letterhead of a new law partnership, Shapiro, Morrison & Shapiro, but the address is still 320 Broadway, New York. A reference in the fourth line suggests that your mother was pregnant, wherefore the time of the writing may have been late in the summer of 1903. The letter reads:

> Hatty Darling
>
> How are you spending your days and *nights*. I want you to get all the benefit out of your trip that you possibly can, as it will serve you well later on. There is so much noise in and around here that one can hardly write and the noise is enough to distract your attention from your writing, but I have only one thought and that is of you: my mind and thought can never be distracted from that thought.
> Hatty Darling tell papa that Harry has made a mistake in his letter to him about a Mr Rosenbaum, he need not answer that letter.
> Hatty Love, Harry has just handed me a piece of candy, and he says it will sweeten the tone and expression of this note. Now I do not think that he is absolutely right. Nothing but my being with you, with you in my arms and your eyes on mine could lend expression and taste to the situation, but will console with your letters in the meantime. Darling Wife, I will close with love and 1,000,000 kisses

to you. Remember me to all at the house Mama papa and children. Good night Darling my love from your faithful and ever loving husband

Philip

4.-A letter dated July 21, 1904

The envelope, bearing a New York postmark, is addressed to Mrs. P. D. Shapiro, Elka View Hotel, Tannersville, Greene County, New York. The enclosure reads:

My dear Harriet:

You have no doubt received my telegram on Saturday explaining the reason for my not writing. The facts were these that all day Friday I was very sick with an attack of the grippe and sore throat & very bad stomach and up to this writing I have not tasted any food since Wednesday night. I have just had a plate of soup for the first time. I am going to see Dr Einhorn tomorrow morning without fail as I can stand it no longer I must attend to my stomach otherwise it will become chronic and I will not be able to cure it.

Don't let this worry you Hatty dear, as I am feeling much better today.

Friday evening I had Dr Braslau and he prescribed for me and Saturday I saw Dr Agatston and he burnt my throat and I feel relieved today.

I presume you have seen Charlie by this time and he has delivered my regards. How did you enjoy yourself at the Ball Saturday night. I hope I did not interfere with your going to and enjoying the affair as you have looked forward to it with some pleasure. I was sorry I could not have seen you that evening, as you surely must have looked "it".

I presume you got the package I sent you up alright it cost 2.50 for both bottles with 16¢ postage.

How is the little darling getting along? He must really look splendid now, as the weather must be fine and he finer and sunburnt.

I am going to close with many kisses to you and the kid from your ever true and affectionate and loving and dear

Husband Phil

Give my regards to all. Folks send regards to you and kid.

5.—A letter dated Aug. 9, 1904

Mailed in New York, it is addressed to your mother in Tannersville. It reads:

My dear Hatty:

Did you really consent to write after all you had firmly determined not to for several days. It must have been quite a sacrifice on your part to overlook the great crime that I had committed and to suspend punishment in that fashion. I must say that you are quite merciful, not to say charitable; think of the enormity of the offense that I had committed—did not write a letter one single day because I was ill and therefore unable to do so, and in place thereof sent a telegram just to let you know that I was a little better and explaining why I did not write. Don't you think that I have committed a grave crime and one for which I ought to be punished with such a severe penalty? Why is it that you are so quickly offended; that no matter what happens you so readily begin to look around for some chance to find fault when the person means no offense and does not mean to hurt you in any way. Why don't you rather find a mitigating circumstance or try to think that probably the person meant no harm or could do no better and overlook it.

I wrote you yesterday that I went down to see Dr Einhorn, but to my sad disappointment found that he was on his vacation and will not return before the 15th of September, so I went and saw some other physician who gave me some nasty medicine to be taken every 4 hours.

Hatty dear I received the two photos this morning and laughed quite heartily over the kid's picture propped up and supported in the chair.

The weather in New York is very cool and at night it is necessary to cover with blankets. How is it in the mountains. I suppose it must be colder, but I suppose we will have warm weather yet.

Aaron got back last Sunday morning.

I do not care to go to Saratoga and if I take any vacation at all or go anywhere I suppose I will come out to see you but I don't know when.

I am going to close with much love very much love and many kisses very many to you and the baby. Good night Hatty dear with love from your ever devoted husband

Philip

6.—A letter dated Aug. 11, 1904

Third and last of the Tannersville letters, it reads:

My darling Hatty

Received your letter this morning and was very happy to hear that you & Jule are well.

This will inform you that I am coming up to see you tomorrow (Friday) on the 3.25 train arriving in Tan. 8.11. I have no doubt that you will be glad to hear this and see me, as I will be happy and delighted to see my darling and lovely wife.

Hatty dear I will not write you a long letter tonight as I am overwhelmed at the shortness of time between now and 8.11 tomorrow so will close with much love and many and many kisses from your darling husband.

Hatty darling I feel quite well now but can't write as the pen is very bad and I must write standing.

Kiss the little darling for me.

Philip

7. — A letter dated June 15, 1909

Sent from New York, it is written on the stationery of Shapiro & Levy, Counselors at Law, 119 Nassau Street, and addressed to your mother at 189 Garfield Ave., Long Branch, N. J. It reads:

Dear Harriet:

You will doubtless be disappointed that I did not come out last night — probably not — but nevertheless the reasons for my not going were twofold. In the first place, my absence is not caused by any desire to remain in the city, or any lack of desire to be with my family, but it was occasioned by reason of the fact that the long postponed and much heralded suit of clothes was bought by me today in Rogers & Peet, and it has to be altered a little, so that it will not be ready until tomorrow at 12 noon — a thing which I do not regret, because the truth of the matter is that I have not yet scraped together the necessary coin. In the second place, I have an appointment in the office tomorrow at 1 p.m. with a guy who has postponed the making of a contract until tomorrow at 1 o'clock, when he has time. So you can see that it will be about 2 p.m. before I will be able to leave the office.

You know Hatty dear that today is the sixth anniversary of our wedding, and it pained me very much indeed that I was unable to be with you on that day, and especially not to be able to remember it in some way, but you see that a person's wish is not always guided by his own desires, and there are times when he must forego pleasures and acts by reason of stress of circumstances, much to his chagrin and regret, but I suppose that in the course of human events, such things go to make a person try all the harder.

It has often occurred to me that disappointment and ill luck is what goes to make a person successful, for if a man or even for that matter a woman, should always get and obtain everything he desires and imagine that everything comes to him without any exertion or effort, then he will surely not strive to obtain it, but if he is unsuccessful, he will try to rectify the wrong and try to correct the evil and remove the obstruction; so you see there is some satisfaction and some consolation to be found even in adversity.

I don't want you to infer that I am trying to be a preacher or a moralist, but it has occurred to me that not to be able to be with you and to honor the 6th ann. is disconsolable. However that may be, I am sure there are scores of these anniversaries to loom in the future, and that those to come will be fraught with greater rewards; that the near future will install the beginning of a life unburdened with the cares of financial and domestic adversity; that you and the dear little children of whom there are none to excel, will be always well and happy, and that the path of life in the future will be strewn with the blessing of the Almighty and that there will be many happy and prosperous returns of the day. Kiss the children for me and give them my love. I remain your loving husband

Phil

8. — A letter dated Jan. 2, 1912

There is no cover for this letter, but from a reference in the one that follows, it is plain that your mother received it at Lakewood, N. J. It reads:

My Dear Harriet:

I must confess that I am guilty for not having written to you sooner, but I assure you that it was not for lack of desire or absence of affection or minus a regard but it was simply one of those lethargic spells that usually over take me when I have to write a letter, especially when I must answer it by inclosing check. You know that I am always silent when it comes to handing out (but not to you). However, I know that you will forgive me and since I know that you feel well and are enjoying yourself, you should not be burdened by reading nonsensical missives from home, for when one is away on a pleasure trip his mind should not be burdened with such trash. There is nothing new here in town. I took Julian home yesterday and he certainly had one fine time and he looks it for he has a marvelous appetite. I took him in to Ike's store and had him shod for he had no shoes left. Ruth is fine and wild and is being taken care of nicely. I was over to see Grandmother on Sunday and she is feeling much better. I am glad to learn that you are sensible and have changed your hotel for I am sure that you can be accomodated much better in a small place than in a large cold hotel where you know no one and have to be afraid to ask for anything, besides the food as far as you can eat it is better at a small place.

There is nothing else of interest Hatty dear and will therefore close with best wishes for your complete restoration to absolute health for the new and coming year, leaving behind the past one which as far as we are concerned has been fraught with many hardships and has produced much sadness and gloom, but I have been taught to understand that God is good and merciful and I know he will have in store for us a good and prosperous and bright New Year.

Enclosed you will please find check as requested.

Your loving and affectionate
Phil

9. — A letter dated Jan. 3, 1912

This is the first of three surviving letters from your mother to your father. It is written on the stationery of the Lakewood Hotel, Lakewood, N. J., and it reads:

My darling Phil —

Received your letter and needless to say that it gave me much pleasure. A letter is quite a treat from you. I know that you do not care to write but there is no excuse when it comes to me as you know that it gives me so much pleasure.

Well dear I was very fortunate in changing from the above hotel to Shapiro's as I met some very nice young people here and we manage to have a good time. We went automobiling yesterday to Asbury Park and we were driving today, we went as far as Lakehurst.

I received the enclosure in your last letter and it has already been passed to a third party. Money has a tendency to melt in this neighborhood.

I am very lonesome for you and the children and I think I will start for home on Saturday or Sunday so if you will send me a signed check I will be able to settle my bill.

The Shapiro's are lovely people and they do their utmost to cater to me. The meals are absolutely perfect and the loveliest women are stopping here. The climate is very mild and I am feeling very good.

Love and kisses to you and the kiddies from your ever devoted

Hatty

10. — A letter dated Jan. 3, 1912

Written by your father in New York to your mother in Lakewood, it reads:

My darling Harriet

I hasten to write this letter, having heard that you and Ray intend coming home on Monday, Harry having told me so. While nothing would afford me more pleasure than to see you and have you with me, still I am satisfied to forego this pleasure for your sake, by *urging* you to stay another week, for I know it will do you a world of good. You know that there is nothing so good for you as rest and since you are away for a rest you might as well take a good one, and when you come back you will be good and strong.

Every one at home is well and you need worry about nothing. Julian and Ruth are fine and you want to forget about home entirely. Just think of yourself and your health. So I will close by advising you to stay as long as you can.

With love and kisses to you I remain

Your loving
Phil

Regards to Ray

11. A letter dated April 7, 1914

The second of the three letters from your mother to your father, it is written on the letterhead of the Hotel Islesworth, Atlantic City, N. J., and it reads:

Dearest Phil—

"Moving day" As usual we were "foiled". Phil dear, I would have remained at the other hotel but it was really impossible as the food was abominable and the quantity was very scant. Otherwise it was a nice place but as I am down here to regain weight and strength I could not do so on their board.

This place is entirely renovated and under new management and we are very well pleased with the change. We even have better rooms and the rates are the same. I had to borrow twenty dollars to pay my part of the board at the other place so please send me a remittance for the amount.

Miss Jais is coming here tomorrow to stay another week.

With love and kisses from Julian and

Your loving wife

I spent the entire morning on Heinze's Pier and just baked in the warm sun and I took a wheeling chair in the afternoon. My spending money has reduced itself to five cents.

12. — A letter dated April 9, 1914

This is the third and last remaining letter of all those written by your mother to your father during the eleven years of their relationship. It too is on the stationery of the Hotel Islesworth, and it reads:

Dearest Phil —

I received your letter with enclosure and I thank you for same. However, I still remain without one cent as I gave Ray the check for twenty dollars as I wrote you I had to borrow it from her to pay my part of the board over at the other hotel.

I do not like to take advantage of your good nature and I already feel that you have given me more than you can afford, but this is an expensive resort and spending money is a positive necessity so please try to let me have ten dollars more so it will last until the end of my vacation.

I am much pleased with the change that I made and Miss Jais is here with us.

Julian is having a lovely time and he eats enough at each meal to last a human being for a week.

Write me about Ruth and let me hear from you each day. My feet bother me a little but I think it will pass away as I have the pain in the mornings only. Love and kisses from your loving

Wife

13. — A letter dated April 13, 1914

This is the last known writing of your father to your mother, now about to return to New York from Atlantic City. It reads:

My dear Hatty

Enclosed you will find check for $32 as you request.

Am glad that you are coming home. Will be glad to see you hope you feel well.

With love and kisses I remain

Phil

SCENE 60

THE LAST SUMMER OF CHAI ESTHER (1914)

Until that time, her parents had been little more than names. They'd always been around and about you, enwound with the air like smoke, but they'd been presences only, with only such form as the form of the air. That summer, though, when they brought their daughter home, they assumed shapes of their own, acquired faces, voices, textures, became factors instead of spaces known as Grandpa and Grandma Nevins. You can see now what they saw then, that your mother was dying: she'd be dead soon, their Chai Esther, she'd die at some table as a stranger passed the bread, in some hallway while a stranger stared or read the papers, in a rented room on a rented bed. So they intervened and brought their Ettie home, and you and your father and your sister too.

There were nurses now, and you saw little black satchels come and go, and medicines observed the doings from the windowsill. You remember a fan you liked to play with near your mother's bed, the lever that controlled its speed, and the wind that was made by the blades, as if you were moving and the world was still. On her better days, your mother would watch you from her chair, but if you were aware of her, it was as the origin of a slow voice, an occasional tired cough. And you remember consultations where specialists spoke gravely, shook hands or bowed, and took leave with their fees but left behind their special language: *Staphylococcus pyogenes*, they'd declared, *a bacillus microscopically revealed as groupings of red dots, not unlike clusters of grapes, which, once seated, form granulations—that is to say, vegetation—on the valves of the heart and prevent their proper closing, a stenotic condition resulting in regurgitation of the blood.*

Being in the way, you were sent off to the country in the keeping of a friend of your mother's, a schoolteacher named Pauline Simon, and the place she chose was Pine Brook, where you'd spent the summer two years before. On your return to the hotel, you may have thought of the slaughtered Leghorn, and your misplaced faith in the god of the winds, and you may have found new things to do and think of, played new games, made new companions— but whatever your round, new or old, surely it was fun, surely the sun was warm and sleep sound, surely you were unprepared for rain.

On a day late in July, Mrs. Simon tracked you to wherever you may have been, collecting bottlecaps near the pavilion or wading in the stream, and she told you she'd just had a call from your father, and you were to leave for the city at once. You can recall nothing of the train-ride except a single glance through a window, as if no more than one were allowed, and what you saw was a glaring square of trees and grass and then a black blank that lasted until you reached the flat on Washington Heights. There you were met by your father, and you can still hear him asking whether you wanted to see your mother then or in the morning. You chose to wait—you knew even then that you were afraid—and morning came too late.

THE COLOR OF THE AIR, VI

A MEXICAN SHEPHERD—1836
UNDER A LONE STAR

In a hollow on the plain of St. Hyacinth, a shepherd knelt before a swamp-grass fire, and looking up at faces like paper lanterns against the evening sky, he said *Me no Alamo! Me no Alamo!*

All day he had heard the sound of guns. It had come up over the savanna with the dawn and with black smoke, and the sun had seemed to be going down in the morning, and all day the guns had spoken and darkened the prairie air. And then it was dusk, and still the shepherd could hear the carbines talking across the ravines and bayous of the San Jacinto, and a wind came with the smell of blood, and the ewes were restless, and to quiet them the shepherd ran the risk of a fire. A small one, it was, hardly more than a hat would span, and flaring up, it died quickly down, but it brought the faces, the paper lanterns, and they glowed.

One of them said *Remember the Alamo, you greaser son-of-a-bitch!* and the shepherd was afraid, and he said *Me no Alamo! Me no Alamo!* but they shot him.

SCENE 61

JULY 29, 1914

No one woke you. You awakened yourself, and you remember that you seemed to do it slowly, as though in sleep there was safety. You were alone, you found, and wanting to postpone what you feared (*what* did you fear?), you lay still for a while and listened for sound outside the room. *Died,* someone said (to whom?), *died during the night,* someone said to someone else. When you opened the door, your father was standing in the hallway, just standing there and crying.

You were taken from the house by your Uncle Dave, who walked you to Trinity Cemetery several blocks away. There he sat you down (where— on a bench, a vault, a headstone?) and told you what you already knew—that your mother was dead.

Did you speak, you wonder, and if so, what did you say, and how did he reply? Did he spell out the meaning of *dead,* tell you what it meant to die? Did he make you turn to a nearby cross or a hooded urn, did he read you granite dates and granite names and use them to explain? Or did he merely state the fact and no more and then watch you watch a starling on a grave? What did you say and do, loving son Julian, how did you respond to your Uncle Dave? Or did you not respond at all, did you stare at the ground, did you simply look away?

SCENE 62

BY AUTOMOBILE TO BROOKLYN (1914)

Acacia Cemetery was close to Jamaica Bay, but of the twenty-mile ride on the day of the funeral, you remember only a roundabout gloom that made the sunlight dreary. The bright sky, the glass-flash, the glare, all of it seemed only to add to the sadness, even to sadden you. You had no mood of your own: the one you put on belonged to others, and you wore it as borrowed clothes. For all you know of the burial, you might've arrived late, after the services had come to an end. Mourners were taking up handfuls of earth and trickling them into the grave, and it was then that you made a blunder so stunning that it stayed with you for life. You thought what the people were doing was useful work, and you thought you could be useful too. You even had a notion that they were playing some sort of game, and saying *I'll do that, papa,* you moved toward a spade planted in a mound of fill. You can still hear yourself saying *I'll do that* and your father saying *No.* He held you by the hand, you recall, while a digger shoveled the dirt and stones, and that too you still can hear, a fall of pebbles and clods until the coffin was out of sight.

SCENE 63

MOURNER'S *KADDISH* (1914)

When the funeral was over, eleven months of mourning began with a period called *Shibbah* in Hebrew, otherwise The Seven Days. During that time, you and your father and your mother's family remained at home, where, performing no labors, you wandered shoeless from room to room or sat on crates and planks instead of chairs and recited prayers for the dead—*Chai Esther, may her repose be ever peaceful*—once at sunrise and twice each afternoon. Without shoes like the rest, you went about dressed in clothes rent like those of Jacob at the news of Joseph, and at someone's nudge or someone's nod, you read the English interlineations of the Aramaic *qaddish. Yisgadal,* you said, *v'yis-kaddash sh'meh rabbo,* but you didn't know what the words meant or whether they were merely sounds and had no meaning at all. There were no explanations. You weren't told what you were doing or why it was being done—still, at someone's glance or someone's touch, once each morning and twice each afternoon, you said *B'olmo di'vro kir' useh v'yamlich malchuseh,* while all your elders cried.

When The Seven Days ended, the raw wood seats were sent away, and with the sheets taken down from the mirrors, again you could see and study yourself, again you would wonder why, though you knew you were moving your right hand, your left seemed to move in the glass. Callers were fewer now, and no more doctors came with their little kits and their smell of soap, and the bedding was gone from your mother's room, and the medicines, and even the fan and its wire cage, and the house would be quiet when you hurried off to *schul* with your torn lapels and the broad black band you wore on your sleeve.

The place of prayer was a store on Amsterdam Avenue, bare except for a dozen benches, and there, morning and evening, a *minyan* gathered, the ten or more males that the Mishnah called for, there thrice a day you prayed for your mother's peaceful sleep. Sleep—you wondered why people spoke of death as sleep. Once you'd thought of it as a running down, like a watch unwound, but you came to think it was more than that and not the same as sleep. If your mother were asleep, she'd still be there, and she wasn't there— she'd gone away. That's what death was, a going away, and for years, you remember, you looked for her wherever you happened to be. *B'chayechon uv'yomechon uv'chayeh d'chol.*

At summer's end, your grandparents moved from the Heights to Harlem, and they took your father and "the children" along. Their new flat—your home now—was only two streets away from P.S. 81 and two in another direction from a *schul,* and most of what you recall of the following year occurred within those limits. Little enough was memorable, for all pleasure was forbidden you, nor was pleasure set before you by your friends. With that mourning band you wore and those slashed lapels, you were marked, even at a distance, as one who could not be counted on to play at games, to join in explorations of the park, to laugh with them in the dark at Flora Finch and John Bunny. You were avoided, or, since you saw no one run at your approach, all too often you found companions absent from a haunt, as if they'd never frequented it, never known it was there. You can see yourself walking the range of your tether, staring at cars, shopwindows, people, you can see yourself in the Model School courtyard (*Childe Julian, Boy King*), you can see yourself in the new *schul* next door to Bergman's pool-room—but almost always, though others were present, you seem to have been alone. *Bes yisroel baagolo uvisman koriv v'imru Omen.*

Ahead lay months of gloom, of your grandma's tears for motherless children, of prayers morning, afternoon, and night for the tranquillity of dead Chai Esther. You never cried, you remember. You went through all those somber days as if no other kind had ever dawned. You went to school and *schul* without joy—*Y'hey sh'may rabbo,* you said, *m'vorach l'olom olmayoh*—but you never cried.

SCENE 64

THE ELEVEN-MONTH YEAR (1914-15)

By the time school opened in the fall of 1914, a war was being fought all across Europe from the Masurian Lakes to the Marne, but if you heard either name, it meant no more to you than any other, and you made your rounds unaware and unaffected. Your boundaries were a classroom in the Fifth Grade, Miss Gibson's, and a *schul* with a file of spittoons, one for each row of benches, along the middle aisle: your home, the center of a new world, was not your home at all; it belonged to someone else.

You'd never been present when the arrangement was under discussion, nor, when it was agreed on, did you ever ask what it was. You accepted it without question, as if where and how you lived were matters for others to determine and none of your concern. Even so, ignorant of what had taken place, you knew your condition had become different, and what you didn't know you sensed. Nothing was the same as before, the atmosphere, the furniture, the food, the faces you saw — you dwelt among the elderly now, and their very sound and smell seemed old.

On the opening day of school, Miss Gibson took you from her classroom to an office across the hall, and there she told you that she'd been informed of your mother's death during the summer. It was a grievous thing to lose one's mother, she said, and she wondered whether you fathomed the depth of your loss. You answered her with silence — it would be years before you could bring yourself to speak of your mother or even to use the word — and you simply looked down while you were given a lesson you couldn't listen to and therefore couldn't learn. *A mother is . . .* , she may have said, or *a mother does . . .* , but whatever it may have been, it was all wasted: it meant less than the dust in the cracks of the floor. *Do you realize, Julian . . .* —the words come back, and you tried to say *Yes! Yes, I do!* but there and vital was that dust on the floor, and all you could do was stare some more. Whatever you may have supposed, though, you realized nothing — and your fifth year of school thus began.

The Sabbath excluded, every morning at six o'clock you were awakened by your grandma and sent off hungry to *schul*. By some rule of religion, you were forbidden to eat before prayer, and as you crossed Seventh Avenue and headed for Lenox, your mind was on food, not on the lamp that hung above the Ark. Through the chanted litany, through the hour-long murmuring of the *minyan,* sometimes from under their shawls, you waited only for a sign to rise and say your *Yisgadal* to the Father of Peace — and then you raced from Lenox back to Seventh, tasting breakfast all the way.

Home. No paper or pictures graced the walls, and there was no library other than the Jewish Year Book, a set of many volumes that matched in all but the date. The beds, one of which you shared with your father, were made of brass, and the springs would jingle when you turned, and the knobs would make the railing ring. The carpeting, a few runners and lifeless Orientals, was merely a lackluster mute for footsteps on the floor. You recall no vases and therefore no flowers, you see no bright cushions, no lamp except a bronze nymph who seemed to be in flight with a streaming scarf and a spray of beaded lights. What color comes back is pale or else no color at all, a grandma in black, a grandpa in gray, a pink-painted wall — home.

And after breakfast, you'd go to school, and soon after that, you'd go back to *schul* — the eleven-month year.

SCENE 65

THE *SCHUL* ON 116th STREET (1914-15)

The *Kalv'riah Schul,* it was called, and so it comes to mind, for you never saw *Kalv'riah* spelled. It might've been a place-name, brought over from the Old Country and kept alive here, or perhaps it was merely a qualifier of the noun, an attributive like white or small or neighborhood. But whatever the word actually meant, to you it stood for an enclosure only a pace or two from a billiard parlor, a space barren of all but a few benches and a chest that held the Torah's scrolls. Its single window cut the altar wall, but the panes were never clean, and nothing could be seen but the rectangular fact of light or dark. A number of elders, a dozen or more, were so unfailingly present that for all you knew they lived in the place, never eating, never sleeping, never changing clothes. They were there when you came and there when you went, always in praying shawls grayed by wear and constant kissing. How could they put the tassels to their mouths, you'd wonder, how could they praise the Lord through grime? And you'd wonder too why no women were among them, why only men could form a *minyan. Among the Jews,* you'd heard it said, *it is the old men who are beautiful,* but you could see no beauty in these long-lived scholars of the Talmud. You saw beards that were combed with dirty fingers and eyes that looked like clams, you saw hair in nostrils, hair in ears—where was the beauty, you thought, how could you think ill-favor fair? You knew that it was their devotion alone that made your *Kaddish* acceptable to the Lord, but even so you felt no bond with them, no warmth for their fidelity. They were strangers, all year long they were strangers, and at the end you failed to thank them, you didn't know their names.

SCENE 66

MARY PHAGAN (1915)

You'd heard the name before, but it hadn't stirred your mind, and by the time it was said again, she was two years dead and gone. Even then, though, not having known she was alive, you didn't know she'd died. On a day still a long way off, the air would be shaken by another name, *Leo Frank,* and with it would come a memory of other vibrations (*Mary Phagan!*), and you'd see pictures made of words unfaded.

You'd find her lying in the cellar of an Atlanta pencil-factory. Thirteen years old and still dressed in her best, a lavender pongee, she'd seem to have been thirteen years dead. Skinned in places, blood-encrusted, black-and-blued, and breaded with splinters, goober shells, and cedar shavings, she'd be half-buried in a pile of grit, paper, lead dust, and dried quids of spit-and-run—trash herself now, with the cores and rinds, the spools of hair and dust, and a few hard stools that no longer drew flies. You'd find Mary Phagan in the basement of your mind.

Leo Frank, someone would say at a street-corner, across a room or a table, from a bench in Central Park. *Leo Frank,* the banner lines would cry, and sometimes you'd see a likeness that was caught on the fly, a grayed print of trees and out-of-focus faces, and a faded something hanging from a rope.

Leo Frank—what would have to happen before you knew how and why a Brooklyn Jew came to die in Georgia? What in your own generation would take you back to his, what would make you read of a Cornell engineer who might've lived to grow old if he'd displayed his degree, B.Mech.E., somewhere else instead of Georgia? What made you care about one who, once he reached Atlanta, had only nine years to go before his neck was broken between the branch of an oak and the ground? One day, the names would come together—

Leo Frank, you'd say, and *Mary Phagan* — and you'd will yourself back to a still factory, to idle machines and vacant aisles, to the cedar fragrance from the stubble on the floor. You'd strain at voices, pleas, cries of pain, the sound of tearing silk. You'd try to be present in a past you hadn't known, to open the closed doors of dark rooms, to summon up a place you'd never seen, an afternoon when blood turned lavender pongee brown while you played in some gutter with a bat and a ball.

SCENE 67

THE FLAT ON 117th STREET (1914-15)

You can see it as you saw it when you were ten years old: all the doors are open, and you know the lay of the rooms. Fresh yet and still familiar, the chairs seem to be where you left them, and the shades, as once, are drawn to the catch. The beaten brass pot and the rubber plant, the *Menorah* on the sideboard, the cut-glass bowl of fruit and almonds, each is still in place. Nor need you be told the number on the phone — *Morningside 1930,* you say in your mind, and in your mind you pass a black box on the hallway wall. You walk there as though the things you recall were as real as ever, the hatrack and its trap-door seat, the Circassian walnut chiffonier. You veer to avoid a table, you close a drawer, you sidle between a crib and the footrail of a bed. What was there once, you think, will be there always, the rugs, the radiators, the medicine-chest — and suddenly you're overtaken by a left-behind word. *Crib,* you think, *crib,* and you realize that it could only have been your sister Ruth's. And now you realize more, that the bed it almost touched was where your father slept — and you! The three of you in the same room? you think, and you try to believe that it wasn't true. But it *was* true, and you knew you must've known it all along.

SCENE 68

THE CRIB (1915)

Once recalled, it grows until it begins to crowd the room. It becomes a great brass cage, and in it you see your sister, no smaller than before but seeming so for the topless bars, the soaring rails. *The Starved Cuban,* you think, and there she is, dark and thin, at your father's feet and yours. How was her presence arranged, you wonder, when and where did she dress and undress, and where and when did you? Did she cry at night or call for Mother, and when carried to the bathroom, did she fall asleep on the seat? Why is the crib so distinct now, why is her face so dim?

SCENE 69

THE SCHOOL ON 119th STREET (1914-15)

You were poor at your studies that year. Earlier, while your mother was alive, you'd been promoted through four grades in a single year, two of them detaining you no longer than a month. But with your mother dead, your impulsion went, as if the wind that drove you had died as well. You were inattentive, there but absent, away somewhere that you could never recall. You learned little that fall and winter. There were no more parties for you in the courtyard where you ruled and romped as king, you won no stars of blue and gold for spelling, fractions, significant dates, and when you raised a hand in class those days, it wasn't to volunteer an answer, but only to leave the room. In the toilet, you'd spurt at a cake of disinfectant, you'd listen to drip-drop in a flush-box, or you'd simply stand and stare — at what? at *what?* — until some pupil was sent to fetch you back. It was a poor fall for you, a poor winter and spring.

SCENE 70

UNCLE DAVE NEVINS (1914-15)

His room was next to yours, and sometimes when he was out of the house, you'd be drawn by an emanation that was his alone, that came from his hair, his clothes, his luggage. You'd wander through his personal air, you'd touch his comb and brushes—*Caramba!* he'd've said if he'd known—you'd poke about in his cupboard, climb a chair to inspect his shelves. And always, from the drawer that held his shirts, from the pages of his books, a flavor—Uncle Dave!—that lasted all your life.

SCENE 71

GRANDPA NEVINS (1914-15)

How neat he was, you thought, and how neatly disposed his things! He furled his ties, and they pressed themselves, his sox were rolled into muffs of cotton, he coiled his collars in a yellow box. His spare shoes, two pair only, stood always at attention, and he folded paper and wound up clews of string. His hats were hard and black, and they exhaled him, the cropped white hair, the faint perfume called clean.

SCENE 72

WHAT THE TRUNK CONTAINED (1914)

Do you remember your mother, Julian? your Aunt Rae would say, and you'd say *Yes* and look away as at private papers in the secret places of your mind. But what, you wonder, if she'd had the power to compel, to make you tell her what scenes had been played in your presence, what you knew that was known to you alone? *Do you remember?* she'd've said, and what reply would you have made?

112

You'd had only ten years of your mother, and for the first five she'd been hardly more than her fragrance; of such days neither motion comes back nor stills of motion, only the glint and silence of space and time. And of the five that were left of her life, how much was left with you? What do you recall as it was, what places are the actual places, what words were arranged as you arrange them now? *Do you remember your mother, Julian?* But you wanted to pretend that there was nothing to remember, that she wasn't dead, and when you said *Yes,* you were answering a different question: *Do you think she's still alive?*

Yes, you'd say, and she'd seem barely out of reach, she'd be rounding a corner, entering the room next to the room you were in, you'd see her in a window, a passing train, a crowd, she'd be a figure across or down the street. You'd know it was she, though in none of your fancies would you see her face: you'd be following always, and always she'd retreat. But not forever would the fiction fly; it was heavier than air, and in the end it fell. Your mother was not turning a corner, she was not in a window or another room or just across the street. She was dead, and then, when asked the question, you knew how little you knew beyond what you'd been told: your past was hearsay well-nigh all.

Off the hallway of your grandma's flat, there was a storeroom that held the seldom-wanted gear of the household, the luggage, the spare bedding, the unseasonable clothes, the holdalls filled with the stowage of the years. In a corner, under a stack of boxes, sat a Saratoga trunk that contained whatever had been saved of your mother's belongings. You'd been told often enough to let it alone, but you'd always known that when the right day came, you were going to disobey: your mother was there, pervading her things, confined with what she'd worn, touched, given her bouquet, and whenever you passed the storeroom, you'd think of her as near instead of far away.

The right day came, and in the trunk you found linens that she'd embroidered, tablecloths, centerpieces, doilies, and there were monogrammed sheets and slips and shams, and among these, between them, beneath them, you found a pair of white kid gloves that once had reached your mother's elbows and a bracelet set with amethysts that once had clasped her wrist, and from the depths you drew a crocodile purse that still spoke of orris root, of keys, of orange sticks, and you came upon a sewing frame with a needle still making a stitch.

And there were photographs in the trunk, and copies of *Felix Holt* and the essays of Emerson, both inscribed by your mother, and, tied with twine, the Furnivall Shakespeare (37 vols.), and among these her paper on Shylock, dated Nov. 1st 1899:

In my estimation, Shylock is more to be pitied than condemned. This might sound rather strong to people living in this present time, still I shall prove to you.

Let us imagine ourselves as people living in Shakespear's time, the time when jews were held in great abhorence, the time when jews were subjected to the cruelest persecutions, the time when most all legitimate means of obtaining a livelihood were closed to the jews; and can we not then find an excuse for Shylock? Was not that the only way in which he could secure for himself immunity from poverty? Also to gain somewhat the tolerance at least of his gentile neighbors. For did not the lending of his money aid him?, and how many of us living in the present civilized age, do what Shylock did then but in a different manner. We have all no doubt heard of the giving of a bonus for the use of money which actually amounts to an extra six percent.

Cannot we also find an excuse for his hatred to Antonio who took away in some measure his means? True it was a most cruel and barbarous thing for him to persist in exacting the pound of flesh, but again there was the loss of his gold and daughter which weighed sorely upon him and there was that desire for revenge.

The jew, for years crushed, downtrodden, insulted and spat upon turns on his persecutor and trys to make him feel the pangs he has so often been made to feel. Perhaps this desire for revenge is not commendable, no doubt it isn't, but can we not find some excuse for his revengeful feeling?

How many of us living in this present enlightened age, hearing and reading of good and noble deeds would not also have these same feelings, but of course not give way to them. There would be no excuse for us if we wished to have our revengeful desires gratified as we have been taught differently; yet what teachings, what examples had Shylock. What had the Christian world in which he was living done for him in the way of education and teaching him the sublimity of that biblical passage "If thine enemy smite thee on right cheek, give him the left," no, they left him in utter darkness, never dissilusioning him of the wrongfulness of his motto, "an eye for an eye, and a tooth for a tooth."

Even Shakespeare finds an excuse for Shylock's conduct when he puts into the mouth of Shylock this wonderful speech which must appeal to all. "Hath not a jew eyes etc." If the time allowed it I am most positive Shakespeare would have more openly espoused the cause of the jews, but it was all his position was worth to take the part of the jew as he certainly does in the above passage.

114

And somewhere in the depths of the trunk, you came upon a letter of your father's dated January 12th, 1903, the first he ever wrote to your mother:

Dear Miss Nevins: I should be very pleased to escort you to the theatre on next Friday evening, provided you are not otherwise engaged.

Hoping that this invitation will prove acceptable, and that I will be favored with an early reply, I am

Very cordially yours
P. D. Shapiro

And you found an announcement-card printed in Old English:

Miss Harriet E. Nevins
Mr. Philip D. Shapiro
Betrothed
Sunday March 13th   1770 Madison Ave.
6:30 P.M.   The "Avon"
at home

And you found a telegram from Pittsburgh, dated March 15th, 1903, and signed by Dr. and Mrs. Lieber:

Of love, true friends always get their Phil. Accept congratulations.

And you found a telegram from Brooklyn, dated June 15th, 1903, and signed by Felliman & Weiss:

Wishing you happiness and joy in a year a little boy.

And you found a three-line clipping from the *New York Times* of June 1st, 1904:

Shapiro — To Mr. and Mrs. Ph. D. Shapiro (née Harriet E. Nevins), No. 2 West 120th St., a son.

Do you remember your mother, Julian? — and there in that trunk, you found her little history and a paling two-word reference to you.

SCENE 73

THE THREE BLOWS (1914-17)

Through the years, you were chastened by your father three times only, and on each occasion, a single slap sufficed his anger.

115

At ten, you were a reader of Tom Swift, of the Rover Boys, of Frank Merriwell, often to the neglect of such matters as valences, decimals, the position of adverbs, and your father, with uncommon discernment, always seemed to know when your brain was filled not with participial phrases, gerunds, and the causes of the war with Spain, but with flying machines and the double-shoot, the pitch that Frank, and Frank alone, could throw. Again and again he urged you to give your mind to your schoolbooks, and again and again you promised to abandon the husks and cleave to the grain, and again and again you broke your word. In the end, you were forced to dispose of Tom and Dick and Frank—that is to say, you hid them and then told your father they'd been given away.

In your room one night, with your lessons unlearned, you were deep with Tom in his submarine or on high with Frank in Peru when slowly you became aware of a presence behind you, and, turning, you saw your father gazing at you from the doorway: he'd come home early, and you'd expected him late.

Remaining where he was, he said, "What're you reading, Julian?"

And you said, "I am reading a book about arithmetic."

"Would you say that if you were under oath on the witness-stand?"

"Sure I would," you said, "because it's the truth. I am sitting here learning about arithmetic."

"I ask you to state the nature of your learning."

"It's about square roots," you said. "About the square root of 36 is 6, and the square root of 49 is 7. Things like that."

"What about the square root of 625?"

"That's harder. It comes on another page."

"What's the square root of lying?" he said and then he crossed the room and took the book from your hands. After a glance at it, he said, "What's Frank Merriwell doing in Peru—lying, do you think, like you?" And then he slapped your face just once and went away.

That was the first blow.

§

You'd bruised an index finger somehow, and the result was an inflammation of the joints. The doctor called it whitlow—a felon, that is—and you were required to soak it in lead water several times a day, a treatment that stopped the suppuration but caused you to lose the nail. For weeks thereafter, you favored the finger whenever you used the hand, and, exempted from all work, it became the weakling child in a family of five, a poor pale misfortunate thing, and eventually you might've forgotten you still possessed it had your father been less aware. From the start, he'd noticed your desistance, and when it became plain to him that you regarded the finger as invalid for life, he intervened in behalf of the derelict sickling.

"Use that finger, Julian," he'd say.

And you'd say, "What finger?"

"That one," he'd say, and he'd touch it with a finger of his own, or a fork, if you happened to be at table, or a pencil, or a matchstick, or whatever else he had in hand. "That one right there."

"But I am using it," you'd say, and by way of proof, you'd make it perform a task. "See that? I told you I was using it."

"Only when you think of it," he'd say. "When you aren't, it does nothing. In time, it won't work even when you want it to."

"What can I do?"

"Think!"

And whenever you did, the finger would respond, rejoining the family circle and doing its rightful share. But it wasn't the finger that failed, it was you, and when you found that you could think you were thinking when you had no thoughts at all, you let the finger have its withering way.

"Use the finger, Julian!" your father would say. "Use the finger!"

But it was irksome to think of one particular finger on one particular hand (the right, was it, or the left?). There were other things to think of (what were they? you wonder, what other things?), and they occupied your mind until one day your mind was cleared by a slap across the jaw.

That was the second blow.

§

At the time of the third, you were thirteen, and you can see yourself walking with your father on Lenox Avenue near 117th Street. Only a moment earlier, you'd left Ricksecker's Drug Store, where someone had photographed you in the doorway—you know what you were wearing, you know it was a summer's day. You couldn't've gone far when the third blow fell with overwhelming suddenness. Fell, you remember thinking, as though dropped from a height, and having struck you, it fell further to lie broken at your feet. You were so stunned that you've never been able to recall what you'd said or done. What request had you refused, whom had you slighted, what secret had you peached? All you know is that you walked with care for a while, as if you too might break.

§

Three blows—there were no others.

THE COLOR OF THE AIR, VII

ELIJAH P. LOVEJOY—1837
A ROUND TRIP TO ALTON

Nobody cared a pinch of water for the man, neither the Pukes of Missouri nor the Suckers of Illinois. He was a Presbyterian minister, that Elijah P. Lovejoy, and it was common opinion he should've kept his bill in the Book. Instead, he stuck it into other people's business— slavery, for instance—and that didn't go down in St. Louis, where slavery was, or across the river in Alton, where it wasn't. Nobody liked him on either side of the stream, and the abolition he put in that paper of his, the *Observer,* was liked even less, and one fine day a bunch of people tore his press out of the floor and distributed his type in the Mississippi. He didn't learn a thing from that, so when he set up a second press, the same or similar people pitched it off of a bluff and into the channel for him. It's a plain historical fact that the fool went and bought himself a third press, and, by God and Christ, that one got a drowning too. He must've been dense or else deaf to reason, because when his fourth press came, the only switch he made was to ferry it over to the east bank, and there, from some warehouse in Alton, he kept right on with his abolitioning. The people, a great big bunch this time, well, they just naturally went a-ferrying too, and when they caught up with that crazy-ike preacher, you know what they done? They killed him.

SCENE 74

THE NEVINS HOUSEHOLD (1914-15)

It was an odd ménage, and you sensed it from the start. In others, the generations were successive; here there was a breach, a missing step in the stairs. The connection had been Ettie, and with Ettie gone, "the children" were asked to stretch beyond their reach, and though your sister may have felt she succeeded, you always knew you'd failed. Between you and your grandparents, there was space: you touched nothing, and nothing touched you. Your grandma acted as your mother at a remove, and though she was much too old for the role, you gave way and let her play it. But that meant allowing your grandpa to fill in for your father—and your father still was there. Unable to comprehend the real relations, you felt misunderstood yourself, and you went about wondering why your behavior so rarely seemed to please. But it could not have pleased, no matter what.

By taking "the children" in, your grandparents must've thought they were preserving Ettie, and in their view, perhaps they did: she wasn't dead while you lived. In fact, however, she was in the grave, and no transfer made in fancy could bring her back to life. You had no mother, and your grandma could not take her place. She tried, but from where she stood, above the missing step, she could not descend to you. There was never a great disagreement: no voices were raised and no blows struck. But there was a simmer, minor and constant, a disturbance seemingly of the surface only, and it was dismissed by all as normal, the mere effect of the young on the old. It began deep down, though, and the force at work was major.

SCENE 75

A NEW MEMBER OF THE FAMILY (1880?-1935?)

When your father and "the children" were invited to reside with your grandparents, a housekeeper was engaged for the additional work. On your return from school one afternoon, there she was, a homely little woman with red hair, a shapeless nose, and thick dry lips that seemed to make a sandwich of her tongue. At ten, you were almost as tall as she at thirty-five, but you sensed in her stunted body an outsize will, and you drew this from her at once, that over her dominion—the kitchen and the pantry—the Nevins flag no longer flew. Her name was Ellen Lang, she said, and she came from County Sligo.

She must've thought you knew the place—*Sligo,* she said, as if it were only across the river or just beyond the park. *I come from Sligo,* she said, and the word was so laggard, so loath to be uttered, that its sound stayed on the air—*Sligo,* she said, and one day she'd tell you of the Slieve Gamph Mountains, of the Moy that rose in Mayo and wound northward to the bay. *Sligo,* she said, and you can still hear her say it, as if time and distance had not yet dispersed its waves.

You were told privately that Ellen's religion was different from yours—Catholic, it was called—and since religion was a personal matter, it might be better if you didn't discuss it or compare her belief with your own. But it was only your religion that was secret, you thought; hers was there for all to see, hanging on the wall. Beside her bed, where she could touch it lying down, where she could adore it and even kiss it, was thorn-bled Jesus, dying on the Cross.

Her church was straight across the street from the house, scarcely a moment's walk, but had the weather been bad and she ailing, had the distance been great, an hour's journey, still would she have attended Mass, and Confession too, nor was anyone allowed to hinder her devotions. On the days of Ellen's Lord, your grandma assumed her chores and helped her prepare for the sacrifice of the Body and Blood in the guise of bread and wine: she tugged the strings of Ellen's corset, she chalked her gloves, adjusted her hat, and sent her on her way. Those were loving things your grandma did, and for all such the fat mick loved the fat Jew back, and throughout twenty years, the two were as thick as sisters. They both spoke a broken English, but each seemed to understand perfectly, like birds, and when you heard them from another room, indeed you might've been listening to some parley in a tree.

How, you often wondered, how did two so far apart manage to draw so near? How was Suwalki made to border on Sligo, how was the map of Europe changed? Sometimes you fancy you know, and sometimes you're in the dark, but always they sit there in your mind, their heads together over tea or a task, and a trill seems to come from between them—nothing for you, though; you're not equipped with wings.

SCENE 76

SARTOR RESARTUS IN HARLEM (1914)

In photographs taken of your sister before your mother's death, no change is more apparent than the one she reveals in her clothes. When your mother lived, there were coats of black or blue serge, there were Leghorn hats and button-up shoes in patent leather, there were kidskin belts and lace collars with cuffs to match, and there she stands, your sister Ruth, in velvet sleeves with her hands in an opossum muff. Eight pictures remain of the time, some in wicker wheelchairs and some in parks and streets, and always she appears to have been dressed with care, with regard to her size, the shape of her face, and her coloration. But beyond such matters as your mother's judgment and its manifest vindication is the gladsome effect she had on Ruth: those eight surviving scenes, in each she shows her pleasure.

But when your mother goes, so too her pretty fancy: clothes become clothes, become feathers instead of plumes, and beauty gives way to the weather's demands, the wool of winter, the cotton of cotton's season. And your sister sits, leans, rides in the snow or reclines in the grass, all in garb that fits her ill, too small, too big, too loose or long, too free of decoration, and that pleasure of the other days is where her mother is, in the early pictures or the grave. There's no sign of it in the pale round face below a hat that was made for your grandma, none in the way the eyes seem to look beyond you at something moving away, something dwindling in the distance and also from the mind.

SCENE 77

THE SILVER SON-IN-LAW (1914-15)

Your father's fountain-pen, a gift from your Grandpa Nevins, was made of sterling silver, knurled all over the cap and barrel except for a smooth oblong in which the name *Philip D. Shapiro* had been engraved.

At the time, it was beyond you to know, even to ponder, the relation between your father and your grandparents, nor, had you tried, would you have

121

understood that it was merely an affinity. His blood met theirs in you and your sister, and it went no further, and had both of you died when your mother did, there'd've been no connection at all: son-in-law Phil would've been a stranger. You could not have grasped that notion then—you'd've supposed a tie that didn't exist. In truth, your father was there because of you, and had you been aware of more than yourself, had you been concerned with even the small room you lived in, let alone the world, you might've seen or sensed the fragile apposition of the household. Your father was a member by courtesy only; he could not have paid his way with coin. You admire now an arrangement made with so much delicacy and played with so much grace. If money was ever mentioned or money ever passed, you were never present to see or hear of it, and you assume that your father, being your grandpa's attorney, rendered his legal services free to requite his obligation for the freedom of the house.

He entered it at the age of thirty-six, a vital and vivid man whose mere presence was enough to revive the air: where he came, he brought no gloom, and what was there he took away. No one frowned when he appeared, no one found an excuse to leave. He talked little and prated never, and he listened to others with care, followed their unsequential thoughts, made sense of their maundering, and so well did he follow that the ignorant were saved from seeming thick: no one lost his cloak to your father, no one felt exposed. His wit was bladed, but he used it on himself, and the blood it drew was his own. The upward comparative meant nothing to him —*more* profit, a *better* seat, *greater* power—and he was always content with a lower place at table and smoking a cheaper cigar. He was most honorable, but he made no more of it than he did of his pulse: it was simply systemic. And the worst you ever heard him say of another was this: *He has a cold eye, Julian.*

The pen your grandpa gave to your uncle was the same as your father's except for the name *Harry W. Perlman* and the fact that it was made of gold.

SCENE 78

POOR MISFORTUNATE BOY (1914-15)

While the family was at supper one evening, the doorbell rang, and you were sent to answer it. When you opened the door, there in the outer hall stood your Uncle Romie, back from a farm in Dakota or a reform school in

122

Vermont, back from somewhere out-of-the-way and hidden from sight, home your Uncle Romie, stained, foul, grinning through the pile of a golden dusty beard. *Come on in,* you said, *we're eating,* and you preceded him to the dining-room, where knives and forks were suddenly couched and china encounters ceased. Your grandma rose, pushed a spare chair toward the table, and then led Romie away to wash. Poor misfortunate Romie was home again from the world.

At the age of ten, you couldn't understand that Romie's existence was a diminution of your grandpa, that his presence alone was a reproach. Here is your fathering, his being seemed to say, a full-grown man half-grown in mind — behold this son you begot, this chimpanzee in shirt and pants. At ten, you couldn't know that to your grandpa, Romie was an unnatural and lackwit thing with his name, his looks, his genetics, that having made a monster, he was thought a monster himself.

To you, he wasn't a monster at all. He was just an intent and gentle fumbler, happy always and always forgiving, and you rather liked to watch him at his footling and fruitless concerns. One of these was a craze for what he called "sending away." Day after day, he'd clip squares from the papers and the pages of magazines (*send this coupon plus a 1¢ stamp,* they'd read, *and receive a trial-size* this or a sample of that), and he'd affix the stamps and send them away. You couldn't seem to learn respect for that particular passion. You'd tease him about it, warn him that he was just sending away stamps, that he'd never get what the stamps were meant for. And then in would come a tide of little boxes, little tubes, little jars, little packets, toothpaste, oint-ment, cereal, soap — a tide! And when it receded, there was the result of his sending away, a display of miniatures that might've been made for a doll-house. Still, when he began another round of sending away, you'd jeer and say. . . .

SCENE 79

THE *FRESSER* (1914-15)

There was a void in you that year, and you tried to fill it with food. You didn't know you were doing that, you didn't even know the void existed: you ate, you supposed, because you were hungry. You were, of course, but not in the way that food could quiet, and therefore, feeling hunger although you were full, you kept on cramming, and in no long time you were fat. The *fresser,* you were called, meaning the devourer. It was your Aunt Rae who gave you the name, and so relentlessly did she use it that you became uneasy when eating in her presence: Julian the *fresser,* she'd say, even when food was not in sight. She could be avoided, however, but there was no avoiding the fit of your clothes. Suits barely six months old might well have been bought for someone else, someone more favorably formed, and no further moving of the buttons could make them ever again yours.

One day, your father took you downtown to Eldridge Street on the lower East Side, where his brother Charlie owned a small store that sold clothing for men and boys. Uncle Charlie reminded you of doctors who could make you feel better just by entering the room: they seemed to bring the open air with them, and there was no need for medicines and those things they put in their ears. Uncle Charlie could make you well with his laughter. There were some who said that he was laughing his life away, but you didn't know what they meant, and when he told you one of his jokes, you laughed your life away too.

It was a narrow little place, that store of his, and day barely reached it from the street, touching only a few front feet and no more. For the rest, there was a green-shaded bulb that hung from the ceiling on a cord, and it served poorly: the single aisle between the two racks looked like the entrance to a mine. From this tunnel of textiles, Uncle Charlie produced a jacket of tawny tweed, and you tried it on before a mirror that showed you back a blur on blackness. To the feel, the size seemed right, though, and being handed the pants, you put them on as far as they'd go. The waistband failed to meet by the breadth of a hand, and below it yawned an isosceles triangle of fly. Uncle Charlie made light of the difficulty. He knew a certain man, he said — it would be defamatory to call him a tailor — he knew a man of genius, he said, a wizard of the needle. Come back tomorrow, your uncle told you, and you will be able to button the pants.

You were there on the morrow, and even as predicted, the pants that would not button before buttoned now — indeed, it would have been calumnious to call that wizard a tailor! — and the waistband that would not meet now met and more, nor could you detect a gaping fly. You were so pleased that when you'd changed into your old clothes again, you took the new to the light at the front of the store, that you might enjoy the tawny tweed as it would appear to others in the street. Alas, the magic could not stand the test of day.

What the tailor had wrought—he was wizard no longer—was an abomination. He'd closed the pants at the front by opening the back, and the breach was spanned by a gore of black satin—a black wedge in a field of tan. You heard your uncle laugh as you ran from the store. He's laughing his life away, you thought.

Julian the *fresser*.

SCENE 80

SOL Y SOMBRA (1914)

When your father came home from the office one evening in the winter of that year, he told your grandma that he was going to Syracuse for a day or two and that you'd be taken along. You were to go by train from Grand Central around midnight, he said, and early in the morning you'd reach Albany, where you'd meet the steamer *Adirondack*; your Uncle Jack would be aboard, and so would his Ford automobile. From the dock, you'd head west through the Mohawk Valley, following the Erie Canal, and you'd pass through Schenectady, your father said, and Herkimer, and Little Falls, and Oriskany. You knew the names from the history book your mother had given you, and as you heard them spoken, you thought of blockhouses ringed by palisades, of pen-and-ink forests with painted faces among the leaves. From Albany westward, you rode every mile in the rain, and though you saw nothing through the windshield and the curtains, those pictures were on the move in your mind.

Uncle Jack's *stuss* house had been lost, and he was in the punchboard business now. Twice each month he made the rounds of his territory to pick up the played-out devices and replace them with new hives of treasure. These days there were no packs of yellowbacks; there was only silver to collect in the rain. Halts for that purpose were made in Amsterdam, Canajoharie, Utica, Rome (on the shady side of the street? you wondered), and then evening came on, and both sides were shaded, and you were in the city of Syracuse.

Uncle Jack stopped before a small frame house in the downtown section, and you can see it still, two stories of clapboard painted gray, and it has stayed with you that there was no stoop, no step, even, only a door at the level of the flagstone sidewalk. The rain had turned to snow, and it fell on a wind-blown slant across all you could see of the world—a sphere of space near a

125

lamp-post. It grained the air, the siding of the stepless place, a swinging sign that read *Rooms and Meals* in gilt on black.

You know now that you weren't there by chance: your Uncle Jack hadn't simply punched a hole in one of his boards. And you know too that the woman who brought you food was more than a wayside waitress he'd never seen before: her name was Helen, and she was your uncle's girl. At the time, you saw only that she was pretty, quiet, and deft, and knowing more than he let on, your father called her *Miss.*

It was still snowing when you went upstairs to bed, and even with the gas-heater burning, the wood-walled room was cold. But you and your father were tired, and adding your overcoats to the blankets and the bedspread, you soon fell asleep. If you had dreams, nothing remained of them by morning, none of their black and white shapes, their unheard sound, their tanglefoot motion, and when you rose and dressed and went downstairs, you were unprepared for what happened in the diningroom. Your father crossed to where Helen stood, and after embracing and kissing her, he invited you to do the same. *We owe her our lives, Julian,* he said.

You learned then that she'd risen during the night, and having to pass your room on her way to the water-closet, she'd detected the smell of gas, and opening the door, she found that the heater had blown out while you slept. After that, there'd been alarums and excursions all through the house, but no memory of the excitement survived the moment, and when you kissed Helen, it was for her prettiness alone. At breakfast, Uncle Jack leaned toward your father and whispered in his ear. *That was one lucky piss,* he said, and no one knew you'd heard.

Inhaling the heater gas had given your father a headache (why not you?), but even so, knowing that you had *Kaddish* to say, he sought and found you a *schul.* It was a long walk from the boardinghouse, and there wasn't much to see when you got there, only a small white building ill-defined against the snow, but it served, that evening and the following morning, for your *Yisgadals.* Not long later, you and your father were headed for home on the Empire State Express. His headache had not abated, and for most of the journey he stood in the vestibule with his brow pressed against the pane. You sat watching the flight of towns and trees, of slush-gray clouds and snowed-on roads.

At Albany, the train crossed to the east bank of the Hudson, and some way downriver, your father took a seat for the first time. The headache was still with him, though, and again he tried to chill it away, and at length he fell asleep. Sitting on the aisle, you gazed past him at the broadening stream, and somewhere beyond Rhinebeck, you saw a band of open sky to the west, just above the lilac Catskills. Soon the sun descended into the clear and fired a salvo of light across the frozen snow-still country. The colors stirred you—so many kinds of blue! you thought, blue snow and lavender shade!—and thinking of nothing else, you tugged at your father's sleeve, saying *Look, papa! Look at the sunset!* But, roused, he turned to you, not to the ravishing sun and shade, and he was angry, and in anger's colors, the excursion came to an end.

SCENE 81

THE NEVINS HOUSEHOLD (1914-20)

It was a flat of seven rooms laid out in line, a railway flat, and though you called it home for all those years, you knew even then that nothing there belonged to you: it always seemed that you were on a long stay in the home of someone else. You were sheltered in those four-walled spaces, you were fed, guided, cherished, but every such favor was extended through your mother, you thoght, and it reached you secondhand. Only two of the rooms had an easeful air, the one where food was prepared and the one where it was eaten; the others were mere containers of bedding, chiffoniers, and vitreous china strung on a hallway bare except for a Persian runner.

No Steens or Hogarths warmed the walls nor gleaming Meissoniers, no tinted light streamed in through leaded panes, no pots of copper glowed. The parquet flooring and the linoleum were of an undistinguished pattern, and the sink beside the stove was crazed. The diningroom with a seven-branched *Menorah*, the kitchen with a hanging pot of Wandering Jew— your grandma's realm, those two rooms were, and there she ruled supreme. The laws imposed were those of Moses. As one of the children of Israel, she said, you were to eat only of such beasts as parted the hoof and chewed the cud, for only they were clean, and of the fishes of the sea, you were to partake of them that boasted fins and scales, all others being an abomination. Banned, therefore, were the things that dwelt in the mud of the land and the ooze of the deep, turn from the swine, she said, refuse yourself the eel, nor might you touch creatures known to creep, the serpent, the snail, nor them that fed on flesh, as the raven did and the gier eagle. And should you fail to heed, she said, should your mouth ever know the meat of the hawk or the flavor of the hare, you yourself would become

127

unclean, an abomination even until the evening of the day.

You didn't know what an abomination was and had no wish to be one, but since no forbidden foods defiled the house, your grandma's rules were observed with ease. She had others, though, and these required more of you than obedience when it was impossible to disobey. The pantry contained two sets of dishes, one for meals at which meat was served and one for those of the dairy. *Fleischig* and *milchig,* they were called, and woe to him who confused them. If caught by your grandma, you'd be read a lecture and made to witness the ceremony of purification, but if you fell to Ellen, her little mick deputy, you'd be rapped on the head with whatever you'd tainted: be it cutlery or crockery, she'd snatch it away and knock your block with it, crying while she did so *You sinful cocklebrained boy!*

It was years before you understood the origin of her fury, and by then both she and your grandma were dead. At the time, you were unable to measure the depth and reach of their relation, and you'd wonder, when you came upon them together, when you found them hovering above some chore at the sink, the range, the drainboard, what bound them as fast as blood. They'd seem to be less at work than conspiring—the Jew and the Catholic, the Litvak and the mick from Sligo, what burned so bright between them, what light did you fail to see? You know now that in some transcendent way, it *was* blood. They were no witchwives bent over devildoing. They were mother and daughter, and at the sink and the stove and in their separate rooms, it was love that lay between them, and it lies there still, between their separate graves.

SCENE 82

WHITE BREAD (1914-20)

Bread! What you remember best is bread!

Until then, all food had seemed the same: you ate what you were given, and you had no favorite flavors, textures, colors, kinds. You knew, or you'd been told, that your mother had worked no wonders at the stove, but however put before you, food there always was, and as such it always served. On becoming hungry, all you were aware of was a certain slowing down, rather like a mutoscope when you forgot to turn the crank, and then, having been fed, you'd see the pictures pick up speed. . . . But your grandma's bread! What better rained the Lord on Moses, what better brake his son at the Supper?

Every Thursday evening, after the dishes had been washed and put away, there was a long and intense to-do in the kitchen. You were forbidden the area on pain of being laid about by Ellen, but well back from the door, you'd loiter and observe, and week after week, it was a work of magic that you watched your grandma perform. Aided by Ellen (the stage assistant, you thought, in black silk tights and glittering spangles!), she dipped flour from a sack and sieved it onto a table-top until a foot-high cone had grown before her. Making a crater at the summit, she filled it with a dash of water from a pitcher that Ellen brought her, and into the pool she dropped guesses of salt and crumbled leaven. You saw no measures dry or measures liquid, you heard no mumbled numbers. She kept no count you ever knew of: there were only surmise handfuls, pinches added and pinches taken away; nothing was done by weight or grain or calibration. And yet you had this certainty, that after the kneading of the dough, after the night-long rise and the baking, seven loaves would emerge from the oven that had no equal in the world, nor would they have until the following week. There was never a failure. Never were the ratios wrong, never the sprinklings too fine, the pinches scant. Each Friday morning, seven loaves of bread would be born in fire to live as long as you did. When you forgot their taste, you'd be dead.

SCENE 83

SISTER RUTH AND BROTHER JULIAN (1916)*

Christmas 1916

The holiday meant nothing to either of you. It belonged to *others,* you'd been told, and therefore once each year, you watched what *others* did, saw through wreathed windows their sweet and solemn joys. In the street, little evergreen forests made you breathe deep on your way to school, and displayed in many stores were the toys that would go to *others,* the boys and girls called *others,* and except for that one year, none of them was yours.

That year, your Uncle Dave sent you a letter from faraway Peru, and along with the letter came a ten-dollar bill, half of it for your sister, he wrote, and

---

* This piece first appeared in *To Feed Their Hopes.* It is reprinted here with minor changes and a new heading.

half of it for you. He directed that the money be spent on Christmas presents, one for her and one for yourself, and being the elder, you were to choose them both. You were to use care and good judgment, he said, and for once, as though you were *others,* there'd be presents for the Jews!

Not far from where you lived, no further in fact than the corner, there was a shop called Peck's, where candy could be bought, and school supplies, and pipes, and snuff, and cigarettes, but in season its shelves and showcases were dense with playthings, and you'd wander among them in a state of wonder, awed by a Flexible Flyer, agape at a set of trains. Never before this, though, had you stared at such as a buyer, one who might pause, point, and acquire; now, with a yellowback in your hand, you were a customer! and you equaled the seller at last.

On entering the store, you'd gone straight to the counter that held a magic lantern, and you'd stopped before it, fingering the red enamel on the chimney, the slide-holder, the tube containing the prism and the lens. You could see, even then, even there, postcards glowing on a plaster wall—balsa boats on Lake Titicaca, Mount Illimani, and a *chimba-chaca,* as your uncle called it, a rope bridge over a gorge. A magic lantern, you thought—but it was the magic, only the magic, that your five dollars bought.

Now came your sister's turn, five dollars' worth for your sister Ruth. What she wanted, and what you knew she wanted, what long she'd longed for, lay ineluctable near the stereopticon: a doll house. With its front lowered and its furnishings exposed—beds the size of dominoes, peewee chairs and sofas, minim chiffoniers—it sought you out and mutely dunned your eyes. You remembered how your sister had yearned through the doorway, drawn by the toy as it now drew you, and you knew, *knew,* how raptured she'd be when, as though you were Uncle Dave, you brought it home, not from a shop at the corner but from faraway Peru.

You were about to buy it when what light there was in the store seemed to converge on one particular object, and in a surround of gloom, it grew luminous, as from some quantum within. You peered into the candescence, and at its core you found what caused it—a sun, a burning mass, a brass and blazing motorboat. At once, it became for you the prime marvel of the pastime world. Gone your memory of a sister's hunger for a small-scale house and its scaled-down wares, gone all thought of her foreknown bliss. Entranced yourself, you bought the boat for your sister Ruth. . . !

Christmas 1976

Sixty times since then, Bethlehem has toured the sun, sixty rounds the radiant manger, and still you can hear the way your sister cried, still see her face change as fancy shrank and hope died — sixty years, and still when you think of her shrunken face, you shrink too. She got the doll house, of course — your father was there, and he simply stared you and the boat out of the flat and back to the store — but it made no difference. You hadn't known what the day was for. It belonged to *others,* just as you'd been told.

SCENE 84

BENEATH A TIFFANY CHANDELIER (1914-20)

It was a bell-shaped spread of leaded glass, its little panes making a show of grapes and leaves, a green and purple scene. The piece was suspended above the circular board in your Aunt Rae's diningroom, and many a time you'd sat there marvelling at the jigsaw vineyard, but if you reached up to touch one of the amethyst clusters, you'd be told to keep your hands away. You learned later of *l'art nouveau,* but at the time all you knew of it was a pendent lamp that threw a cloth of light over a table of mahogany. Where you lived, there was nothing like it, no art new and no art old: your grandma's house was the place where you ate and slept and changed your clothes; it was bare of decoration. You've never forgotten that lamp; it still sways slightly in some room of your mind, still turns on those twisted stems, still glows.

As a companion of your cousin Jassie, you were often in his home, and once in a while, if the hour was late, you'd be asked to stay for supper. In that household, none of the rules of *kashruth* held, and your Aunt Rae's fare was a very bill of abominations. It offered the flesh of swine and of beef and lamb the forbidden loin, and you saw, through quilts of cream, the lobster claw, the crab, the shrimp, and hung meat too was seen, the shot deer, the high bird, the iridescent hare. Abominable, these things were, and hateful to the Lord, yet there they were, steaming and savory, beneath the Tiffany chandelier.

Strange to say, you never desired them. Of your Aunt Rae's cuisine, the only real allurement was what you called the *frankfooter.* The deviled Chincoteague drew you not, nor did the *moule marinière,* the scrapple, the oyster

131

gumbo—nay, it was only the little pink link—the dog. Frankfooters were presented once each week, on the maid's day off, and if your aunt chanced to note your avid look, that was the day you made five of a family of four beneath that Tiffany chandelier.

You'd be seated thus, your uncle facing your aunt and your cousins Jassie and Gladys between them at either hand. Your place was always at your Aunt Rae's side, almost directly across from her husband, and from there you could watch him without his knowing, because he never then, nor ever after, took you in or let you catch his eye. For all you knew, he may have thought that your chair was vacant, that you weren't there. But he was, and sometimes, for moments on end, you'd study him through the cone of light thrown by the chandelier.

Within his reach, there'd be bowls and boats and salvers of adjunctive foods, of sauerkraut and piccalilli, of green tomatoes in brine, of liquefying Camembert and pork on hills of beans, and there was a trencher too with rye bread slices, gray as ash and moist as clay—and when to all these a tray of frankfooters came, the air grew heady with spice and herb. Served first, your uncle would fall to eating at once, and while you awaited your turn, you'd observe his workman ways. He was a deft and remorseless guttler, eating with his face down, but blind, it seemed, to the victual agony on the plate before him, deaf to the screams, unmoved by the squirting juices, the pleas to the gods of prey—for it wasn't food, nor did he eat it; it was fair game, and he fed.

When your helping came—two frankfooters (two and never more), a lengthwise quarter of a dill pickle, and a modest mound of beans—when your aunt passed you your share of the feast, you'd go at it slowly, chew it well to make it last. You knew that however much you honed—and hone you did!—nothing else would come your way. Of the dozen frankfooters your aunt had bought, two would still be on the platter, and, hopeless, helpless, hungry, you'd watch your uncle take them for himself with his knife and fork (tooth and talon!) and devour them, screams and all. He never offered you one, or even part of one—but how could he have done so? You weren't there beneath the Tiffany chandelier.

SCENE 85

DISSENT (1915)

"Julian," your Grandpa Nevins would say, "do like everybody does. Take butter as much as you want—there is no limitation in this house—but put it on your plate."

It was your inclination to treat the butterdish as part of your table-setting. Others drew on it only for a renewed supply, taking it for what it was, a receptacle to be used in common, no different in nature from a saltcellar or a pepper-shaker. To you in your proof world, it was a private piece of china at the mercy of your knife.

"Food you can have," your grandpa would say, "all a human being could get away with. But when you want butter—and you could have a pound—it's only right you should take it with the butter-knife, not the one you been using on your plate."

You'd hear him, you'd even feel his hand detaining your own, and, more, you'd know it was true that he was objecting to your habit and not to your share—but when the pause ended, and the meal was resumed, again, as though you hadn't been reproved, you'd do the same as you'd done before. Of all those at the board, four, five, and often more, only you would infringe your grandpa's rule, and in a pervious moment, you'd wonder about your self-exemption, about the special rights of Childe Julian. There were none, you'd allow, but at meals to come, or even now, on the heels of a chiding, you'd butter your bread according to your bent.

"Julian," your grandpa would say, "how many times must I tell you. . . ?"

Across that circular field of white linen, a long and indecisive engagement would be fought over food. Daily—aye, thrice daily—there'd be a collision of wills between you and your grandparents, an encounter brought on by one or another of your dietetic aversions. They were many and various, and none could be explained, none overcome. Nothing would persuade you to try certain dishes, neither plea nor threat nor ridicule. Their agreeable taste, their universal edibility, would be made known with rolled eyes, shown to you with licked lips, with sensual purrs and groans, but all such efforts would go to waste, fail and fall away, like a charge against a sunken road, a stone wall, a Devil's Den.

When peppers were being cooked, you could hardly enter the flat. They'd remind you (why? how?) of the sweetsome smell of privet, and at your core you'd feel a clenching, as if your stomach were making a fist.

In the Nevins household, coffee was served with heated milk, but now and then, if allowed to reach a boil, it would form a phlegmatic skin that you could no more swallow than the pickings of a nose.

Fish was a staple. Many kinds were offered, and the offers came in many ways, but rarely would hunger so pang you that you'd try the haddock, the carp, the pike, the halibut ("Take some Albert," your grandma would say), and as for the smelt, how could you have gotten past the name?

"Julian, Julian," your grandpa would say, "use the butter-knife, not your own!"

There were difficulties too with feathered things. Unfit were the neck and the running gear, the giblets and the wings. The remainder, the breast, would be refused unless tendered in prune-juice. Prune-juice!

Of a hard-boiled egg, you'd eat the white, but never the yolk.

If cake came with raisins, you'd pick them out, and you'd do the same with citron, currants, and maraschino cherries.

Watery custard would be rejected — custard with holes, you'd call it — and though you'd down the foam of a lemon pie, you'd never touch the filling.

Cold veal and cold lamb would turn you cold behind your navel, and the smell of saffron would make you sweat.

"Julian, Julian. . . ," your grandpa would say.

And your father would say, "Julian, I want you to listen to your grandpa. Do you hear me?"

What was there about marzipan that put you off, about bonbons, nougat, and blancmange? What made an alligator pear unthinkable, a persimmon, a mango, a papaya? Why couldn't you bear watermelon, dates, figs, rhubarb? Where did the list end — with borscht, schav, lentil soup, with buttermilk, sour cream, sturgeon?

"Put the butter on your plate, Julian," your grandpa would say. "Eat to your heart's content, but put it on your plate."

Strawberry ice cream — you never ordered strawberry in your life! And never having tasted herring, how did you know it would've made you puke? And why no cucumbers, onions, Roquefort cheese. . . ?

"You know what's the trouble with that boy?" your grandpa would say. "He's never been hungry."

And your sister would sit there and laugh.

THE COLOR OF THE AIR, VIII

RALPH A. BLAKELOCK — 1847
A DREAMER PERISHES

In the beginning the end, wherefore he must've been born with signs
on the palm of his hand, islands on the lines, rings, mounts, a *via
lascivia* to give the kind and cast of his mind, a crossing of creases
to betoken his first and last illness — his life. It must've been known,
that history-to-come, it must've shown on his plain of Mars that he'd
bear seventy-some years of pain and die.

From a queer father, this queer son — shy, tight-spun, a ten o'clock
scholar, a lover of olive-green and lonely places, a visioner, a sleep-
walker, a negative in a positive world, and as for his pictures, he'd
be his pictures, he'd be the shaded side of his trees, dappled by his
filigreed suns and moons, he'd be faint little rills, fainter wraiths,
he'd be paint in part and part painter. In time, it'd be only night
that he drew, and sylvan figures dressed in white, fauna, really, as
seen from afar, and no wind would preen the leaves, and even the
streams would seem to have paused, as if he'd invaded a dream and
made it stop.

It must've been there at the start, that his scenes would be hard
to sell. Some palmar arch, some flexion-fold of skin must've told how
he'd hawk them from door to door, a canvasser of canvases, how
he'd trade them for a meal, for a marriage service, display them in
junkshop windows, deal for them in lots, thirty-three once for a
hundred dollars flat, and if that was written, this was too, his madness,
and how the sane would see him in freak clothes snacked with snickets
of trash, how he'd wear a dagger in a beaded sash and tear up blood-
won money, burn it, strew it in the streets.

In the beginning the end: twenty years in an asylum, a wall outside
his wall. There'd be no more trees embroidered on the sky, no more
jabots of running water, no more rounds with rolls of landscape,
and gone the vivid turbans and tassels of defeat — the end, twenty
years of peering into himself, a dim and simple room. He'd be painting money then, million-dollar bills, and he'd be giving them away:
he'd be rich.

135

SCENE 86

HARLEM (1915)

The Perlmans lived only a block or two from your grandma's, in an apartment house called the De Peyster. They were even closer to the Model School, and you'd pass by each weekday morning and again in the afternoon, and you can still remember the iron grille between the sidewalk and the cellar well, the granite pillars at the entrance, the tiled hallway and its dark red rug. You knew many of the tenants, and even now their names come back to mind—Jaffin, Weinstein, Solomon, Henline, Avrutine—but it was to join your cousin Jassie that you stopped there every day.

Somehow, in the games you liked to play, he had become your partner. In such contests as marble-shooting, card-tossing, and pitching buttons at a crack, though he engaged in none himself—could not in fact knuckle an imme—he gathered in your winnings and took his share of all. You never disputed this levy—possibly on some hazy occasion, he'd chipped in with a soiled card or a cracked agate—but you did wonder, and you wonder yet, how half of your kickshaw kingdom could've been swapped for a pistareen.

In truth, the marbles meant little to you, not even the swirling reals, and as for the baseball faces on the buttons, who was Hooks Wiltse, who was Orvie Overall? But in a higher realm by far were the pasteboard chromos that came in cigarette boxes and ever after wore sachet. Two particular series are part of the permanent repertoire of your mind, one of them picturing lighthouses and the other theatres new and old. You can still see the Haymarket as you saw it then, and the Garrick, and the Drury Lane, and just as clearly loom the piles of Minot's Ledge, Fastnet, Ile Vierge, and Alguada Reef. There are no people in those paper squares, and nothing moves, nothing seems alive: the stages are empty, waves are poised at the break, the very gulls are drawn on the sky. The porticoes, the tapering towers, the halted water and the wind—why have you retained them? you wonder. In the still streets, in the soundless cry of birds, was there a loneliness to match your own?

In front of the De Peyster grew a row of elms, and every afternoon, from the open earth at their feet, the shouts of little gamesmen rose—*Dubbs!* they'd call, or *Knucks down tight!*—and nearby on the pavement Thalias fluttered down to capture Globes. On days when you'd lost your stake, you'd stand aside and look about you, at passing people, at delivery wagons, at horses hauling drays, at starlings among the dumplings picking grain, and you'd see awnings ripple and the candy-cane revolving of a barberpole. Sometimes, in the doorway of the De Peyster, you'd find a boy you knew, Nate Weinstein,* who played no games at all. Older than you by a year or more, he took no interest in the coveys in the dirt before him — to his mind, you thought, they and you were like those starlings in the gutter — and he'd loaf there on the stoop, his arms adangle as if his sleeves were stuffed, and you'd wonder how he could appear to shamble while merely standing still. Natchie, his mother called him, but his name was Nathanael, he'd told you — Nathanael von Wallenstein Weinstein — and the Nathanael was spelled with an *a*. But whatever the name and however he wrote it, to you he was a big-eared and homely boy, a lurcher in his way of going and out of sync at rest. Never, though, did you find him ungainly in the mind.

It would kill him one day, that discord. There was something wrong with his neural wiring, some defect in the fibres, the sheathing, there was a short, a shunt, and what began as a command to slacken would end in still more speed. The impulse was always right; the response, at a certain time and in a special place, would be fatal. That time and place were then three thousand miles and twenty-some years away. On a day in a far December, at a roadcross near the Salton Sink he'd instruct his foot to press a brake, and instead it would tread the gas, and there'd ensue a great smashing of wood and glass and metal, only the start of which he'd hear, and within an hour the unhandy boy (the one on the stoop grown older) would be dead.

But all that was unknown on those afternoons before the De Peyster, and someone would cry *No heistings!* and with your knucks down tight, you'd shoot your red and blue real.

SCENE 87

THE WIDOWER (1914-15)

The world grew greatly different for you that year, became indeed another world, but as you'd been unaware of the old, so were you unknowing of the new: you still went about within yourself, still began and ended in your skin. You were in a room called you, walled in even from your father, and

---

* Later, Nathanael West.

you spent your days strangely, as if you were living out some novel calendar. What did you miss, you wonder, what were the doings you never knew of, what was said that you never heard? You try to put time aside, to fly back in fancy.

What were your father's days? What thoughts did he have through all those mornings among dusting lawbooks, what was he told by the brethren posed and dead in the steel engravings, by the slow-motion smoke overhead? Where did he while away the afternoons, on what bench in what park? And how did he make the evenings go—in a small-stake game of cards? a walk in the dark with a last cigar? or did he find other ways to go pleasuring that you were blind to at the time?

Had there been women—but how could there not have been women? How could cards have beguiled him, street-corner talk, the bulldog edition of the *Times*? At thirty-seven, how could he have abstained for phrases in front of a drug-store, for another Between the Acts, for a meld of the jack of diamonds and the black-eyed queen of spades? You allow now what you'd've denied then, that he didn't always stare through his office window, didn't always square the block when he went for a breath of air. At the end of the stroll, had there not been a woman waiting? And if so, had your mother known her, had she been a neighbor once, a guest on occasion, a summer acquaintance, had she been someone that you yourself passed in the street? Or had she been a stranger, met by chance in some corridor or conveyance, during an intermission, at a counter in a shop, and had she lasted long, you wonder, or been one of a succession?

Your father resided with you at your grandparents' home for six years, until the summer of 1920. In all that time, never once did he fail to come home for the night. It was a point of honor, you thought.

SCENE 88

SON-IN-LAW PHIL (1914-20)

After your mother's death, your father resided with her parents. He'd spent all he possessed on her illnesses, and for him the home-of-his-own was gone, and with it the rosewood upright, the shelf of Shakespeare (37 vols.), the Holsteins agraze on the wall, and out of reach as well the boardinghouse of Mrs. Behr and even the cheap hotel. Later on, he rarely spoke of those times, and since you, for your part, let them be, they seem now to have been uneventful, like some era free of war and revolution, of famine, panic, pestilence. If there was discord in that household, it was never shown or known to you.

You've never forgotten that long-ago day when you tried to throw earth into your mother's grave, and you still remember how your father drew you back and cried, but there, beside that mound of fill, the day seems to end, as though nothing more occurred to store away in your mind. You know now that another age began when you left the cemetery behind, but all you saw then was what you passed in the Brooklyn streets—signs, shops, lines and lines of windows gaping back at you.

From the car, your father must've seen what you did, the same trees and trolley-wires, the same people in the same doorways, but you've always wondered what he was thinking of—the hard times coming, or the good times past. Did he dwell on the bread of benevolence, did he dread what he'd receive because of his wife, or did he rewind his life a dozen years and stand once more under a canopy of blue and gold, did he bring back the face, the flowers, the form of his bride, did he hear the Rabbi intoning before them, did he hear the questions and responses, the benediction, the sound of breaking glass? Did he recall the precise music, the initial round that he and your mother waltzed alone? And after the feast and the toasting, did he rise to read from the yellow papers he held in his hand, telegrams from Oakland, Shreveport, Pittsburgh, Little Falls

May your future be as bright as Edison's electric light
May happiness be your share, and may you never know the word despair
Best wishes for a long lifetime of married happiness

and did he rue the yellowed hopes, the good will of no avail? A long lifetime, he may have thought, from Vienna Hall to the grave in something short of a dozen years. As the car crossed one of the bridges to Manhattan, he must've known that the hard times coming were already there.

For six years, he was beholden to your grandparents, and in all that while you never heard from him or them a raised voice, a refusal, an ill-tempered word. It was their house that your father lived in, and he and his children were only tenants at will, but so well was their gift bestowed that it could not fail to be well received. And for not being made to lower his head because of his empty pockets, your father honored your grandpa and grandma as long as they lived, and thereafter as long as he did.

SCENE 89

GUMMELAPPEN (1914-20)

Years earlier, in their lower East Side butchershop, the Shapiro family had used the word to describe the cut of beef between the ribs and the hip, a shallow layer of meat that stretched across the bones in thick elastic strings. Its texture was tenacious, breaking down slowly and holding little fluid or flavor; when boiled, however, when seethed in seasoning with the proper greens and herbs, there came a time when it seemed to relent, to yield juices long withheld, a succulence concealed. All his life, your father would smile when he spoke of *gummelappen*, because the word meant rubber bands.

In the Nevins household, the same cut was known as *flanken*, and no figure of speech ascribed to it the qualities of another object: there your father alone enjoyed his joke about rubber bands. Even so, whether the meat was *flanken* or *gummelappen*, your grandma's skill with it was supreme, and if your father's allusion was beyond her, his relish for her cookery was plain. On such days as soup was part of the fare, he'd come home from the office, and without waiting to put off his derby and chesterfield, he'd rush into the kitchen, gaff some meat from the pot, and wrap it in bread, and then, derby-hatted and velvet-collared, red with the winter wind, he'd stand there eating, occasionally breaking off to exclaim *Gummelappen! Gummelappen!* and though neither of them understood him your grandma and Ellen would smile.

SCENE 90

ZOOLOGICAL GARDENS (1915)

zo-ol-ogy: the branch of biology dealing with the animal kingdom

Your mother used to take you there from Harlem, and as you rode down Fifth Avenue on the deck of a coach, you'd call off the mansions as you passed them by, Carnegie's at 91st, and Frick's, and Phipps', and Tiffany's, and then you'd be at the Zoo. As you went from cage to cage, there too you'd recite what you knew, and reading from the plaques as well as you could, you'd say *Vulpes fulva*, and *Ursus maritimus*, and *Procyon lotor*, and from red fox, polar bear, and raccoon, you'd proceed to *Pecari angulatus.* To you it was *Pessary angulatus,* and you were unaware that nearby conversation ceased and women turned to stare.

One day about a year after your mother's death, you found yourself alone in your Aunt Rae's flat. You no longer know the reason for your visit, nor can you recall why no one else was there. Where was your Cousin Jassie, you wonder, and what of his sister Gladys—were they still at school, and if so, should you not have been there too?—and even less accountable was the absence of your aunt. But however it may have come about (some crisis, was it, some devil to pay?), the household was away, and you were by your lonesome.

No voices, no tin and china frictions, no running water, no footfalls to hear but your own. You wandered from room to room, fingering mahogany, ivory, jade, bronze, and even the colored glass of the chandelier, drifting, drifting along the hall—and all at once you were drifting no more. (*I was looking in my mother's dresser,* Jassie had told you, *not for anything paticalar, just looking, and way back in a drawer, I come across a thing I couldn't figure out what it was, a funny kind of a thing.*) You knew where you were going.

The bedroom smelled of your aunt, you remember, but not of your uncle—of her sachet, of her perfume and powder, of her, and it was she who escaped when you opened a maple drawer. You gazed at trays of pins and buttons, at piles of handkerchiefs, gloves, scarves, and you saw too the jars, the reticules, the orange-sticks, and far back in a corner, you turned up a small and well-worn box. It was shaped rather like a toy hat-box, and indeed, on being opened, it revealed a little hat. (*I was looking in my mother's drawer, and I come across a thing.*) A thing like a hat, you thought, a rubber ring with a rubber crown (*a funny kind of a thing*), dark gray, and it gave when you pressed it (*I couldn't figure out what it was*), and you turned it over, guessed at the top and the bottom, sniffed it for a sign, but in the end you were in the dark, as Jassie had been, and you replaced the hat in the box, the funny thing, the what's-it-for. . . .

And suddenly you knew—you couldn't've explained, but you knew. It had to do with your aunt and uncle, it was something they used in a secret way, something for the dark, the bed, the room that smelled of orris root and not of sweat and cigars. . . .

At the Zoo, you kept on reading the contents of the cages. *Lynx canadensis,* you'd say, and *Equus zebra,* and *Pecari angulatus*—still *pessary* to you, though not to those nearby.

SCENE 91

LONG BRANCH, N.J. (1915)

There was no cottage that year; instead, early in June, your Grandpa Nevins took the family to a summer hotel. Miller's, it was called, and it claimed to be *kosher*, or else your grandma would never have gone there and surely never have stayed. As you recall it, there were two stories to the place, each so trimmed with fretwork that they seemed to be draped in lace. It was on North Bath near Second, adjoining a small white *schul*. A month or so of your *Kaddish* remained, and you hadn't far to go.

Your father came for the weekends. You'd meet him at the depot, a little shed, really, almost lost in a bower of privet, and two days later you'd see him off, stare down-track at the last car (it looked like an angry face) until it was out of sight. Those weekends were your weeks. No sooner had your father gone than you began to watch for his return, and day after day you'd wait for hours beside the rails, sometimes talking to the gateman, sometimes merely gazing along the shimmering right-of-way. There were bees among the yellow-green flowers of the hedge (did the humming come from the flowers or the bees?), and the only other sound came from telegraph wire being tuned by the wind. You felt sheltered there, as if you were looking from a cave at falling rain. And then Friday would come, and a distant whistle — two longs, two shorts — and you'd see a high-stacked American running toward you up the track, and soon your father would be letting you carry the basket of peaches or plums he'd brought for your Grandma Nevins.

On one such Friday, when your father reached the hotel, your Aunt Ida introduced him to a cousin named Adele, a visitor from Duluth — and only later did you see what he saw then, a gift, the gift of peaches, the gift of plums. As you remember her, she was a plain and pleasant woman, a little younger than your mother would've been, and having few accomplishments, she pretended to none at all, wherefore she was thought to have many more than she did. You see her vaguely as someone in white, but it was summertime, and every woman dressed in white. You rather liked her.

Your father liked her too, but not for a wife. He was courteous, courtly, even, but whatever your grandparents may have intended, it came to nothing. Adele stayed for a week or two, and then she went back to Duluth. After that, there were many more Friday afternoons, many more arrivals with fruit.

SCENE 92

AND GRANT THEE ETERNAL PEACE (1915)

One day, near the end of June, your grandma told you that your year of mourning was almost over, that you'd honored your mother with your prayers and won everlasting repose for her soul. You were a *goldene Kind,* she said, and she wished for you a long life and a descendant to be proud of, as she was proud of you. When you returned from *schul* that night, she said, the eleven-month year would end. And then you left the lacework hotel and went toward the corner, where the little *schul* was a white box among the evening trees, and you thought *this is the last time, the last time,* and you felt as though you were coming to the real finish of your mother's funeral—after eleven months, this the final spadeful.

In the morning, you woke to find your torn jacket gone and with it the black armband, and you thought of what your companions would think—that you and they were equals now, that once again you were free to play. But when you joined them out-of-doors, they seemed still to be hampered by your presence, as if you were still in your rent garments, still wearing crape on your sleeve. You came among them now without your signs, you and they were the same to the eye and ear, someone running, jeering, digging down to water in the sand—but they'd always see an armband in their minds.

SCENE 93

BROTHER'S KEEPER (1916)

"None of that, now!" Ellen said.

You'd just returned from school, and, shucking your coat on the run, you left it behind as you sped for the pantry, where, as you knew, Friday's batch of pastries would be cooling on a shelf.

"None of that, you slummocky boy!" she said. "It's devil a morsel your face will know whilst your coat is on the floor!"

143

She picked it up, and, in the act of flinging it at you, she paused to puzzle out its unexpected weight. Suspending it by the collar, she hefted it a few times, as though a jigging in the air would force a disclosure.

"What's in these pockets?" she said. "The sins of all the world?"

And then, spreading the coat on the drainboard, she began to extract its burden—*your* burden, you thought as you watched the search proceed. In single bits, in pairs and pinches, and at last in handfuls, there emerged an embarrassment of trash, your gleanings of a year. Matchsticks, nutshells, twigs, hairpins, and pencil-stubs, all these were drawn by Ellen from your swollen pockets, and these as well, bottlecaps, buttons, rubber bands, box-nails bent and box-nails new.

"What're you doin'?" Ellen said. "Sweepin' the streets?"

The pile grew, and you yourself no longer knew what you'd stooped for in gutters and hallways, on station platforms and flights of stairs. You were shown now: ball bearings were brought to light, and a Sweet Cap box, and hooks-and-eyes, and acorns, and a rock the size of your fist; and fished from the depths were a twist of metal, a spill of paper, a toothpick quill, a yard or more of twine, and a buckle from a shoe. And still the pile grew.

"For the love of the Saints!" Ellen said, "You left no room for your hands!"

Beads, washers, screws, a cork, a spool, a sprung spring, all these were brought from the pockets and added to the finds of before—and then, as you wondered whether there'd ever be an end, the end began to appear. No longer were knowable objects mined by Ellen's hand, no more the keys, the combs, the orange rinds. What came up now was deposit, the dust, the crumbs, the shreds and grains of larger things.

"You must have a hole in your thatch!" Ellen said.

You knew you weren't crazy, but how you have explained what imbued you? How could you have put it? Who would've believed that what you'd seen in that salmagundi of junk was danger to others, the unwary, the unobservant, the many who were dead to the world? Could you have realized for others the stumble, the skid, the fall, could you have described the broken head, the compound fracture, the tumble down a stair? You weren't crazy at all, but that's what you'd be thought if you took the blame for not removing the cause—the stick on which a foot would trip, the pebble, the next-to-nothing that would lead to blood and death.

144

But suppose you *had* been able to speak of the compulsion, suppose you'd gabbed until Ellen understood—what would you have said if she'd asked you this:

"Very noble-hearted, but why didn't you just boot the trouble out of the road?"

How could you have made her see that you couldn't have put the trouble aside, that for trouble there was no place in the world that was out of the road? You had to bear it, and that meant you had to carry it away.

You said nothing. You merely watched while Ellen fetched the garbage-pail.

SCENE 94

DISSENT (1916)

For rebellion is as the sin of witchcraft.
—1 Sam. 15:23

On Saturday afternoons, it was your father's custom to visit his sister Sarah, who with her husband Harris Friedman and their numerous family dwelt in a four-story brownstone on 117th Street near Lenox Avenue. Adjoined by taller buildings, the house seemed to cower in their shadow, its rooms gloomful reminders of man's numbered days. A flight of steps led from the sidewalk to the main entry and an upper hall that gave on a formal suite frequented only on the great occasion. More commonly used was the doorway below the stoop, a dark mouth, and even before you entered it, you'd be met by its breath, an exhalation very near to having substance. It was the almost palpable ghost of saffron, a flavoring that so poisoned the air that you could hardly bear to breathe it.

Before leaving for his office, your father would say, "I'll be at Aunt Sarah's later in the day. I'd like you to join me there."

"I'm suppose to go to the park and play ball," you'd say. "Me and Lenny, we're the Harvard A. C., and we have a game on with the Yale A. C.— that's Jassie and Carl Sloss. They challenged us."

"I think the park will still be there tomorrow."

"But the game is today!"

"My sister is hurt because you see her so seldom. She knows how often you visit Aunt Rae."

"That's different," you'd say.

"Different?" your father would say. "How so? Aunt Sarah is your aunt, and so is Aunt Rae. Where's the difference?"

"The difference is Aunt Sarah is your sister."

Your father would study you for a moment, and then he'd say, "What you mean, then, is that you're a Nevins, not a Shapiro."

"I guess so."

"A bad guess, Julian. Whether you like it or not, you're half-Shapiro — and I wish I knew which half it was. You're one tough nut, do you know that, Julian?" He'd turn to go then, saying, "If you decide to play ball, I hope Harvard wins," and the door would close.

Harvard would neither win nor lose, because Harvard would not play. At the urging of your Grandma Nevins, you and Lenny would seek out Carl and Jassie and tell them that there'd be no game that day. They'd whisper to each other, and then they'd go into another room, where they'd laugh and be silent and laugh some more, and when they returned, they'd hand you a note, and you and Lenny would read: *We are sorry we challenged COWARDS!*

And later, at Aunt Sarah's, you'd sit in the savor of saffron, and still rippling before you, you'd see the note from Yale, a white flag of words, all in blue but the red and capital last: *COWARDS!*

After a time, your father would glance your way, saying, "What made you come? I thought you were a tough nut."

"Oh, I am," you'd say. "I chew Star Navy and spit ham gravy."

And your Aunt Sarah would say, "*Was meint das,* Phil — a tough nut?"

"It means my dear son Julian."

SCENE 95

ON THE WAY HOME (1916)

After leaving Aunt Sarah's, you and your father would walk for a while, sometimes in a winter afternoon. You'd pass huge mounds of snow in the gutters, soiled if they'd stayed there long, gray igloos studded with rinds and bottlecaps and streaked at the base by dogs. But away in the distance, the spoilage could not be seen, and the slopes of the park were lavender in the low-down sunlight and purple in the shade.

And your father would say, "You're quiet, kid. What're you thinking about?"

"Aunt Sarah," you'd say. "The way she looks."

And he'd say, "What way is that?"

"She looks like a Shapiro."

"Well, she *is* a Shapiro."

"The Shapiros look alike," you'd say. "I was watching her, and after a while, she began to look like you. Very fierce."

"Do you think I look fierce?"

"Aunt Rae says all the Shapiros do. They could kill you with their eyes, she says."

"And what do you say?"

"Well, you get pretty mad at me sometimes."

"That's true," he'd say. "But the Shapiros don't kill, and I'm afraid the Perlmans do."

SCENE 96

SEVENTY-FIVE FLIES (1916)

That summer, your grandpa's seashore cottage was out along Sairs Avenue, a dirt road leading from Long Branch to the village of West End. It was smaller than those of other years, and it was plainer too, lacking their fretwork, their bartizans, their windows in the roof. It was simply a white house with shiplap siding, and it comes back as having been narrow, compressed, even though it stood quite apart from everything but weeds. Far back from it, almost against the railroad embankment, the shack where the year-round owner lived rode hull-down in reeds and catkin, and you and your cousin Jassie saw it only when you broke your way to the tracks to watch for Pullmans and call off their fetching names—*Nokomis, Tombigbee, Fallen Leaf.* . . .

It was a season of warnings and boundaries. A case of infantile paralysis was running its course only a block or two away, and you and Jassie were on a short tether: you were barred from crowds and the beaches and restricted as to play: your range was the cattail covert behind the house, and what games you there engaged in were games for no more than two. But half an acre of bulrushes held little to be found after your first-day's hunt. Once you'd discovered the redwing blackbirds and the meager berry-vines, you began to fare further, sometimes climbing to the railroad tracks and walking through the simmer of air above the ballast.

You were caught in that violation, seen by someone and reported, and for your disobedience, you and Jassie were sentenced to still greater isolation: you were separated from each other. He was sent away to the Catskills, where his Grandma Perlman lived, and you remained behind at the little pinch-faced house in the chest-high grass. For an hour after his departure, you simply wandered about, wishing time would pass as if wishing would make it pass the faster. No toy detained your eye, no dido suggested itself, no want cried out to be satisfied: you were emptied of need, and the days that lay ahead seemed gray.

Passing the stoop, you saw what you hadn't seen before—a flyswatter cocked against a baluster of the porch—and it drew you as nothing else you knew of in your uneventful world. Taking it up, you tried it for limberness, cleared its mesh of dried victims, and set forth on a spree of murder. On the white siding of the house, on the window-screens, the wicker chairs, the cane stand, the globes around the lamps, you smashed seventy-five flies before you tired of their red and yellow splotches, some of them smeared with later kills.

Seventy-five. Not seventy-two or seventy-nine, but seventy-five! You've never been sure why you stopped at that number—was Jassie worth neither more nor fewer—nor have you ever known why you began.

SCENE 97

THE FLYSWATTER (1916)

The things of summer were forbidden that year. With infantile so near at hand, just a few doors down the street, your metes and bounds were the four sides of a weed-filled lot, four invisible lines, like those described in a deed. Within that parcel, there were no beaches to be combed for sand-ground shells, no trolleys bound for Pleasure Bay, there were no runlets to be dammed, no games that one could play alone. There was only a house that seemed to cower, as if it too sought to escape disease. A summer that extended like a long still Sunday, you thought, and when there was nothing new within your reach, no field-mouse burrows to excavate, no nests to disturb, no flowers surviving the reeds, you simply stopped moving and sat—what was there to move for?—and watched a new hatch of flies use the air.

Your frame of mind was taken by all to be an ominous symptom, and you were tested for fever, chill, numbness, watched for convulsions and cyanosis, made to swallow, demonstrate balance, report on pain. When nothing more than boredom was found, consultations were held that you heard but faintly, as if the sound you were hearing came from a hive. In the end, it was decided that you were to join your Cousin Jassie in the mountains, and one morning you were put in charge of yourself and sent on your way from the Long Branch station. Before the ten-hour journey was over, you changed cars three times, at Jersey City, at Catskill, and at Phoenicia, where, for the final climb to Hunter, you rode the rails of the Stony Clove division. You arrived at evening, hungry, weary, but once again with your Cousin Jassie.

But alas, alas! the cuisine of his Grandma Perlman was repugnant to your taste. She was kindly, you remember, and she tried her best to please, but the food she set before you simply grew the more unsavory as it lay there growing cold. You watched Jassie across the table, marvelling at his relish for what disinclined you. Was flavor of no matter to him, you wondered, were there no bitter or noisome herbs, was his stomach too low, too far from his mouth, or was he lacking a sense, did his tongue not know what it was sending south? Or was he eating because it was eating-time, was he feeding?

You starved. All you could touch was soda crackers, and when the larder was bare of those, you walked to the village grocery and bought from the first barrel you reached inside the door. Lemon drops—you bought a pound of lemon drops! They lasted for three days; you ate lemon drops while Jassie fed on meat, soup, pudding, and pie. Lemon drops!—and when your pound was down to an ounce or two, you went to the store for more.

Along the way, you were overtaken by the hired man in a buckboard. On the seat beside him was your packed valise, and you were driven to the depot and sent off on a train. Down Stony Clove you went and down Esopus Creek, and later it was Catskill again, and then Jersey City, and in the evening at last it was Long Branch. There you were met (by whom?), hurried to the shrinking little house, and served a Grandma Nevins meal.

The family watched as Ellen brought it. "Lemon drops!" she said. "You witless boy!"

"Why didn't you drink milk?" your Aunt Ida said. "Why didn't you ask for fruit, bread and butter, cereal?"

"Why didn't his honor eat the food they served him?" Ellen said.

"I couldn't," you said. "It was different."

The next day, you killed thirty flies before you put the swatter away for the summer.

SCENE 98

THE PRESIDENTIAL CAMPAIGN OF 1916

It was a fine Sunday morning, you remember, and you and your father were out for a stroll, an excursion to nowhere along Seventh Avenue. As you passed the Owasco Club, you were joined by a friend of his, and with you between them, they exchanged opinions across your head. You paid little attention to what they said, for you were absorbed in your game, taught to you by Nat Weinstein, of identifying automobiles from a distance. He'd instructed you in such details as the shape of radiators and hubcaps, the color and size of insignia, the sound of four cylinders and how it differed from six—*Apperson,* you were thinking, and *Chalmers,* and *Mercer,* and *Marmon,* and then came one that, for all your schooling, you couldn't call. But however engrossed, you did hear fragments of the conversation above you, a word here and there, a phrase, a date, and you made out *Woodrow Wilson* (*too proud to fight,* you thought) and *Charles Evans Hughes* (three plurals, you thought, as if he were several men), and other things descended to your level that you failed to understand—*continuous voyage, strict accountability, contraband.* But you were occupied with testing yourself, and you saw no *Lusitania* sink, only a *De Dion Bouton* stopping across the street.

From overhead came your father's voice. "Who's *your* candidate, Julian?" he said. "Wilson or Hughes."

"My canidate is Wilson," you said.

"Why Wilson?"

"He kep us out of war."

You expected another "That's a good one, kid" from your father. Instead, he laughed, and his friend laughed too.

SCENE 99

THE MICK FROM THE MOY (1916)

She'd take a stick to you at times, a ladle, a broom-handle, a rod for pounding wash, and if you stopped in her road, she'd crack you where the skin was tight, across the knuckles or on a shin—"Out of me trot," she'd say, and out you got. To her, you were a hindersome mass, and, worse, as though you were leavened, you only seemed to grow. Her kitchen was a large enough room, but she'd concede you no square foot of standing space, no corner was yours, no alcove, no place along a wall. Wherever found, you were bound to be in the way—"Move yer larrd," she'd say, "and may God fergive the worrd!"

"If it's the chocolate cake ye seek," she'd say, "you'll not be findin' it this day." Whenever a wedge remained, she'd stash it for your sister Ruth, but in time you grew to know her bunks, and rarely did one of those hidden favors fail to fall to you. "Not this time," she'd say, but you'd stay on the hunt, and late or soon, you'd root out the prize: you were a dog with a sensitive snout. "Ah, the spalpeen," the mick from the Moy would say, "the good-for-nothin' boy!"

In the end, she outwitted you. She hit on a cache that saved a hundred delights for your sister Ruth. You were years at the search, but you never again trove the treasure, and when she revealed the hideout later, she laughed at your cheated look. "Ye niver give a thought to the wash-boiler," she said. "Now, did ye!"

Your grandma tried often, but no persuasion would induce the mick to sit with her at the dining-room table, not even when no one else was there, nor on winter's hot-tea days. Wherefore, rather than be served, your grandma would join the mick in the kitchen, and there, side by side, the two would perch and twitter.

SCENE 100

TWO YEARS AT P.S. 10 (1915-17)

The building, old even then, stood at the corner of 117th Street and St. Nicholas Avenue, diagonally opposite the house you lived in. It was faced by every window of the strung-out flat, and from any room, you could stare across the intersection at the red-brick blur of the school. Always the same scene filled your gaze, and in time you came to think of it as mounted on the panes, in time it seemed to gaze at you. It was a constant presence, but what went on within and without reappears only in separate views, like those in a roll of film: you see phases of motion, frozen goings-on.

You missed the event; you caught the upshot. In the gutter, a few feet behind a delivery-truck, lay a boy who had just been run over. The truck had stopped, and even the running people were only pictures of people running, and in that stuck moment, you thought that maybe the boy wasn't . . . but he was. You heard later that a wheel had crushed his head. His name was Fitzgerald, and he was dead.

Miss Campbell taught English (was it Grace Campbell?), and sometimes she'd read to the class from the *Jungle Book,* and you remember how much you liked her voice, full and somewhat breathless, as if she were speaking through a kiss. And when you think of Rikki-tikki-tavi the mongoose, or of Mowgli, who was reared by wolves, you hear the names as you did before, as if whispered through a kiss.

You remember Flora Goos—Gose, she pronounced it, but the witty boys said *Goose.* She was the German teacher, and she was forced to resign on account of something called *atrocities.* When the time came to say goodbye, she ended with *Glück auf!* which was what she'd always written in autograph books. *Glück auf!* she said, and she was gone.

In the schoolyard one day, you watched a high-jump competition between a Negro named something-Johnson and a white boy named Alvin Rosenstein. Johnson was the better jumper, and everybody knew he was going to win, including Rosenstein. Before every try, though, he'd massage Johnson's legs, and Johnson would massage his. You weren't shocked by Johnson touching Rosenstein, but you were, you remember, by Rosenstein touching him. He touched black skin, you thought, he put his hands on a Negro!

Every spring, a three-day trip to Boston was conducted by Abe Greenberg, the arithmetic teacher. The charge per pupil was $16.50, and when your Cousin

Jassie announced that he was going, you besought your father to send you too. Times were still hard for him, and he was angered by the plea, but he managed to scrape up the money, and you went. You saw the site of the Massacre, you saw the one-if-by-land belfry, you climbed Bunker Hill, you were below deck on *Old Ironsides,* and at Concord you stood on the rude bridge that arched the flood—but though you remembered all, you enjoyed nothing. You knew that when the trip was over, you'd have to assuage anger, and you tried with a souvenir, a match-safe bought at Lexington for 35¢. It went into a drawer; you never saw your father use it.

Dr. Birch was in charge of the Science Class, and for a reason that no one knew, he had a grudge against Miss Benjamin, the History teacher. He made the mistake of calling her a loose woman while Alvin Rosenstein was present, and Alvin punched his nose. Alvin used to walk Miss Benjamin home, carrying her books right up to her flat. He said she wasn't loose at all.

Your Shop teacher was John Linton, and everybody said he was sweet on Miss Hammargren. They couldn't get married, though, unless she gave up teaching, so they lived in adjoining flats. That was sensible, because they could see each other in the hall and save carfare.

Two years at P. S. 10.

THE COLOR OF THE AIR, IX

JOHN JACOB ASTOR – 1848
THE LANDLORD

> *Has Mrs. So-and-so paid that rent yet?*
> —last words

He came from London with seven silver flutes
And some odds and ends of pounds and pence,
And keeping the coin as far as the grave,
At some place en route he gave up the rods.
His taste was for the till, a music-machine
That he could play all day long, never tired
Of the coloratura chime of chink on other chink,
A sound he found sweet when living soured,
And hired help had to haze him in a blanket
To spook the blood in his lukewarm heart.

He died at eighty-four, a few years more
Than were due him by the terms of the Book
And twice what a Sac trapper could look for
If, wambly on *voyageur* whisky or high wine,
He balked at pelt-prices, shorts, and shoddy.
The brave was brave indeed, that or cracked,
Who backtalked a factor or spat in his face
When given a frypan for a brace of blue fox:
Such a one left early, with a ball in his eye,
And over the plains, when an east wind blew,
His blown-out brains ran west with the dust.

Nor was life long for Astor's slow-pay tenants.
They too died in traps, at about the same rate
As the game he took in figure-4 and deadfall:
They died of fevers and of more scenic fires,
Of the shade of plague all the rage that year,
They died of milk-sick, of pox and marasmus,
Of struma, stone, quinsies, and peccant humor,
Of the malady that, when its name became known,
They could've cured *now* — by killing the rich.

But the flutes, what happened to the flutes?
Did he lose them, whose only loss was life?

SCENE 101

GOD HELPING HER, SHE CAN DO NO OTHER (1917)

You were aware, of course, that the country was at war. How could you
have missed the parades, the songs, the posters, how not have seen the razzle-
dazzle ships, the troop-train faces, the Uncle Sam who needed *You*. You read
the strange names of strange places, you saw pictures of streams pontooned
with dead, you had dreams of mud and wire, of *Lorraine Lorraine my beautiful
Alsace-Lorraine,* of dachshunds in spiked helmets, or champagne bursting on
a hull. But what, you wonder, was the war to you, how much of it or little
can you say now that you knew?

In Long Branch one evening, with the family gathered on the porch, Jassie and his father—by agreement, it seemed—walked off along the road in the darkness. You hadn't been asked to join them, nor had they announced where they were going, and an hour passed and more before you heard them coming back. Beyond the cast of light from the doorway of the house, the night was all navy shadow, and they were almost at the steps when you saw Jassie, supported by his father, mounted on a bicycle. They were smiling, you remember, but, glancing at your father, you saw that he was not.

You raced down from the porch, saying, "An Iver-Johnson!" and in marvelment you palmed the handle-bars, the tire-tread, the fresh black paint. "Has it got a coaster-brake?" you said.

"Sure it has," Jassie said, "and a bell," and he rang it, "and tools too," and he tapped a kit that hung behind the seat. "It cost thirty dollars!"

Long after Jassie had crowed himself to sleep, you lay wide awake, thinking of the days to come, when he rode cock-a-hoop ahead of you, and you brought up the rear in his dust. Wherever you went, you thought, he'd arrive first, and whatever sights there were to see, he'd take them in before you got there and be done before you began: he'd lead, you thought, and you, on foot, would have to follow. It promised to be a poor summer. *Lorraine Lorraine my beautiful Alsace-Lorraine.*

And for a week, the summer was poor indeed. You trailed Jassie everywhere, to the beach and the depot and over pathways through the fields, and he kept barely in sight on the boardwalk and out on the country roads. He was borne, you thought, he moved almost without effort, like a hawk, while you stood by on awkward feet. He went, and you watched, watched even when he paused to grease an axle or smear graphite on the chain. A poor summer, it promised to be, with you yearning on the sidewalk and he lordly on the wheel.

Your father spent the week in the city, returning to the shore on Friday afternoon. It was still light when supper was over, and before the Sabbath set in, he went for a walk with a last cigar, and he asked you to go along.

"What've you been doing all week, kid?" he said.

"I went berry-picking," you said. "And I went swimming when the white flag was up. And once when it wasn't. I saw a moving picture with Carlyle Blackwell."

"And what was Jassie doing?"

"He was riding his bike."

Smoke was on the air, and the sweetness of privet, and a mist off watered lawns. "Did he let you ride?"

"Oh, he's not suppose to do that," you said. "Not till I know how."

"When will that be?"

"When he lets me ride," you said, and you laughed.

He laughed too, saying, "My father, *selig,* would've called this *bitter Gelachter.*"

"What's that mean?"

"What it sounds like—sour laughter."

"How can laughing be sour?"

"People don't always laugh at funny things."

"What other kind can they laugh at?"

"Things like Jassie having a bike and you not," he said. "Things like Uncle Harry being flush and me being busted. We laughed just now, but what was so funny?"

"I don't know," you said, and nothing seemed funny now. "It must've been bitter Gelaughter."

Ahead of you, Third Avenue abutted on Broadway, the main street of Long Branch. When you reached the junction, your father stopped, and, roughing up your hair, he said, "Kid, do you think we could find a bike for less than thirty bucks?"

It turned out to be a khaki-colored Pierce-Arrow—and it had a bell and a tool-kit and a coaster-brake as well! It cost fifteen dollars.

Lorraine Lorraine. Of course you knew of the war.

SCENE 102

CLAUDIA MUZIO (1917)

b. Pavia 1889 - d. Rome 1936

When you showed the tickets to your Cousin Jassie, he said, "Who wants to hear a opera singer?"

You said, "My Cousin Harriet was suppose to go, but she can't."

"Charlie Chaplin is always making fun of opera singers."

You tapped the little slips of pink cardboard, saying, "She said it would be a nice way for us to spend the afternoon."

Jassie took the tickets from you and examined them gravely, judiciously. "Claudia Muzio," he read, "I never heard of the guy."

"I never did, either."

"Hippodrome," he read. "That's the place for Barnum & Bailey."

"Well, we don't have to go just because we got tickets. We could do something else. Walk around."

Jassie said, "I heard my father say when you can get something for nothing, you got to take avantage. I'm for going."

156

And you went.

The Hippodrome was on Sixth Avenue at 43rd Street. You'd been there at least once a year when the circus came to town, but it was unfamiliar to you with the tents down and the clowns gone. It was a theatre now, larger than any you'd ever known, and your seat was so high up and far away that you might've been peering down at a doll-size piano on a toy-store stage.

An usher handed you a program, and to show that you were *au fait,* you leafed it aloofly, as though you knew what it contained. You had no notion, though, of the function of a program, and before you reached the gist of it, the list of song-groups you were due to hear, you were caught by a column called *Wit & Humor.* You never learned, therefore, what arias, what Lieder would resonate soon in the gloomy cavern of the Hippodrome. *Muzio,* you thought, and you wondered what the guy would look like (would he be fat? would he have long black hair?) — and then the audience began to applaud, most of them rising as they did so, and a woman in a gown of blue sequins flashed like water as she surged from the wings.

"Guy!" you whispered to Jassie. "Guy!"

When the ovation died down, the woman placed herself at the waist of the piano and nodded to her accompanist. After a few bars of introduction, a voice came from that blaze of blue on the stage, and you were listening to — what? What was the name of the air, by whom and in what language and when had it been written, what role, what opera, what age, and what was its meaning and its mode?

Neither then nor later could you have spoken of pitch and phrasing, of range and timbre, of parlando, bel canto, bravura — you knew nothing beyond the knowledge that you knew nothing. And being in the dark, you grew uneasy, resentful, even, as if diminished by the absorption of so many others — what were they hearing that you were deaf to, or were they pretending, like Jassie and you?

You beguiled yourself with a flight of mind, and it flew at once to a little man at a musicale, Charlie!, uninvited, unwelcome, ordered away, and somehow as he shuffles off, ice cream slides down a diva's dress. From then on, you heard no more in the Hippodrome, and all you saw was film you'd seen before: the singer's surprise, her clutching hands, her staring eyes, and Charlie (or is it four-eyed Harold, or cock-eyed Ben?) trying to reach . . . trying to put his hand. . . . That was when you began to laugh, and you made Jassie laugh too, and then both of you ran for the stairs and the door.

You and Jassie walked uptown through Central Park — along the Mall, across the Terrace and around the Boat Pond — and somewhere near the Harlem Mere, Jassie said, "What was so funny?"

You left him at his door and went on alone to your Aunt Sarah's, where you'd arranged to join your father. In the entry, you encountered your Cousin Harriet.

"What're you doing here so early?" she said. "Didn't you go to the recital?"
"Oh, yes," you said. "I went, and I took Jassie, and then we walked home."
She glanced at a gilded clock on the parlor mantel. "You must've left before it was over," she said.
"A little."
"How little? You've had time to walk four miles and she's still singing."
"I guess we didn't stay as long as I thought."
"And I guess you hardly stayed at all!"
"That's right," you said. "I'm sorry."
She looked at you, shaking her head. "You walked out on Claudia Muzio," she said. "You must be the most insensitive member of the family. Muzio has one of the loveliest voices of our time. She has sung with Caruso and Scotti at the Metropolitan. She has sung at Covent Garden and La Scala. She has sung the leading roles of Massenet, Verdi, Puccini. Her voice floats, floats! But not for my Cousin Julian!" She went past you to the door, and as it closed behind her, you heard her say, "I'm ashamed of you."

You stood there, thinking of the little man in sagging pants (or was it popeyed Buster?), and as ice cream slowly slid off a plate, you again began to laugh.

SCENE 103

THE STEAMBOAT HOUSE (1917)

It was the first of three summers in a cottage that looked like a sternwheeler. The posts and rails of its piled-up decks were hung with curls and scrolls of filigree, an embroidery of woodwork, and sometimes when you saw it from a distance, you thought of it as on the move, sailing toward you across the lawn. If you had nothing you cared to do, as when it rained, the wicker rockers on the porch would become deck-chairs, and you'd sit watching the trees and road, trying to imagine that you were passing along some shore. But not always were you on the river gently, drifting gently in the stream, not always did you pretend to be peering for spars and channel markers, for shifting bars and sawyers — there were days when the sights you saw lay within.

On the top floor of the house, there were four bedrooms off a central hallway that extended from a window at one end to the door of a bath at the other. Two of the rooms were spares, rarely in use during the week; the third and fourth, face to face across a strip of carpet, were yours and Ellen's. You were awakened one night by a sound — something falling, was it, a dog-bark, a broken branch? — and trying to match the sound with a cause, you found that sleep had gone. And then you did know what had roused you: nothing had fallen or broken, and nothing had barked at the moon. Water was running, and you knew where it ran. Ellen was drawing a bath.

You lay where you were, remembering another night, when, half-asleep, you'd gone to the bathroom and tried the door without noting that a line of light showed at the floor. There was an inch of travel in the latch, and a crack opened between the stile and the jamb, and through it you caught sight of Ellen standing beside the tub. She was drying herself, and her breasts, pale and pendent, swung with her swaying, and for a flicker of your mind, you thought of her as dancing. But your eyes would not stay on her moving parts; they strayed slowly down to her thighs and a dripping swatch of bright red hair.

And then you fled, to your room, to your bed, and, soon, to a small warm outpouring in the dark.

SCENE 104

A PAIR OF SHOES, SIZE 2 (1917)

Your mother and her sister Rae were little alike except in blood. Your aunt was darker-toned, more minutely made, and smaller too in nature, but the blood drew you, and she knew you were drawn, not as to your mother in another form, but to her, your mother's sister Rae. She, though, was never drawn to you. A cool room, your Aunt Rae was — *Why did you marry Uncle Harry?* you asked her once, and she said *To get rid of him.* Her only fire was the power to strike fire, a minor gift, but it was enough to kindle you. Only the eyes of your mind ever saw her body: when she passed by, you'd listen for the garment-sound of thighs, and you'd wonder upward from her size-2 shoes to what lay hidden by her clothes.

On one of those summer days in Jersey, some of the family had driven out to the fruit-farms on the Eatontown pike, and others were on the verandah playing whist. You were upstairs (sitting? standing? doing what?) when a draft through the hallway brought a rumor of perfume that sent you to another room, where you stopped before a row of flasks, fragrant soldiers, on your Aunt Rae's chiffonier. In the mirror, you saw the same row facing away, but for an instant you thought of it as separate and scenting a separate room. Impelled by a memory, you found yourself opening a drawer. From it, a breath, an insubstantial Rae arose, and you stared down at small possessions you seemed to have seen before — scarves, gloves, coiled ribbons, a trinket-tray of hairpins, buttons, spools of thread. Far back, almost hidden, was the cardboard box, pale blue once and worn now to gray. Handling had almost erased the print on the cover, and an illustration of the contents had been reduced to a blur. You remembered the little rubber hat with its rolled rubber brim, but you had no desire to see it again.

Why did you marry Uncle Harry? you'd asked, and she'd said *To get rid of him.* But she hadn't gotten rid of him, you thought. The box told you he was still there, still in her room, and somehow you felt betrayed. You closed the drawer and turned away. It was over.

SCENE 105

FEAR YE NOT, STAND STILL (1917)

On fall afternoons, when you returned from school, you'd scarcely have slung your books into some corner before speeding off to join your friends for the usual game of touch football. It was played between two manhole covers on 119th Street, where sides were chosen by a pair of boys whom no one had elected captain but who were nevertheless always the same: they were leaders; they were sought, and you envied them. Because you were a poor kicker and a worse runner, you'd be among the last to be tapped, and when there were more players than positions, you'd not be picked at all.

On one such day, leaving home at high speed, you steamed around a corner and collided with a strange boy steaming in the opposite direction. Chest to chest, you came to a stop and glared — sizing each other up, the act was called.

"Why don't you watch where you're going?" the other boy said.
"How about you watching?" you said.

"I don't have to watch."

"Since when?"

"Since right this minute," he said. "So get outa my way."

"I'll get outa your way when I'm good and ready."

"You better get ready, or I'll spit in your eye."

"I dare you," you said. "I double-dare you."

He spit in your eye.

He spit in both eyes.

You got outa his way.

SCENE 106

MILDRED A. (1917)

You've forgotten where and how you met her—at a party, it might've been, or perhaps someone introduced you on the street—but you know you thought her pretty when you thought of her at all. Pretty in a crayon sort of way, though, low in saturation, slow to come to mind, and quick to fade. Still, you did think of her now and then, and you did recall her yellow hair and her wash-blue eyes, and one day, finding yourself in possession of a few dollars, you invited her to attend a matinee of vaudeville at B. F. Keith's Riverside— eight acts and an overture, possibly from *William Tell*. In accepting, she became, on the following Saturday, the first girl you'd ever walked out with.

And it was a long walk. At 96th and Broadway, the theatre was almost two miles from where she lived, but you walked, you remember, though you don't remember why. It may have been because the subway fare would've drawn too deeply on your reserve for refreshments, or because the cars seemed too common for so rare an occasion—but whatever the reason, you and Mildred walked. Along the way, there must've been conversation, but what it was has long since gone to the limbo of the lost. In oblivion now the wisdom you'd overheard and passed off as your own, and in Lethe too your display of lore (that's a starling, sparrow, maple, elm). Nor can you recall the bill at the Riverside (were there dogs that sprang through rings of fire, were there dancing, comedy, legerdemain, somersaults on a strand of wire?), and you cannot say that the exit music came from *Harold in Italy*. Had you laughed at jokes, you wonder, had you clapped for a feat, and what of Mildred in the seat beside you, had she been amused as well, had she like you rewarded daring? And had there been sweets after all (caramels, chocolate sundaes), and what more had been said on the walk to her home?

The return was made through Central Park, a wooded place then, with dells and granite steeps and even, near the Blockhouse, a languid rill that was one foot wide. Were there more sightings on the way, did you name for Mildred A. the pigeon, the squirrel, the jay, and, again, what subjects did you cover as you climbed up a hill or down a dale, were there further shows of lifted learning? You were crossing a meadow, you remember, rambling toward a path that rimmed the Mere, and the Seventh Avenue entrance would soon be in sight and with it the end of the afternoon.

Reaching a one-rail fence that wound away with the path, you ducked a little to pass beneath it, and then you turned to wait for the miss. She followed suit, bending as you'd just done, but she lost her balance and sank to the ground. As you extended your hand to help her rise, you saw flesh exposed where her stockings stopped, midway up her thighs. You remember still a sense of cold, as if you'd been startled in the dark, a congeal that spread from the inside outward, and you were silent (or did you say much and forget it all?) until you arrived at the place of beginning—Mildred's door. There you said goodbye, and from there you fled.

No more had you reached home than your sister came running down the hall, staring at you as though you'd undergone a change. *I saw you with a girl!* she said. *You were walking in the street with a girl!* Beyond her, standing in the kitchen, your grandma smiled, and hidden around a corner, Irish Ellen sounded her Sligo laugh.

You never squired Mildred again. Everyone thought it was because your sister had seen you, but only you knew that it was because you'd seen Mildred.

SCENE 107

THE POOR MISFORTUNATE BOY (1917)

At a ring of the bell, you opened the door, and there in the hall stood your Uncle Romie. With a shuffle and a flourish and a *Ta-da tsing!* your Uncle Romie was again at home. Once more now, he'd fill the rooms with sack-tobacco and rice-paper smoke, once more he'd send away for trial-size samples (Free!), once more the morning mail would be almost all for him. Each day he'd stand or sit or move about, the spit and image of his father, who'd sit or stand or move about as if he too were on display, as if his son, in exposing himself, were also exposing him. Poor misfortunate boy, your grandma would say, but to your grandpa, the misfortune had befallen him as well, and when he beheld his son, *he* was the one cutting coupons from a magazine, *his* fingers were nicotine yellow, *his* teeth grained with green. A son was the father, he must've thought, and a father was the son.

That return of Romie's produced a variation in the household order. During his stay, your sister Ruth, then nine years old, was almost never to be found at home. For days on end, she'd be away somewhere, now with a cousin and again with a friend, and what appearances she made were merely for a change of clothes. When you inquired into her absence, you were told of piano lessons and parties, of field-trips and visits to the Aquarium and the Metropolitan Museum. You accepted the entire series of explanations until your father took you for a walk in Central Park on a Sunday afternoon.

From a pathway around the Mere, you were watching a flotilla of mallards when he said, "I've heard you asking your grandma about Ruthie."

"She must be having a good time," you said. "All those parties and things."

"There are no parties, Julian."

"But grandma said there was. She wouldn't lie."

"She would, if Romie was in the room."

"What's Romie got to do with lying?"

"She doesn't want him to hear the real reason why Ruthie is away."

"What's the real reason?"

"Romie," your father said. "Romie is the reason."

Two of the cruising mallards suddenly tipped forward, as though going down by the bows, and then, their twin screws thrashing, they righted themselves and sailed on across the pond. "What kind of a reason is that?" you said.

"Romie is a man in body, but without a mind to go with it. He has nothing to stop him from doing bad things. Do you know what stops people from doing bad things?"

"A pleeceman!" you said, and you glanced up to learn whether he laughed.

"That's one of your good ones, kid," he said. "Some people call it a conscience, but pleeceman is better. Romie has no pleeceman. Ruthie is growing up, and we're afraid that Romie might hurt her."

"He's always patting her head, always asking her to sit on his lap. That shows he wouldn't hurt her."

"I want you to keep something in mind, Julian," he said. "When you're around Romie, remember he has no pleeceman."

The mallards were gone. The Mere was calm.

SCENE 108

HOW TO KNOW AND CHECK THE ЈPREAD OF (1917)

On coming home one day, you were handed a large envelope bearing the postmark of the Coco Solo Naval Base in the Canal Zone. It was from Chief Yeoman D.W. Nevins (your Uncle Dave was a Chief Yeoman!), and it contained a letter and an enclosure, a pamphlet issued by the Government. Upon enlistment, your uncle told you, every sailor was given a copy of the pamphlet, he among them, and he was passing his along to you in order to acquaint you fully with what you'd probably picked up in part from your bonehead friends in the street. You were only thirteen, he said, a little too young to go out whoring (he'd spelled it wrong, you thought; it should've been *whooring*), but you weren't too young to think—and since thinking led to doing, you might as well know what might happen if you ran into some hard luck. The pamphlet described with great clarity what those penalties could be, he wrote, but for numskulls like you and your friends, there were pictures to go with the words. He didn't often give advice, but you were his favorite nephew, the only son of his dear sister, and he was duty-bound to warn you that the water was deep; so read the pamphlet, he urged, and the day would come when you'd thank your Uncle Dave.

Of the text of the pamphlet, you recall almost nothing, a word or two first heard from your simpleton friends, a flagrant but freezing phrase; but once seen, the illustrations, most of them photographic, simply pasted themselves in your mind, became part of a fadeless album you'd leaf through with dread for the rest of your life. On those perennial pages, you see now, as you saw then, naked men and women posed with the signs and stages and results of disease: sores on lips and tongues and areolas and on the tips of pendent things, monstrosities of stricture and distention, specimens of paretic change, of gonococcal blindness—a crooked generation! You stared at exposed bodies that seemed equally exposed within, and you thought then and think still of broken furniture in a vacant lot, sprung chairs, horsehair boiling from a split mattress.

The day will come when you thank your Uncle Dave, he wrote, but if you ever did, it wasn't for that—a fear that never left you, that for some later generation, you yourself might be on display; you might turn up in another pamphlet, you might pose for a snapshot of the clap.

164

SCENE 109

YOU AND YOUR BONEHEAD FRIENDS (1917-18)

You seldom had much to say at their musters in front of the candy-store or on this one's stoop or that one's roof: they were drier behind the ears than you, older dogs, and you'd listen, pretending comprehension, while like adepts they spoke of arcane things. It was as if they belonged to a secret order, communed in code, gave signs of the hand and countersigns, and for all your show of *savoir-faire*, you knew they knew you did not know. Still, fearing derision, you could never own that you were in the dark, you could never ask a question, never join their worldly crowd.

"If you do it too much," they said, "you can get feeble-minded." Do what? you'd wonder, but they'd always use the neuter pronoun, not the word for the act or thing, and you were left to seek what you couldn't name. "That's why they have asylums," they said, "For people that do it too much." You thought of your Uncle Romie, and you wondered whether he'd done it too much, whether those schools and farms he was sent to weren't schools and farms at all, but asylums that people went to when they were feeble in the mind.

You were tantalized by their secrets. While in their company, aping their poise, or while off somewhere on your own, you sometimes sensed the nearness of understanding, but ever as you strove to attain it, ever it drew away. "It feels good when you're doing it," they said, "but it's better for your health to have an octurnal Seminole omission." What was an octurnal omission, you wondered, and what did the Indians have to do with it?

You were at high school then, De Witt Clinton, and during a study period one day, you sat in the almost deserted auditorium. You weren't preparing for some class to come, though, you weren't trying to prove a theorem or memorize a stanza of Gray's *Elegy*. You were simply staring across several arcs of seats, at the organpipes, perhaps, or at the folds of the platform flag, and if you were thinking at all, it was of an adolescent nothing—you were merely a break in a vacant row. A classmate passed behind you and dropped a book in your lap, saying, "Take a look at that," and you watched him move to another part of the hall.

Without touching it, you looked down at the book. It was old, and its title, if it ever possessed one, was indiscernible, as if use had rubbed it away. The spine and covers were soiled and the edges of the pages grayed, and it was with distaste that you regarded it, as you did drinking-cups, door-handles, public-toilet seats.

You opened the book—the *earth*!

At your feet, a void gaped to the depths of space, and on the very edge stood you. It was a book of photographs, all showing naked men and women, but unlike those in the pamphlet sent by Uncle Dave, none was a scientific specimen, a hang-dog victim with lesions and malformations—none was on view to dismay the headlong. In pairs and trios and cavorting quartets, these subjects were happily demonstrating the many varieties of union—all were of good cheer, winking at the camera while filling someone's mouth or being filled both front and rear. There was no text, and there were no captions to accompany the poses—there were only photos by the dozen of bizarre junctions, of hair and orifices and swollen parts, of cocked legs and spread buttocks, of privities now private no more.

How quick your heart as you turned the dingy pages, how shallow your breathing! And between your thighs, you felt a soft trifle grow, rise against the weight of the book, and still turning pages, still staring at double and multiple coupling, you pressed the book down while you strained yourself upward, and soon you knew the coming forth of a warm wetness that cooled too fast, alas, that all too quickly grew cold.

And then the hour-bell rang, and your classmate returned for his book, and you remember how he looked at you, how he seemed to search you, and you remember looking away.

"If you do it too much," they said, "you can get feeble-minded."

SCENE 110

DICTATORSHIP OF THE PROLETARIAT (1917)

Newspapers, you thought, were printed solely to bring you word of Krazy Kat, of Silk Hat Harry and Eaglebeak Spruder; they were for picture-puzzles and the doings of favorite teams. You were aware of their front pages only on days of calamity and disaster (*Lusitania Torpedoed Bomb Kills 10 at Asian Parade Czar Abdicates*), and even then your eyes were drawn by the size of the type, by maps and photographs, and not by the weight of the event. You knew of the war, but only as a distant occurrence, a game played somewhere else. You heard slogans (*Make the world safe*) and epithets (*The Beast The Hun*), songs (*Lorraine Lorraine*), and you saw cartoons of a long low dog wearing a spiked helmet, but all such things were part of the game, like the cheering of a crowd, and soon someone would win and someone lose, and there'd be another game in another place on another afternoon.

You'd sit at the dining room table, where you prepared your homework for the following day, and there too some of the household would gather, your Grandpa Nevins, your Uncle Dave, if he happened to be home from Paraguay or Panama, and once in a while your father, who listened more than he spoke while he mulled the air with the smoke of a cigar. Your absorption would be with who and whom, with logarithms and square roots, with the formula for acetylene, and what entered your hearing would leach through the lessons you were trying to learn, reach you drop by drop, like a distillation, and into your world of equations and metrics, there'd come tidings of the world outside.

Your grandpa was in favor of someone called Kerensky, and your Uncle Dave was for something that sounded like Bullsheviki, and that's how Grandpa would pronounce it.

"The Bullsheviki," he'd say. "The Bullsheviki."

And your Uncle Dave would say, "It's Bolsheviki, papa. Why do you keep on saying Bull?"

"I say Bull because that's what such lowlives are full of—Bull!"

"This Kerensky you think so much of is only a bag of wind. What he wants to do is sell out the Revolution. He's a windbag, and one of these days he'll blow away."

You thought of a balloon shaped like a man, inflated till its fingers and feet were stiff and its belly bulging, and you saw it tugging free in the breeze, rising above the trees and buildings, turning and tumbling in the air, disappearing in the distance—blowing away, as Uncle Dave had foretold.

"Bullsheviki," your grandpa would say. "What's yours is mine, and what's mine is my own."

And Uncle Dave would say, "Kerensky is a traitor to the Revolution and the workers. His aim is to hand Russia over to the landowners and the middle class. Czarist Russia without the Czar!"

Your father would take neither side; he'd merely listen and smoke his cigar.

"The Revolution," your grandpa would say, "you're always talking the Revolution."

And your uncle would say, "It's the only way to end slavery."

And your grandpa would say, "What would the slaves be after they got free?"

"They'd be the masters!" your uncle would say.

And your grandpa would say, "And would *they* have slaves?"

And your uncle would say, "Damn it, papa!" and run from the room. Sometimes he'd run as far as Ecuador.

SCENE 111

THE YEARS AT DE WITT (1917-21)

In your day, the high school was located in a section of Manhattan known as San Juan Hill. It stood at the corner of 59th Street and Tenth Avenue, a six-story building with the stepped and windowed gables of the Dutch, and in its rooms and through its halls and up and down its glassed-in stairs, you whiled away four years of your life. You see them now as having been little used or not at all, and you think of the time as a tide-washed beach, where hardly a mar remains to show where you were or wended, and you find yourself wondering whether it was all a fancy there on San Juan Hill, only a dream that you left behind—what was real, what was in the mind?

Jesse Whitsett, you think, and you dredge up his Chem Lab and his Bunsen burners on counters of zinc. And was there or wasn't there a Mr. Barras who tried to teach you French, and did or didn't you call him Bare-ass with the rest of the class? And who was it that wore a built-up shoe on a shortened leg—Mr. Westphal in English or Mr. Frank in Math? And among the boys, were there such names as Cullen, Trilling, Meeropolsky, and what was the meaning of those *Arista* badges of red and gold? Were you caught reading smut on the lunchroom walls, and at Julian's on the Circle, did you try your skill with fifteen balls? Was there a Mr. Biggs, a Miss Garrigues, a Harry Penhallow, a teacher called Schoenchen? . . . Oh God, Schoenchen . . . !

On your way to school each morning, you passed the College of Physicians and Surgeons on your right and Roosevelt Hospital on your left, and on your way home in the afternoon, they exchanged positions, and the hospital lay at your right and the college at your left. Between those two crossings of 59th Street, there were six hours of school that seem to have elapsed in rooms and corridors thronged with sensation but otherwise unfrequented, as if classes one and all had been dismissed. You were aware of almost no one: you heard footsteps, voices, bells, you were jostled, herded, hurried along, you endured outlandish smells, but few and fleeting were the faces you saw and fewer the days enjoyed. Schoenchen, you thought—Schoenchen!

He gave a course in English. Grammar, it might've dealt with, or poetry, or composition, or Elizabethan drama, but whatever its burden, it was more than you could fathom from the start. Words were used that dazed you (preterit, gerundive, syntactic), and if there were quotations (*the curfew tolls the knell*), they seemed to come from nowhere, a gust of birds. Others fared well in that strange country, but you fell behind on the first day and more so ever week until (was it compassion? disgust?) Schoenchen ceased to call on you, and you were left to sit beside the road while he and the class marched on and disappeared (*a lowing herd among the murmuring pines and the hemlocks*).

Why had you become so impenetrable? When your mother was alive, you'd been open to the world, absorbent, but in going, she took that quality along, as though it were a part of her, not you, hers all the while. In its absence, you became denser, and much that touched you remained outside. You didn't know then that Childe Julian was of your mother's making and that her dying had been the death of you: the Boy King too was dead.

As the end of the term drew near, it grew ever more certain that you'd fail the course ("You failed in English?" your grandma would say. "What are you, a greenhorn from Ellis Island? A Galitzianer? How could you fail in English—your own language?"). You thought with dread of the final exam, then but two weeks away. What did you know of attributives, moods, copulative verbs? What soliloquy could you quote from, what stanza of what poem, and who pleased most where most she satisfied? You'd learned nothing —nothing had gotten in!—and you knew you were due to fail.

Schoenchen, Schoenchen! You can still see yourself in his classroom, still feel as you felt then, that you were listening to a language not your own, that the phrases, meanings, rhythms you heard were peculiar to another people, that you were alone among a strange company. But their sound became ever fainter, as if those who made it were moving away, and presently nothing reached you but the drone of the distant (*the lowing herd winds slowly o'er the lea*), and then truly you were in a foreign land forlorn.

Cheating was your only hope of avoiding failure. In the final fortnight before the exam, you gave all your thought and effort to the preparation of a trot. You devised a palm-sized book of india-paper, and on its half-pint pages you inscribed mites of information minutely drawn—examples of the fused participle, the omision of relatives, subjunctives contrary to fact, of the trochee and the dactyl, of assonance, alliteration, onomatopoeia, of what was a simile and what a metaphor, and you included tables of tenses (shall and should, will and would) and quotations from the speeches of Cassius, Enobarbus, Lear. While gathering such lore, it never occurred to you to make it learning. You were a transcriber only, as though strictly following some command to lift knowledge from here and set it down there, taking none for yourself on the way: you were not to swallow the diamonds you'd mined.

It was a long exam, consuming most of an afternoon, and though at the start you had little faith, at the end your heart rode high. Somehow you'd managed to supply yourself with answers relevant to the questions asked, almost as if you'd known what the questions were to be. When the bell rang, all you had to do, you thought, was remove the trot from the exam booklet — but, alas, you never did. The bell was still ringing when Schoenchen, his hand extended, reached your desk.

"I'll take that paper," he said.

"I have to arrange it first," you said.

"It's arranged," he said. "It's been arranged for hours."

"I've got to number the pages," you said.

"I'll take the paper, Shapiro, and the pony too! You must think I'm a fool!" You gave him the booklet.

"And I'm going to enter this on your record," he said. "The record will show that you're a cheat."

You waited for him in front of the Clerk's office, and when he came along, you tried to detain him with a plea, with an explanation (what was there to explain?), but he refused to stop, and you watched him open the door, and then you watched it close.

SCENE 112

WELL, ROMIE IS HOME AGAIN (1917)

That's what someone would say as soon as you came through the door — whoever answered the bell would tell you of his arrival, fulsome and lousy, grinning through a beginning beard, happily back from an exile year. *Romie is home,* you'd be told by your grandma or Ellen, and in you'd go to greet him. By then, he'd be shaven and clean, dressed in his father's castoffs, and absorbed in clipping free-sample coupons from some paper or magazine. *Julian!* he'd cry when he saw you, *my darling nephew Julian!* and he'd clasp you close and hold you long.

You wondered then, and you wonder yet, why you welcomed his presence. Others deplored it: to them, he was one of life's hindrances and almost always in the road, an obtrusion but not quite an intruder, hard to bear and harder to put aside. You seem to have viewed him as a diversion, an animal pursuing a zoic round, and you can remember watching his engrossment in a small endeavor, as if he were a cat licking kittens, a monkey picking nits. But you knew there was more to it than that, and though you couldn't say what it was, you could sense it in the air. Merely by being in it, he rarefied its gases, made them less sustaining and more likely to explode.

170

Explode? you thought, and wasn't it he that might explode?

It was, but your grandpa always made it happen far away. He'd allow Romie to remain for weeks on end, but he'd be observing all the while, listening, even, as though to hear the ticking of his son's deficient mind; and finally the day would come when he'd nod to your father, and your father, for the dozenth time, would perform the office of betraying Romie's trust and handing him over to the law. Poor Romie, he was always accepting your father's offer of a visit to the circus, the zoo, the Statue of Liberty—delights that invariably ended at some school or farm or asylum a thousand miles from home. There was a factor in his nature that laid him open ever: he believed what he was told. Again and again he'd been deceived, and still, childlike, when the next time came, he'd let himself be guiled.

The lure once was a trip to Coney Island, rides on the roller-coaster, and a ticket to the Steeplechase, and there'd be salt-water taffy, your father said, and there'd be ice cream sandwiches, and there'd be . . . , but nothing more was needed: Romie had been snared. Poor Romie, you thought, as, eager but docile, he left the house with your father, bound not for Coney, alas, but for an unknown destination, for somewhere out of sight.

When your father came home that evening, you kissed him first, as you always did, but there was no kiss for you in return, and saying nothing, he went along the hall to his room. You followed and watched him put away his hat and coat, after which he washed his hands and then stared at them, as if to see whether they were clean—or was it whether they'd been washed at all? Whatever it may have been, he washed them again before noticing you in the bathroom doorway.

"What did you do today, kid?" he said, and he trailed a finger through your hair.

"Nothing much," you said. "Except I was thinking about Uncle Romie."

"What were you thinking?"

"About what he was thinking—that he was going to Coney Island."

"And all along, you knew he wasn't?"

"Yes," you said. "How did you get out of it?"

"You don't really want to know that, do you?"

"I do want to know."

He gazed through the narrow little bathroom window, a frame for one of the red brick gables of Public School 10. "I took him down to Grand Central Station in the subway," he said. "He had no idea where he was. He probably thought the waiting-room led to the roller-coaster." And he was still looking out at the darkening sky when he said, "I guess it did lead to a ride, at that."

"What happened in Grand Central?"

171

"I'd arranged for a plain-clothes guard to meet us at the Information booth, but as soon as Romie saw him, he knew there'd be no Coney Island. He'd've known even if the guard was naked."

"What did Romie do?" you said.

"Nothing, really—he let the man lead him away. But as he was going, he turned to me and said: 'But you promised, Phil, you promised!' " And now your father turned to you, saying, "Ice cream cones. Salt-water taffy," and then he began to cry.

"Why did you do it?" you said.

"Who else could've done it?"

"Grandpa! Uncle Dave! Anybody!"

"Could *you*?" your father said, and you didn't answer. "*You* couldn't. He's your own blood."

SCENE 113

THE MANLY ART OF SELF-DEFENSE (1917)

One of the marble-shooters in front of the De Peyster was a boy named Harold Schnurrer, or, as your Aunt Rae pronounced it, Schnorrer. In Yiddish, a *schnorrer* was a beggar, the word deriving from *schnurren,* echoic of the musical humming that once accompanied a plea for alms. Harold Schnorrer, your aunt would say—Harold the Beggar. You remember him as no great marvel with the migs, but he did lose quietly, and, if winning, he'd always *give you a show,* which is to say he'd keep on playing till you got even or ran out of bottle-caps or campaign badges or whatever else was coin that day. Being only a middling hand yourself, you rather liked to go against him: you knew you'd probably wind up with the same sack of glassies, the same packet of pictures, give or take a few. Why did your aunt call him a *schnorrer?* you'd wonder. He wasn't a beggar at all.

The eastern side of Seventh Avenue was the gentile side. Several of the shops were owned by Germans—Hess the upholsterer, Bachrach's ice cream parlor, with its pewter molds in the window, Kuck's beer-hall where, in a print above the bar, Custer was forever firing at Indians who forever fell. There were trees on that side too, each with a square of earth for games, but it was a rare day when a Jew crossed over from west to east or a Dutchman came the other way. In the life and times of Harold Schnurrer, you remember two such days.

On the first of these, he was playing marbles with a blue-and-blond boy you'd never seen before, and between them on the ground his steelies were deployed against the stranger's glassies. It was Harold's turn to shoot, and as he kneeled and knuckled with his real, he saw a shoe step on each of the glassies and press them out of sight—one by one, while many watched, the glassies disappeared—and then many jew-brown eyes moved upward to the owner of the shoe, blue-eyed Georgie Kuck.

Harold rose, saying, "Whatsy idea?"
Tapping the strange boy's shoulder, Georgie said, "Me and my cousin Alfred, we want to see how good you shoot."
"Howm I going to shoot after you went and stepped on his immes?"
"That's your lookout, Jewboy."
"I wouldn't call me a Jewboy if I was you," Harold said.
"You want to make something out of it, Jewboy?"
"Call me that again, and I'll roon you."
"You and what army, Jewboy?" Georgie said, and Harold swung and missed, and then Georgie swung, and Harold fell among his marbles in the dirt. "Right on your Jewboy ass!" Georgie said. "Come on, Alfred. I never seen a Jew could fight worth a piss." And back they went to the gentile side of the street.

Coming from Eighth Avenue a few weeks later, you met Harold, who was just emerging from Billy Grupp's, a gymnasium for boxers. He fell in with you, and as you crossed 116th Street, you asked him how much it'd cost him to watch the fighters train.

"It don't cost me a cent," he said, "because I'm not watching. I'm training too."
"You're going to be a price-fighter?"
"I'm taking lessons. I'm learning how to defend myself."
"Against who?" you said.
"When I told my father about Georgie Kuck, he got sore and said no son of his was going to get licked a second time. And right off, he took me to Billy Grupp's and signed me for ten lessons. He paid twenty-five dollars."
"I thought you said it didn't cost a cent."
"The twenty-five is for learning, not watching."
"What're you learning?"
"Well, the first thing they teach you is how to croush. You got to croush down, so when your adversory swings, he'll go over your head."
"You're not going to win any fights just by ducking," you said.
"Tell me something I don't know," he said. "You ought to see me jab. I never could jab before. And I can hook. And I can right cross. And an upracut—an upracut is my best punch."
"How many lessons have you got left?"
"Two," Harold said. "After that, it's goodbye Georgie Kuck."

When you reached Seventh Avenue, you said, "Well, I have to go home now."

And Harold said, "Me too."

Not long afterward, while you were practicing with a new agate near the De Peyster, Harold came from the doorway and headed straight for Kuck's saloon across the street. Following him into gentile territory, you saw him stop at the swinging bamboo doors; opening one of them, he called in for Georgie Kuck. In a moment or two, Georgie appeared, attended by his cousin Alfred, his fat father, and three or four bar-flies carrying steins of beer.

"What'll you have, Jewboy?" Georgie said.

"An apology," Harold said. "And if I don't get one, I'm going to mobilize you."

"You wait till I apologize, you will not be a Jewboy any more. You will be an old Jew*man*."

Harold jabbed, Harold hooked, Harold crossed, and then Harold tried his best punch—the upracut. The only blow he landed he landed with his head: he struck the ground with it.

Right on his ass, you thought, and when Harold was able to stand, you helped him back to the Jewish side of the street. That was the second crossing.

You left him at the De Peyster, and when you were alone, you laughed, but you've never known precisely why.

THE COLOR OF THE AIR, X

AT HARPER'S FERRY—1859

OH, DEAR DANGERFIELD

> *If you do not get me somebody else will. Come this fall without fail, money or no money I want to see you so much: that is the one bright hope I have before me.*
> —Harriet Newby

Dangerfield was her husband, half-nigger and half-Scotch, six-two barefoot and both feet free to come and go: if he wore a collar, he also wore its key. But she was still a slave, his Harriet, and about to be sold down the Rappahannock, and she wrote *Buy us soon, dear Dangerfield,* and his own bright hope became old John Brown.

A Mr. Richard Washington shot dear Dangerfield in the yard of the Armory at Harper's Ferry, using a rifle that fired a six-inch spike. It took out gullet, jugular, and part of the jaw, opening the throat in a grin like a broken watermelon. For souvenirs, a mob cut off dear Dangerfield's ears, and then they cut off twos of anything else he had no further use for.

SCENE 114

HOMAGE TO JACOB MENDELSON (1916-17)

Mr. Mendelson was a teacher of Hebrew, a meager little man, poor, precise, and exuding always the sweetness of some gum or resin, some myrrh or powder of the East. You remember him best for his constant hunger, a desire so fervent that eating seemed only to heighten it, as if food merely fueled the fire. At the same time, quite as clearly do you see him affecting a distaste for the table, an aversion, almost—bread and meat were obnoxious, he'd pretend; he'd dined within the hour, he'd claim, and there was a limit to what his body could contain. But there *was* no limit! and when dishes were set before him, he'd demur (*a mouthful for politeness,* he'd say) and never lean back till they were clean.

By arrangement with your Grandma Nevins, he turned up twice a week to prepare you for your Bar Mitzvah, still a year or more away. You'd be thirteen then, a man according to the Talmud and answerable for all your acts. For the ritual, you were expected to learn of Mr. Mendelson the language of the Torah, from which you'd be required to read when the solemn day came. Your studies began with the new alphabet, twenty-two letters strange in themselves and stranger still in formation. Spread across a page and read from right to left, they seemed always to be in motion, as if to evade your mind, to spite your comprehension—and largely you did not understand, not even after many months of Mr. Mendelson. Again and again, he'd arrive overfed, as he protested, yet ever underfull. *The sight of food, Mrs. Nevins, I'm afraid would make me ill,* and then, as though only to stave off illness, he'd stow it out of sight. And later, folded in his sweet-gum fragrance, you'd try to read writhing letters with vowels like the cast of worms. In the end, for all his patient lessons, you'd learned little, a word here and there, a phrase or two that you'd memorized—*Shema Yisroel, Adonai elohenu, Adonai echod!* Why, you asked him once, was *Jehovah* pronounced *Adonai?* and you were

175

told that you spoke of the Tetragrammaton, the four consonants of the incommunicable name—J H V H—which no Jew was so impious as to utter.

In addition to making you ready for the ceremony of recognition, Mr. Mendelson instructed you in the use of phylacteries, or *tephillin,* as he called them. These little leather boxes, he said, held bits of parchment bearing excerpts from Exodus and Deuteronomy, wherein man was exhorted to love the words of the Lord and to wear them for a sign upon his hand and as frontlets between his eyes. He produced a pair for demonstration, and you watched him enter upon an orthodox sequence of steps that ended with one of the boxes strapped to his arm and the other to his brow by a band around his head. Removing them, he made you repeat the procedure and, at certain stages, recite the appropriate prayers. After your Bar Mitzvah, he said, excepting only the Sabbath, you'd do the same every day of your life. . . .

The cards your father sent were inexpensive and poorly printed. They read:

Mr. Philip D. Shapiro requests
your presence at the Bar Mitzvah
services of his son Julian to
be held at Congregation Mount
Zion No. 39 W. 119th St. New York
on Saturday June 2nd 1917 at 9.30 A.M.

You remember the day with shame. You wore a new suit, a new hat, and a white and zion-blue praying-shawl, the gift of your Grandma Shapiro, and as you sat waiting to be brought to the altar, you tried to recall the passage of the Torah that you'd gotten up by rote, to summon the speech written by someone else. *Dear Father,* it began, *dear Grandparents, dear Friends and Family, on this day I become a man. . . . ,* but the rest resisted you. You could see the words, dim as within a cave, you could even reach in and touch them, but when you sought to draw them out, they seemed to claw at cracks and corners, and when nothing came, you thought of running.

But you didn't run, you stayed, and, called forward by the Rabbi, you made your way to his side, and there, facing the congregation, you let him, guide you through the mysteries with a nod, a sign, a whispered word. Kindly man, and you so far from manly! *Dear Father,* you said at last, *on this day . . . ,* and glancing down, you saw him weeping. For your mother, it may have been, or because he knew your way was long.

176

SCENE 115

THE FISHES AND THE FEITS (1918)

Irving Fish and Sam Feit had married sisters of your Uncle Harry, and, like him, they were building contractors. Their field was limited to row houses of brick and brownstone, walk-up flats, and renovations. For all these small-scale ventures, their chosen sphere was Bronx County, and by careful planning and constant vigilance, they managed to extract modest gains from Stebbins Avenue, Southern Boulevard, and West Farms Road: they saw to the pennies, and pennies they remained.

Sam Feit was a round little man who made you think of those weighted toys that, when knocked down, always returned to the vertical. He smiled without end, as if capable of no other expression, and when you saw him in your father's office, he'd rock as if about to return to rest. His clothes were off the rack and ill-worn, and often they were splashed with plaster and streaked with tar, and often too they were torn. He spoke with a foreign accent, thick and permanent, and you can still hear him say *Mr. Sapira, now I'll gonna tell you something.*

Irving Fish was stooped and thin, consumptive thin, and he never smiled at all. His face was drawn tight over its base of bones, and his skin was so sheer that you wondered how it held his blood. He too dressed poorly, wore any old thing in any old way, and the splash that had speckled Sam Feit seemed also to have spotted him. He too smelled of mortar and cellars and pipe-joint compound, and he too spoke in broken English: *in better vords,* he'd say, and he'd call deeds and mortgages *documents, legal documents.*

Your Uncle Harry had nothing in common with his brothers-in-law and hardly more with their wives, who bore the smell of saffron and reminded him of Minsk. He sported shirts with monograms, and from a banded pinkie a yellow diamond flashed. The Fishes and the Feits, with their *legal documents* and their kitchen-flavored women, were never invited to his home. To your Aunt Rae, they'd've been out of place, offensive to her sense of order, they'd've been loose shoes left under her baby grand. There was small danger of a casual call, but she so feared a ringing doorbell (*we just happened to be passing by*) that she tried to forestall it by jeering at her relatives and joking about their names. *The Fishes and the Feits!* she'd say, *the Feits fish, and the Fishes fight!* and whenever you thought of the fishing Feits and the fighting Fishes, you couldn't help but laugh.

They'd long been clients of your father, and their trust in him was as absolute as that confided in a Rabbi, and, what was more, they seemed to enjoy being in his presence, as if there they were nearer the fire. You met them often in his chambers, in the law library and the outer rooms, and always when you saw them, you'd recall your Aunt Rae's derision— *The Fishes and the Feits!* —and you'd size them up on the sly, hiding your amusement while you graded them in your mind.

One day, after the offices had emptied, your father called you to his desk and invited you to sit down. He put a match to a cigar and tilted back in his swivel-chair, and then, after studying you for a moment, he said, "Tell me what you think of when you look at those men."

"What men?" you said.

"Mr. Fish and Mr. Feit."

"I don't think of anything."

"I watch you while you're watching them," he said. "You're thinking, all right."

"Well, maybe I am," you said. "I'm thinking of the funny way they talk. In better vords, they say, and Mr. Sapira. And documents—they always say documents."

"What else do you think?" your father said.

"That they're always dirty. Mud on their shoes. Plaster."

"They speak with an accent, and they're dirty. Are there any other counts in your indictment?"

"No," you said.

"Those are your reasons, then, for feeling superior?"

"I didn't say I felt superior."

"You say it every time you look at them," your father said, "and what's worse, they hear you. You think they're a pair of greenhorns, insensitive and illiterate, and yet they can read your foolish mind. Yes, they do say documents, and they do call me Mr. Sapira, and it's true that they come here with black fingernails and soiled clothes. But, my dear stuck-up Julian, I'll gonna tell you someting—no finer men ever lived! Your Uncle Harry and your Aunt Rae hold them cheap, and it's from them you've been taking your opinions. In learning from small minds, you can only become small-minded too. I love Sam Feit and Irving Fish. They're your Uncle Harry's relatives, not mine, but I love them, and it shames me that you judge them by things that never measure the man—dirty hands and dirty clothes. By my standards, Julian, they're superior to you." He turned his chair to the window then and spoke to your transparency in the glass, saying, "And now you may go."

SCENE 116

EPISODE IN A BATHROOM (1918)

While undressing one night, you glanced at the mirror and saw on your shoulder what you took to be a fly, a moth, a spider. In revulsion, you flirted it away, but as you removed the last of your clothes, you became aware of a crawling on your chest, and looking again at your reflection, you found that a rill of blood was running from the spot you'd flicked with your hand. It seemed to flow in spurts that kept time with your heart, and when you pressed the fount with your fingers, you merely felt your pulse; you bled from the cracks between them, and soon there was red on your side and leg and around you on the floor. It was as though you were pumping yourself dry — stand there long enough, you thought, and you'd well away and die — and now the shivers began, and you shook until your image blurred in the glass.

And then your father was in the doorway, home from somewhere, a card-game at the club, a walk in the dark; his coat and derby still gave off the outdoor chill and his nosegay mix of Havana, bay rum, the winter open air. He'd help you, you thought, he'd stop the blood, and time rewound to a fall while running and a gash above your eye — he'd saved you then, you thought, and now he'd do the same! And even as you believed, it was done. He used a chunk that he knocked from the ice-box block, and wrapping it in a towel, he rammed it against the bloody issue, and as it began to congeal, your shakes began to subside.

"You scared, kid?" he said.
And you said, "Yes."

He was still wearing his coat and derby.

In the morning, there was a rough wart-like scab on your shoulder, and without touching it, you thought back to your thought of the night before — a moth, a tick, a bottle-fly — and one more time you shuddered. The family was gathered in the dining room, and with them, seemingly only to bring you breakfast, was the mick from the Moy, thick-lipped Ellen. While you ate, you heard flittering bits of conversation about the weather, the war, the Red Revolution (*Bullsheviks,* your grandpa said, and your Uncle Dave was angry). But when you'd eaten, you were stopped from going to school: instead, you were told, your uncle would be taking you to see Dr. Walsh.

"Who's Dr. Walsh?" you said.
"A surgeon," your father said.
"I don't want to see any Dr. Walsh!"
"That thing on your shoulder has to be looked at."
"I looked at it this morning," you said, "and that's all it is—a thing."
"You're no doctor, Julian."
"But I have to go to school!"
"The great lumpish boy!" Ellen said. "Suddintly he's a student!"
"Get up off your fat ass!" your uncle said. "You're going to Dr. Walsh!"

You remember well where his office was, in his home near Mount Morris Park, but of your visit that day, only a spoken suffix remains in your mind. -*oma*, you heard someone say, something -*oma*, but not even now do you know the rest. *Fibroma*, it may have been, *lipoma*, *epithelioma*, but whatever the word, it's over the dam of time. That same afternoon, though, your Grandma Nevins delivered you into the hands of the Sisters at St. Vincent Hospital, and on the following morning, Dr. Walsh cut you loose from the -*oma*: he showed it to you afterward, a red half-ounce of tissue rather like a stepped-on worm. You recalled your trembles of the night before, and you trembled again as the morsel of meat was taken away.

SCENE 117

MENS SANA IN CORPORE SANO (1918)

At De Witt Clinton, a course in Hygiene was conducted by a man whose name, whenever you try to recall it, eludes you among the amassment of the past. Always you feel that you're about to lay hold of it, only to find that you've caught at its sleeve, at some assonantal syllable, and that your grasp, being partial, has let it get away. The truth may be that you have no real wish to remember it, that you're content with its escape into the accumulations of the mind. There are times, indeed, when you think that you haven't forgotten so much as buried it, put it where it can't be summoned to attest your shame. But even so, ten minutes of one long-ago day remain with you, and to make yourself bleed, you know that you need not know the name.

You'd gone to see the teacher when school was out for the afternoon. The three o'clock bell had rung moments before, and there was no spate of sound in the hallways now, there were no cries, laughter, scraping feet; it was quiet when you reached the room and opened the door. He was at his desk, facing thirty-six empty seats, and though he heard you enter and said, "What do you want?" he continued to work on a pile of papers that lay before him.

You thought of saying, "Excuse me. I didn't know . . . ," and quickly going away, but instead you said, "A friend of mine sent me. Someone in the class. He wants me to talk to you for him."

"Why didn't he come himself?"

"I guess he don't want you to know who he is."

"And he picked you as his emissary. Is that it?"

"I don't know what an emissary is."

"You're his John Alden."

"No, sir. My name is Julian Shapiro."

"What does this friend want you to talk about?"

"The lecture you gave the other day," you said. "The one where you warned us about certain things."

"Go on," he said.

"Well, this friend of mine does one of those things."

"Which one?"

"The one where he abuses himself."

He looked up now, staring at you but saying nothing, and as though forced to speak by his silence, you said, "My friend would like to stop doing that thing. He would like to stop self-abusing himself, but he doesn't know how."

"There's only one way to stop. Stop!"

"My friend says he done that, but he started again."

"Tell him to stop again."

"It isn't easy, he says. Once you start, it's hard to stop."

"Your friend's trouble isn't the stopping—it's the starting. Tell him not to start."

"My friend says he sometimes don't even know when he's self-abusing. He only finds out when it's over, and then it's too late. He sits there thinking about something else, and there's nobody around, and it's quiet, and its's almost like he was falling asleep, and all at once the thing is happening! it's happening! My friend says."

He went back to his stack of papers. "This friend of yours," he said. "Tell him. . . ."

But you didn't wait for the rest. You left the room and walked the length of the corridor to the stairway, and on one of the landings, you stopped and spoke to yourself. "Your friend!" you said.

SCENE 118

THE PAINTED WOMAN (1918-20)

You can't recall when it all began, just after the war ended, perhaps, or possibly just before. It seems to drift into being in wisps of awareness, and you see a face, a form, a color, a glance, each for an instant a mere cast on the mind, but more and more the shadows gather and longer and longer they stay, and in the end they turn to mass, become actual, and then they will not pass away. *The painted woman,* your Aunt Rae called her, and when you thought no one was looking, you sought for signs of what she meant. You saw a faint down of powder and through it a flush that some might've said was not her own. She was beautiful, you told yourself, and you remembered plumes in a hotel hallway, and your Aunt Rae said *Your father knew her while your mother was still alive.*

On intermittent Sundays, your father would take you for a morning's walk, and along the way, on a bench at a certain corner or seated in some cafe, you'd come upon the woman of plumes and glinting jet, of white skin and black hair, and she'd kiss you more than kindly, press you close, hold you by the hand. *The painted woman,* you'd think, and you'd try your best to fault her when you could bring yourself to stare. But she was living, and your mother was dead, and that was her only flaw. Her name was Josephine.

And when you came home, your aunt would always be there, and she'd ask *How was the painted woman today?* and *What did she wear, Julian?* and *Julian, what did she say?* But you'd not be able to speak, and you'd trace the figurations of the carpet, turn your face downward while she let her hatred pour. *Your father is going to marry her, Julian,* she'd tell you. *She's going to take your mother's place.* Your grandma would try to stop her, saying, *Let the boy alone, Rae. What does a child know of such things?* but Rae would go on with her aspersion of the painted woman, and in the end she'd always show that your father was the mark. *Do you know that your father killed your mother?* she'd say, and you'd hear your grandma's *Rae, Rae,* but Rae would be in motion, and she'd say *He put her in the grave!* and then Childe Julian would go to his room and shut the door.

SCENE 119

GREEN MOUNTAIN CAMP (1920)

In the early summer of that year, your father sent you to a camp in Vermont. It lay along the shore of Lake Hortonia in the foothills of the range for which it was named. Of the weeks you spent there, seven photographs remain, nearly all of them mottled where the emulsion has peeled away. In one, you're carrying a bat and wearing a baseball shirt and cap; in others, you're lounging in a field or on the steps of a raw-wood bunkhouse; and in the rest, to your lifelong dismay, you're shown in comic poses with a bow and violin.

For all the unease caused by those speckled images, for all the times you've wished them away, they show you as you know you were, one of the many and unimbued with a wish to be otherwise. You gaze at those seven faces of yourself, five of them caught with a smile, and you wonder what beguilement lay before you: was it the prospect beyond the camera, was it a wag with his thumbs in his ears, or were you amused by some misfortune that for a while assuaged your blues?

Your father may have written to you more than twice that summer, but only two of his letters survive their journey on the Rutland and the dispersions of time. In one of them, he wrote

Julian dear, I suppose you have heard that I have, since you left the city, been married. This event I presume does not come to you as a total surprise, for it has been common gossip and knowledge, has been in contemplation for some time.

and he wrote

I hope and trust, Julian, that this change in the life of your father will not reach you with any measure of disappointment, for you as my son should not form any personal conclusion or conviction about this important subject, but abide by the wish and will of one who, in all your future life, will be your guardian and counsellor. I assure you that this change will not affect you in the slightest degree, but on the contrary, your interest will be just as safely guarded as before.

and he wrote

Julian dear, if you have any personal ideas or prejudices on this subject, you should subordinate them to the paramount wish and will of your father.

183

Julian dear, I do not have to tell you that my wife is now entitled to the respect and esteem due to a person so closely related by ties to your father.

and he wrote

Your loving father.

How did you reply, you wonder. Did you tell your loving father that he had a loving son? Did you say you honored him that your days might be long upon the land and would do the same though you knew your time was short? Did you say, Julian dear, that your father could do no wrong? Or, sitting in the mess hall or on the dock or under a tree, did you read the four pages and put them away, fold them at the creases and turn your mind away?

His other letter reached you toward the close of the summer. In it, he wrote

My dear Julian, while your correspondence is somewhat infrequent, it is nevertheless very welcome. I suppose you may make the same complaint about me, but you must take into account the fact that I have a few more things to keep me preoccupied than you have.

and he wrote

I receive an occasional letter from baby and she is having a wonderful time and I presume you know that I was up to the camp to see her and that I found her looking like a miniature hippo.

and he wrote

Julian dear, I have taken an apartment on the "Heights," but it will not be ready for moving in until Oct. 1st and until then we will have to camp out, but we will do the best we can. The room assigned to you is one with a private bath.

and he wrote

Julian dear, there is one more thing that you have omitted and which will make me happy and that is an occasional note or card to my wife. She will esteem it and it will be greatly appreciated.

and he wrote

With love and affection from your Father.

Between then and now, sixty years and more have come to intervene, a swirling smoke of time, but through it all you see that summer loom, you see that pair of letters, you see your room on the "Heights." You see those

184

seven faces of Julian dear, five of them smiling at what in the world outside of you or what in the world within? You think of your loving father, and you know you could not have made him happy with a *note or a card* to his wife. You know you turned away.

SCENE 120

JULIAN DEAR, HE WROTE (1920)

I want you not to forget that I am still as fond of you as I always have been, and that nothing you may do or say will ever make me lose the affection which a father has for a son, excepting only when you show me that you have lost the paternal affection and respect due me.

When you returned from Vermont, you went straight from Grand Central Station to the Jersey Central pier, and there you took the *Sandy Hook* or the *Monmouth* for the Highlands and the boat-train down the shore.

and he wrote

I did not think that you would postpone seeing your father after an absence of ten weeks when a 5¢ ride would bring you to him. I can only judge your inclination by your action: you had your mind made up to leave direct for Asbury on your arrival, else you would have come to the house.

It was to your Aunt Rae that you went, fifty miles away, and not to your father, who awaited you in Harlem, a 5¢ ride uptown. If it misgave you that he knew your mind, you put your disquiet aside, left it behind you on the beach, lost it in the Barrel of Fun at the Steeplechase, forgot it at the cottage pianola in the swing and sway of *The Blue Danube.* You had an Indian summer fortnight still, and you thought it would never end. You swam in the Natatorium on the boardwalk (you can smell the steamed towels, hear your voice roll back from the dome), and you rode the Deal Lake launches, watched baitmen seine for mullet and dories return from the nets. It would never end, you thought, but having kept your father's letter, you knew otherwise all along.

and he wrote

I have taken an apartment on 177th Street and Audubon Avenue, where I will be located on and after Oct. 5th. You can judge for yourself where your future home will be without any urging or suggestions from me. I write in this strain because I am afraid your immature impressions may be the result of imaginary prejudices.

But they weren't imaginary; they were real, and they'd been put where they were by Aunt Rae. *The painted woman,* she'd always say, and in those two weeks at Asbury, she insinuated more. In avoiding your father, you'd supposed yourself safe for the while, but having fled him, you were exposed to her, and you weren't safe at all.

and he wrote

If there is lurking in your heart any antipathy for me or anyone else, I want you to eradicate it, as that is attributable only to your extreme youth. I hope and trust as you grow older and your mind and understanding develop, that you will live down those prejudices, if any exist. Unless I am very much mistaken, I do not believe that you will be anything but a faithful and dutiful son.

Your father had married a divorcée, your Aunt Rae told you. The word meant a woman whose marriage had been dissolved in a court of law; it also meant that her husband was still alive. In marrying again, therefore, she'd done a shameful thing. She was revealing to a second husband what she'd vowed to reserve for the first, and from being a fast woman, she'd become a loose one. A shameful thing, your Aunt Rae said, and it was made all the worse because your stepmother had a child of her own. *You have a stepsister now, Julian,* she said, *and first place goes to her.*

and he wrote

There will be awaiting you a comfortable home, pleasant surroundings, and love and affection from me and my wife. There is nothing in the world that I am able to afford that you will not have. In return, I and my wife expect very little, and that is honor and respect.

Don't live with him, Julian, your Aunt Rae told you, *stay with your Grandma Nevins.* And you'd go down to the cellar, where all those old newspapers were piled, and you'd read of Tige and Buster Brown and Happy Hooligan and Marcelline the Clown, and then you'd go upstairs again and play *Velia O Velia, the witch of the wood,* and rapt in such pursuits, you'd let the fourteen days run out.

A FAITHFUL AND DUTIFUL SON (1920)

Only the closing of Aunt Rae's summer cottage made you quit the Jersey shore. No letter from your father could stir you, and no one else's urging, nor were you moved from deep within you, where inwit sleeps. There still were days to be spent on the sand, cool now in the shade of the pavilions, and there were new birds to be seen as the season changed; more windows were shuttered and more blinds drawn, and you saw fewer people on the porches, and often you were alone in the roads, wading through fallen leaves, brown and upturned, like sunburned hands. There were days left, you thought, there were days still to come—but then the last of them came, and with it one more weather-tight house and one more withering lawn, and you watched from the train as the summer fell behind.

There will be awaiting you a comfortable home, your father had written, and soon, that very afternoon, you'd be called on to say where you meant to reside. Would you go with your father and the painted woman, you wondered, would you leave places and people long familiar, would you turn from your friends and your usual ways, would you be a faithful and dutiful son, as your father had surmised? In a little while, you were due to join him at his sister Sarah's, and there the questions would be put to you, and the answers would have to be made. Your Aunt Rae had been at your grandma's house all morning, and as you moved toward the door, she said *He gave her your mother's diamonds, Julian. Your mother's diamonds are on her hands and in her ears.*

Your Aunt Sarah lived in a row house a block away from your Grandma Nevins. It was a four-story granite-front, one of a dozen or more and distinguishable from the others only by the number above the door. A semibasement held the areas of the household that were used daily—an eating room, a kitchen and pantry, and a scullery. One flight up, below two floors of sleeping quarters, was a parlor with furniture of gilded wood and rose brocade, and adjoining it at the rear, equally severe in its cut crystal and mahogany, lay an equally ceremonial dining-room, dimmed almost always by its crimson portières. It was there, at a great circular table and half-lighted in the skirt of a chandelier, that you found your father, and with him sat his sister Sarah.

Your aunt was the first to speak. "Julian," she said, "we asked you to come here today so that we could possibly help you make a very important decision that would involve your whole future life. The decision is about where you are going to live. Your father wants you should live under his roof, under his control, where a young boy like you belongs. If I thought he was wrong, if I thought you would be better off with Mr. and Mrs. Nevins, I would tell him so. But he is right that a boy should have the advantage of a father's experience, a father always being there to help and advise in time of need. You don't know the ways of the world, Julian—a *bitter Gelachter,* this life can be—and a boy can get in trouble without a father to protect him. I say nothing against your grandparents, Mr. and Mrs. Nevins. They are the finest of people, and it was a *mitzvah* what they did when they took in six years ago a son-in-law and his motherless children. A *mitzvah,* and God will reward them for it, but the time has come, Julian, when you should be in your own home, not in the home of somebody else."

You never looked at her while she was speaking. Your eyes were on a small quadrant of table-top, on the high gloss of the fine-grained dark brown wood. At the limit of sight lay a flint-glass bowl aglint with rays of light from above. Your gaze was downward. Never once did you raise your head.

"Let me say a word, Sarah," your father said. "I think Julian is old enough to be told why I accepted his grandparents' hospitality. It was the wrong atmosphere to bring children up in—I knew that, Julian, but I was helpless. To save your mother's life, I spent every dollar I owned in the world and all I was able to borrow. When she passed away, I was so deep in debt that I couldn't raise money for food, for clothing, for rent. To use an expression you'll understand, I was broke—worse, because I owed—and when grandpa and grandma offered us a home, I was only too glad to move in. But things have been changing, Julian. My law business is better now, and I am able to provide for you and your sister in the way that I have always desired. I want the two of you, my two children, to live with me. I love you both with all my heart, and I want you near."

Did you respond then, did your eyes meet his, did your own heart rise—or did you greet his plea unmoved, and had you been hard from the start?

"People come to me," your Aunt Sarah said. "Friends, I couldn't mention their names, it wouldn't be right. And they say Mrs. Perlman, Rae, they say, she is going around circalating stories about your father, that no better man ever lived. She is going around, Julian, I don't know why, and she is saying he gave your mother's jewelry to his new wife, her engagement ring, her bracelets, her lavalière. What jewelry? There was no jewelry left. Your father pawned them for doctors' bills, for nurses and medicine. Your father is not such a man that would give what belonged to your mother away."

"There have been many stories, Julian," your father said. "They come back to me from clients, from other lawyers, from men I play cards with at the club. One of those stories is that I knew my present wife while your mother was still alive. I don't deny that. I did know her. But what Aunt Rae leaves out is that your mother knew her too. We all lived at the same hotel, Stein's, and it was only natural for two women, having children the same age, to become acquainted with each other. I would not deign to explain this to anyone else but you, but I care what you think, and I want you to know the truth. Another story, and just as false, is that I 'arranged' my wife's divorce. I did no such thing, Julian. True, I represented her, but a lawyer doesn't 'arrange' a divorce. He applies for it only at a client's request. . . . But there's no use raking up these matters. Let it suffice for me to remind you that, just as in a courtroom, there are two sides to every controversy, and both are entitled to be heard. I ask you, as my dear and only son, to consider my side, to hear me as you seem to hear Aunt Rae."

At times, they spoke to you directly, and at times, though always for your benefit, they addressed each other. They were patient, they were mild, they appealed to your sense of duty, your devotion, your faith in your father's judgment, and while you may have seemed deaf because you stayed mute, you heard it all, heard their every word. Their efforts went for nought: as well might they have sought to persuade the cut-glass bowl between you, the table, the chandelier.

"He sits and says nothing," Aunt Sarah said.
"You're an intelligent boy," your father said. "You know very well how to express yourself. Why won't you tell me what's going through your mind?"

Nothing was going: your mind was still. It had come to a stop somewhere, gotten stuck — when? why? There were no thoughts to convey: you weren't thinking.

"He sits and says nothing," Aunt Sarah said. "He just sits, Phil. Sits and says nothing."

You were there for two hours that afternoon, and never once did you look up at them, never did you say a word. In the end, your father rose, came around the table, and stopped behind your chair.

"All right, Julian," he said, "if it'll make you happy, stay with your grandpa and grandma. My home will never be closed to you, and the day may come when you change your mind."

He didn't touch you, as you hoped he would. He merely stood where he was for a moment, saying nothing more, and then he left the room and went downstairs.

"With such a father," Aunt Sarah said, "how could you be so cold? You didn't get that way from him, I know my brother, and you didn't get that way from your mother, I knew her too. It must've come from somebody else, God forgive her."

And then she too was gone, and you sat there alone, a faithful and dutiful son.

§

Aunt Rae was still at your grandma's house when you returned. "Well," she said, "what did you tell them?"

"They tried to convince to go with my father," you said. "To go and live in his apartment."

"And what did you decide?"

"To stay here with grandma."

"How did they take the news?"

"I didn't give them any news. I didn't say anything."

"Then how do they know?"

"They know," you said.

"Enough, Rae," your grandma said. "You done enough. I want you should let him alone."

But Rae had not done enough, and she said, "Do you remember your mother, Julian?"

"Yes," you said.

"The way she looked? The sound of her voice?"

"Yes," you said.

"Never forget there's no such thing as a second mother. A stepmother isn't a mother. Your mother is dead."

"Enough is enough, Rae," your grandma said.

Ettie, you thought, Chai Esther, Harriet—but after that day, the word *mother* was harder than ever to say.

SCENE 122

WHILE YOU LOOKED THE OTHER WAY (1920)

two men were shot and killed on a street in South Braintree, Massachusetts. The victims, Frederick Parmenter, a paymaster, and a guard named Alessandro Berardelli, were murdered while transporting a shoe-factory payroll of $15,000 in a pair of metal boxes. Others would know these facts, but not then you, and they'd know as well the weather of the day, the sun's inclination, the shape of the clouds, if any, and the whence and whither of the wind. What had you been doing while they saw and heard such things—if gazing from a window, what had you seen; if walking, where had you wandered; if running, had you been pursuer or pursued?

Not yet you, but others would know that two Italians were arrested on a trolley-car bound for Brockton. They'd know that the officers' names were Connolly and Vaughan, and they'd know what each of them said and what their prisoners said in reply. You, though, you'd go your blank and aimless way while the Italians were indicted and tried for the Braintree murders, while they were being convicted (*one looked like a regular wop,* a witness would say), while lawyers argued and the pile of pleadings grew—and not a phrase spoken or written would reach you, not a date or a photo or a name.

Nor would you be aware of the motion for a new trial, of supplementary motions, of supplements to the supplementary motions, of appeals taken from the denial of all, of the briefs that were filed, of the hearings, of the petitions for writs, stays, clemency, of the protests and demonstrations and the pleas of noted men. For seven years, you'd be aware of nothing, nothing all through the *much we have suffered during this long Calvary.*

And then the seven years would come to an end. It would be a late-summer night, and you'd be with some of those others who'd known what you had not, and a certain hour, they'd fall to speaking quietly while one of them listened to sound-waves on the air. You'd be dwelling on—what? On Mr. Prufrock? On *Exagmination Factification Incamination?* On the untranslated French in *Tristram Shandy?*

And then there'd be a silence, and into it someone would say, "Well, they burned 'em."

And into a second silence, you'd say, "Burned who?"

And someone would say, "Are you serious, Julian?"

And you'd say, "Yes."

"Because if you're not, it's a poor joke."

"I'm serious," you'd say. "Who burned?"

"Do these names mean anything to you—Sacco, Vanzetti?"

"No."

"You've never heard of Sacco and Vanzetti?"

"Never."

And someone would say, "You just finished law school. Your father's a lawyer, and you're with lawyers all day. All around you, there must've been talk of Sacco and Vanzetti. And you never heard of them?"

"No, I told you."

191

And then someone else, someone who hadn't said a word, would say, "Well, then, Julian, you're one ignorant son-of-a-bitch."

SCENE 123

THE RIFT (1920)

Early in the fall, you began your final year at De Witt Clinton. Your father had removed to his new home on the Heights, and the room with the pale pink walls was yours now, yours the single pennant (Minnesota, why Minnesota? Where was Yale?), the brass-railed bed, the mirrored chiffonier—all such things were yours. Within that pastel realm, and without as well, you were under the supervision of your Grandpa and Grandma Nevins, both of them past the age of sixty and too old to pursue you for the broken resolution, the idled hours, for truancy and halfdone homework when done at all. At sixteen, you were very nearly your own guardian, and the rules you imposed were few.

Before you left for school one morning, your father telephoned to summon you to his office when classes were over for the day, and at midafternoon you were on your way downtown. At City Hall, you crossed the park to Temple Court, a red-brick building not far from the abutment of Brooklyn Bridge. As usual when there were no other passengers, the elevator-man let you haul on the cable (Rocco! His name was Rocco!), and up went the cage to the tenth and topmost floor. There, facing you through the grille, was a door of translucent glass bearing the gilt-bordered black letters of *Philip D. Shapiro* and *Counsellor-at-Law*. Rocco, you thought, and you wondered whether Rocco was a first name or a last.

At that hour, there were no clients in the chambers, and you found your father at his desk, gazing at something distant without seeming to be blocked by a wall across the way. He was humming, a few tuneless notes more like those of a sigh than a song, and he knew you were in the room only when his cigar-smoke surged on the air. After you'd kissed him, he motioned you to a chair and tapped a slip of paper lying in a green clearing on his blotter.

"Read that," he said. "It's about you."

Taking up the strip, torn rather than cut from a sheet, you saw that it carried a one-line message for your father, though it lacked both a salutation and a signature. *Your fine son*, you read, *came home at ½ past eleven last Monday night.*

"That's grandpa's writing," you said. "I reckonize it."

"What else do you reckonize?" your father said.

"He forgot to write *Dear Phil* at the beginning."

"Forget what he forgot. Is it true you were out until almost midnight?"

"Yes, but he shouldn't've squealed on me."

"That's where you're wrong. He was bound to tell me you were out that late. You're in his care, and he wants you to do the right thing."

You glanced away at the janitor's flat on the far side of the air-shaft; in one of the windows, a curtain moved. "He didn't have to say *your fine son*," you said.

"What should he have said?"

"If he meant bad, he should've said bad."

"How could he ever call you bad?" your father said. "You're his favorite."

"I don't think it's right to spy on me and then send a nonymous letter." Moving again, the curtain parted a little, and through the opening, you saw the half-hidden face of a very young girl. "A milkman gets better treatment than that."

Your father blew smoke at the girl in the window, and she quickly disappeared. "I'm afraid my standing isn't quite as high as a milkman's," he said.

"Another thing," you said. "He didn't have to write. He could've told you when he came to the office."

Your father turned back to the room and studied you for a moment or two, and then he said, "He doesn't come to the office any more, Julian."

"Then where do you see him?" you said. "A client is suppose to come to the office."

"He's not a client any more. He sent for all his papers, and he took his business elsewhere."

"You mean you don't repasent grandpa any more?"

"He has a new lawyer now. A man named J. Sidney Bernstein."

"I know him!" you said. "He lives in Uncle Harry's house!"

"He's your Uncle Harry's lawyer."

"Why did grandpa go away? You're the best lawyer there is!"

"I don't know about that, kid," your father said. "But I did represent him for seventeen years—from the time I met your mother. It hurt me to lose him, but he wouldn't stand for my marrying again, and he hasn't spoken to me since."

You looked at the scrap of paper, saying, "I guess that's why he didn't write *Dear Phil*."

THE COLOR OF THE AIR, XI

ABRAHAM LINCOLN – 1862
AT THE TELEGRAPH OFFICE

My God! What will the country say!
— A. Lincoln

He couldn't stay away from the place. Day after day, he'd put on
that tweed shawl of his and that tall black hat and cross the street
to the War Office, and there he'd be when news came in — from
Malvern Hill, it might've been, from Antietam, Shiloh,
Chancellorsville. He'd be standing at a window or folded to fit a
chair, but wherever he was, he'd be silent or saying little sadly when
the sounder began to play in code. Somewhere, in a wagon or a tent
or the open air, a hand on a key would be making and breaking a
circuit, sending word in Morse for a loss of lives, for death at a stone
bridge, at an unheard-of church, or where two roads met in a wood.
And to the man at a window or choked in a chair, it would be as
if he were with those dead as each one died, and each on going left
less of him, and the day would come when the last of him went,
and he'd die there, in the war being fought in that room.

SCENE 124

TO JOIN THE GYPSIES (1920)

The train, the Washington local, left Pennsylvania Station at one o'clock in
the morning. Coming out from under the shed, it cruised the open yards
to where the sidetracks merged with the two main lines, and there it entered
the Hudson tunnel. Just outside your window, a transparent car ran at equal
speed on a concrete wall, and seen through glass, it seemed dimmer than the
one you rode in, as though its world were less well lit. In that see-through
region, you too were indistinct, and you saw your image as strange, as someone else's reflection somehow switched with your own. You put your hand
up and touched the hand beyond the panes, and then, chilled, you drew it away.

194

In a few more hours, your note would be found pinned to one of your pillows, and the lines you'd written on foolscap would be read (by Ellen? by Uncle Dave?) to a still of gaping faces above the undisturbed cover of your bed. You tried to recall what you'd said, what message you'd left behind, but it was as if the yellow sheet were blank, for only its color came back to mind. What had become of your recital of slights, you wondered, your list of grievances, your bill of rights denied?—it was all there, you knew, but in disappearing ink. And you knew further that even if it reappeared, it wouldn't reveal the truth—that you were running from you and in particular from your fist. You had four dollars in your pocket, and your ticket was good to Baltimore.

The train expelled itself from the tunnel onto the Hackensack Meadows, a vast tidewater blue with moonlit snow. Though lights were strung on far-off rises and scattered on the flat, little could be seen but an occasional glassed-in mass bright with the passing train and then dark against the night. At Manhattan Transfer, there was a power-change to steam, to a black Pacific with a red keystone on its boiler head, and then came stops at stations that seemed to be spaced by the mile. Who got aboard, you wondered, who was left in the Rahway, Metuchen, New Brunswick dark? But you wondered more whether distance would diminish the attraction of your fist. You thought of four dollars, of a ticket to Baltimore, and then you fell asleep.

Your flight seemed dreamsome even when you woke (where?) to frozen creeks, bare trees, and a sky of dirty rags. You'd come from a night filled with a strife of faces, voices, colors, into a still and silent country no less frightening than the scenes of fancy. Beside you in the windowpane, faint against the unclean clouds, rode your self of the dream, a transparent you, four dollars rich and headed for a place called Baltimore.

You never knew why you'd said *Baltimore* when the agent said *Where to?* You'd read no maps or travel brochures, you'd made no inquiries, laid no plans—*Baltimore,* you said to the agent, and money became a ticket that would carry you two hundred miles from home. Now, soon after dawn, your train was coasting over the city's shopworn snow. You heard *Baltimore! Odenton, Bowie, Washington the next!* and you thought of staying aboard, of riding as long as your four dollars lasted—but in another moment, you were standing on a platform along with an extra self, a haze of transient breath.

In your hand, you carried a small satchel of black fibre. You could hardly recall what it contained—clothes, you supposed, but which? and the trinkets you'd treasured from the past, the trove of gutter and sidewalk and diggings in the sand. You looked down at it, thinking of the schoolbooks it once had

195

been laden with, the lunches, the overshoes for the rainy day, and you knew that whatever it held now would wear the flavors of rubber, fruit, and herbs. For a reason you left unexplained, you wished you were rid of it.

And then you were out of the train-shed and on the street, walking past shops still shut, past hurrying people, past bundles of the *Sun* lying near the curbs. As in some hallucination, you seemed not so much to be going toward as going away; you were moving with no aim but the motion itself, as though you could only misstep by standing still; and on that endless way, there were no faces that you ever remembered, only a whirl of places that you might've seen from a carrousel

flashes —
a trolley-car to Pimlico
(why Pimlico?) and
a chestnut horse in a bank of snow,
the Virginia end of Arlington Bridge,
a ride with a man who drank paregoric,
a night's sleep in a railroad shanty,
a meal for thirty cents,
another ride,
and another ride

and all the while, you were unaware of signs reading Manassas, Chancellorsville, the Rappahannock, Drewry's Bluff, and then you were in Carolina, riding with a man who said

Where you from, son?
and when you told him, he said
You ever been at the South before?
and you said
No, only to Washington,
and he said
Washinton is North. This heah is South,
and then he said
What you think of the South, son?
and you said
I like it. All but the lynching.

(Leo Frank, you thought, a name you hadn't known you knew.)

and the man said
What did you say, son?
and you said
Lynching,

196

and he stopped the car and said
Out, you Jew bastard!
and out you got, and he drove away,

and then, with only half a dollar left, you began to beg at back doors (you remember a cold veal sandwich) and to sleep in ricks of hay, and, one night in the Durham YMCA

ptomaine!
with vomiting,
abdominal pain,
and the running squitters,
and someone
(who?)
sent a telegram to your father,
and, shivering when you thought of
cold veal,
Jew bastard,
and Baltimore,

you went home.
Somewhere along the way, you lost the black satchel and all it contained, the clothes (which?), the prized possessions, the smell of fruit, books, rubbers for the rainy days, but you still had your fist.

SCENE 125

THE DOTEY SQUAD (1921)*

At one of the tables in the Clinton lunchroom, you sat looking out across the Hudson at docks and ferry-slips, at the houses of Weehawken, at clouds going downwind over the state of New Jersey. You wondered where their rain would finally fall, and for no reason that you knew, the name *Musconetcong* came to mind. Turning away from the scene outside (what and where was *Musconetcong?*), you absently eyed a scribbled-on section of plaster wall, where a tangle of graphite slowly evolved into words:

Poor Alice, you read, *she gave away two hundred dolars worth before she knew she could sell it.*

---

* In *A Man Without Shoes*, 1951, this actual happening was treated as fiction and ascribed to another.

197

"What're you doing?" a voice said.

Alongside the table stood a boy with his jacket unbuttoned to display, on one of the points of his vest, the black-and-red enamel of a Dotey Squad badge.

"I'm reading what it says on the wall," you said.

"Which part?"

You put your finger on it. "This part here."

"*Poor Alice*," the monitor read, "*she gave away two hundred.* . . . That's smutty!"

"What's that mean—smutty?" you said.

"If you read the posters in every hall, you'd know about the Anti-Smut Campaign. A smutty thing is dirty. It's smutty."

"Instead of putting up all those posters," you said, "they ought to wash the walls."

"You admit, then, that what you read was smutty."

"Sure. But I had to read it first to find out."

"You should've known it was smutty before you read it. It was on a wall, and anything on a wall is smutty."

"How about posters?" you said. "They're on a wall."

"What're you?" he said. "A wise guy?"

"I know my rights. My father is a lawyer."

"You're going to need him. I'm running you in."

You were tried, convicted, and sentenced to spend ten hours in the Squad Room, to be served in equal stretches on five successive days. When, on the fifth day, the bell rang to end your confinement, you waited for the Squad Master, Aaron Dotey, to dismiss you. After several moments, he raised his head and took notice of you.

"Shapiro," he said, "your time is up."

You rose.

"I haven't told you to go."

You sat down.

"Your time is up, and your offense has been paid for. But the Dotey Squad is never interested in punishment as such; it is concerned with reform. No boy ever leaves here without being asked the question that I ask you now: What have you learned from your experience?"

You weren't hurting anybody, you thought. You were just sitting there doing nothing, and accidentally you read that Alice thing on the wall. But nobody would listen when you tried to explain, and you got punished just like you were the guy that wrote it. What could you learn from that?

"I'm waiting," the Squad Master said.

Talk about justice. Where was the justice in convicting you for reading something you didn't know how it was going to end? Justice! That wasn't justice. It was *un*justice!

198

"Shapiro," the Squad Master said, "I asked what you learned from your experience!"

"Oh, I learned a lot," you said.

"That's fine. That's what we like to hear."

Only you didn't teach it to me, you thought.

SCENE 126

HIGH SCHOOL ON 59th ST. (1917-21)*

In your time at De Witt, there were two blacks, or two you knew of, among a thousand whites: for all those rooms and halls and flights of stairs, all those books, boards, and windowed walls, you were aware of only two. You never wondered, meaning you never cared, about the black multitude that stared at the doors from Harlem, half the town away. Through some seepage or intromission, you sensed their presence, but they were still somewhere else, present *there,* and it didn't pertain to you that but two of their number found the way to San Juan Hill.

About one of them, no more than a particular remains in your mind, a single point, a brass tack, less than his name and only this: he came to class one day with a pistol. Memory of him begins and ends there, on the selfsame downright fact: the pistol. The ins and outs, if ever they were known to you, are gone now, why the gun was carried and why and where drawn, whether it was loaded and, if so, whether it would shoot, gone such things, along with how the news was spread (by a rumor running the corridors? by a stir that sped the stairs?), and gone as well the punishment—death, was it, or did they let the nigger go?

You never said the word, but in your head, you never used another. There in your sequestered self, it was always nigger, soundless since there was no ear. All the same, the Clinton pair seemed to hear the slur you cast in secret—a current, it must've caused, and when they entered your galvanized sphere, you could almost see them stiffen. They knew, they knew: one of the two brought a pistol to school.

The other** tried to sing, to soar on lyrics till the pull of g was nil, and he lost the need for feet. Up there, he'd find no white realms where his image

---

* from *View from This Wilderness,* 1977.
** Countee Cullen (1903-46).

was refused by your eye, where no passion was, no dispassion, no hand for
and none against him, no place for him to be or not to be. He'd find no
color in space but his own. Up there, he'd fly!

His songs were heavier than air, a mourning more than music, and they
never set him free, never flew him. *To make a poet black, and bid him sing!*
he said—but was it black that weighed him down, or was black made heavy
because of such as you?

SCENE 127

CHILDE JULIAN: WORKING STIFF (1921)*

In your final term at De Witt, you received a failing grade in English. You
were therefore ineligible for graduation in the company of your classmates,
but the English Department granted you permission to take a re-examination
in the fall, and on condition that you passed it, your diploma would be awarded
then. You had two full months in which to prepare, and having obtained
a waiter's job at a summer camp, you proposed to study there in your spare time.

Julian dear, your father wrote, *I hope that you will keep your promise to devote
some time to study and not in tomfoolery, for you have something to make up before
Labor Day, and I know that you can do it. . . .*

§

Camp Wakonda was in the foothills of the Adirondacks on a small and
nameless lake three or four miles from the village of Pottersville. In the
mornings, the water would wear a fleece of vapor that the sun would shear
away, and you'd hear a bugle-call and its echo and then a rise of voices from
the cabins, and a day in the woods would begin.

"Say, Clem," you said, "could I talk to you a minute?"

"At Camp Wakonda," he said, "a counselor is called Mister."

"Mister, then," you said.

"Get it over with, Shapiro. I'm in a hurry."

"Well, us waiters kind of count on the time between meals. It's our only
chance for hikes and fishing—things like that."

"What's your point?"

---

* from *A Man Without Shoes*, 1951.

"Breakfast is supposed to be from 8 to 9, and you don't show up till 8:50. I never get out of the Mess Hall before 10, sometimes later."

"And you'd sooner be out fishing or hiking—things like that."

"I'm glad you understand, Clem," you said.

"Mister," he said. "I'm a counselor, and you're a waiter. A waiter waits. Look for me tomorrow at 8:59!"

At times, when the lake was still, a cloud would lie poaching in a reflection of the sky, and then a wind would come, and the cloud would disappear.

The kid said, "I want to use the handball court."

"Wait till we finish our game," you said.

"I want the court now."

"But you're all alone. You got nobody to play with."

"I'm going to practice for the turnament. I want the court, and I want the ball too."

"Waiters have rights, you know."

"Not when a real camper is around," the kid said. "Ask Mr. Greenberg. Ask Mr. Squires."

"Look" you said, "this is a challenge-game for twenty cents."

"I wouldn't care if it was for the champeenship of the world! I want that ball!"

"Here, you stinker," you said. "And you can stick it up your ass!"

In the afternoons, the whine of reels as line unwound, the pound of running feet, the retch of oarlocks, the sound of water on water as schools of swimmers thrashed.

"I been looking for you, Jerry," you said. "I wanted to tell you about that tray of dishes I busted yesterday. They fined me a buck for it."

"Tough titty," he said. "But why tell me?"

"I tripped on your foot."

"You should've kept your eyes open."

"Your hoof was in the aisle. It belonged under the table."

"It belongs wherever I put it!" he said.

"Next time it's in the aisle, I'm going to piss on it."

"Say, you're talking to a camper!"

And the days would spend, and as the sun went down, the pines laid purple shadows where thrushes played their flutes.

It was your turn to wait on the waiters, and at the end of the meal, you took a tray to the bakery and said, "Ten big portions for the proletariat."

The bake-chef shoved a pie-tin at you, saying, "Cut it ten ways!"

"One pie for ten toilers!" you said. "Nix on that!"

"Nix is nix."

"How come campers get seconds, and waiters hardly get firsts?"

The bake-chef laughed, saying, "You ain't organized."

In a ring of flame-lit faces, a campfire burned on the beach. Songs were sung to its commotion, and recitations were made and stories told across the blaze, and when there were only rippling embers, the powwow ended, and the faces went away.

In a pine-grove near the boathouse, the ten waiters of Camp Wakonda were bedded down in needles. "He was only being funny," you said, "but a Waiters' Union wouldn't be a bad idea."

Vic Sabin said, "My father don't like unions."

"When we signed up," you said, "they told us we'd be treated like regular campers, and we're not."

"My father says if you want to stay out of trouble, stay out of unions."

You said, "They told us we could use the facilities just like anybody else, but that only holds good for the toilets. We start to play handball, and any midget snotnose can kick us off. We go out in a rowboat, and we got to come in for whoever hollers. We get docked for broken crockery, and we only eat good when a meal is bad and something's left."

"We're supposed to get a hundred bucks for the summer," Earl Sultan said, "but nobody said a word about deducks. Fourteen bucks for railroad fare!"

Pete Swann said, "What about laundry? Two smackers a week! There's sixteen more!"

"And breakage," Marty Solomon said. "That'll come to plenty!"

"You know something," you said. "We're going to land back in New York without a cent."

"What about tips?" Vic Sabin said.

Joe Geiger said, "Tips!"

Solly Fishman said, "Tips!"

Stan Vogel said, "What tips?"

Ed Oliver said, "There ain't no such a word!"

Vic Sabin said, "There is for me. I'm in fifteen bills so far, and I'm going to triple it."

"No wonder you don't want a union," you said. "You'd have to cough up for dues."

"Tips!" Wally Willard said. "I ain't seen no tips!"

"We ought to stand up for our rights," you said. "All those for having a union, say Aye." There were ten Ayes, nine strong and one weak. "The Waiters' Union of Camp Wakonda is formed. Now we get up a committee."

Vic Sabin said, "I nonimate Julian Shapiro."

"I second the motion," Ed Oliver said.

Vic Sabin said, "I move nonimations be closed."

§

"What do you want?" Mr. Squires said.

"The Waiters' Union elected me to be a committee and talk to you about the camp rules."

"So the waiters have a union. When was it organized?"

"A few minutes ago," you said. "The rules we don't like are the ones that take away the money you promised. All those deducks."

"Who was the leading spirit behind the union?" Mr. Squires said. "Whose idea was it?"

"Mine," you said. "The way we figure it, we're hardly going to make a cent after you take off for carfare, laundry, and like that."

Mr. Squires opened a ledger and added a column of entries. "You've earned forty-six dollars so far, Shapiro, and the charges against you come to forty."

"Forty!" you said.

He took two bills from a box, a five and a single, and, pointing, he said, "Sign there."

You signed *J. Shapiro* near his fingernail.

Handing you the six dollars, he glanced at his wrist-watch and said, "You have one hour to pack and get off the grounds. You're fired!"

"I'm going to tell the union!" you said, and it was a long time before you learned why he laughed.

"Beat it, you little pissant!" he said.

§

Julian dear, your father had written, *I hope that you will keep your promise.*

§

A milk-truck took you to Pottersville, and from there you hitched rides through Lake George and Glens Falls to Saratoga Springs, sixty miles away. At the desk of the Grand Union Hotel you asked for your father and were told that you'd find him in the card-room. At one of the many tables, he was playing pinochle with three of his friends.

After you'd kissed him, he said, "What brings you down here, kid? The races?"

"I got bounced," you said.

He closed his cards and put them on the table. "With only a week to go?" he said. "What for?"

"I organized the waiters."

He scanned the other players and then returned to you. "To protest what?" he said.

"They were rooking us out of our wages."

"Were all the waiters fired?"

"No," you said. "Only me."

"Why only you?"

"I was the spokesman. The union elected me."

"Did anyone support you?" he said. "Did anyone quit to back you up?"

"No one even said goodbye."

"Well, kid," he said, "I hope you learned a lesson."

"Sure he did," said one of the players. "That it's easy to agitate when your father's at the Grand Union."

Your father pushed his cards to the center of the table and stood up. "You can go to hell, Sam," he said, and then he took you by the arm. "The lesson is this. People are only people, Julian, and sometimes they'll let you down. . . ."

SCENE 128

HOW FAR FROM THEN FORETHOUGHT OF (1921)

I hope, your father had written, *that you will keep your promise to devote some time to study, not tomfoolery. . . .* In Columbus Circle, you were standing before the Monument, watching water in the fountain pour. You'd just come from De Witt, two blocks west on 59th Street; you'd just seen your last of its halls and oaken woodwork, its trophy-cases and shrunken footballs, its view of Jersey and blue and bluer hills. It was all in the past now, your four years of going to and fro in snow and heat and rain, of bells and books and changing classes, of tests and grades and the shame of desperate guessing when called on to recite—four years spent in a daze.

Only a few moments earlier, you'd turned in the paper you'd written for your second try at the English final, and you knew, you knew! that you hadn't passed. *Devote some time to study,* your father had urged, *devote some time,* but instead you'd whiled away two mindless weeks at the shore. With Lenny and your cousin Jassie, you'd gone crabbing in Shark River and the Shrewsbury, you'd tomfooled around on the beach and the boardwalk, you'd seen derring-do on the screen at the West End open-air, you'd japed and jawed as though unaware that your books had gone unopened and your day-dream days would end.

You watched water fall in quarter-circles that seemed to buttress the column on which The Navigator stood (*In 1492,* you thought, *he didn't know what to do, so he sat on a rock and scratched . . .*), and then you were walking northward through Central Park. It was four hundred and twenty-nine years later now, you thought, and you wondered what *you* were going to do, what lay in store for *you*. How far from then forethought of that you'd one day write a blues for two greenhorns. . . .

Their faces were just faces, you'd say,
and if you saw them in the street,
you'd forget them as soon as they passed.
But if they happened to be talking,
those sinful ginnies,
then as long as you lived,
you'd think they'd played you a score.
It wasn't English they spoke,
or even broken English;
it was the kind of language
the dumb might mumble
and the deaf might hear,
the kind a saint might use with animals
and animals understand.
But whatever it was,
nothing so eloquent
had been heard around Boston
since the witches reigned,
and when those wops opened their mouths,
they worked such wonders that words,
like birds,
took wing and flew.
We no want fight by the gun, they said
(to the pure, that was pure diablerie),
and for refusing to fight
for Who's Who and the Board,
they were burned alive
a mile or so from Bunker Hill.
Not their words, though—
the words turned out to be fireproof. *

How far from then forethought of! as you went toward Harlem through Central Park.

---

* from *A More Goodly Country*, 1975.

SCENE 129

FIRST SEMESTER AT LAFAYETTE (1922)

We'll gather in the twilight's glow

At Lafayette, the only college that would admit you on Regents' credits alone, you were enrolled in the class of 1925. You were told that, having missed the previous semester, you'd be on probation, and for failure to maintain a passing grade in any course, you'd be demoted to the class of the following year. From the start, the caution went for naught. It was as if you hadn't heard, as if the Registrar had spoken to an ear with no tympanic membrane, no auditory nerve, as if he'd made no sound in your empty room. Within a month, you'd squandered every allowable cut, and, summoned by the Dean, you were shown a letter he was about to send to your father *devote some time devote some time.* Though you still couldn't hear, you were able to read: one more cut, he'd written, and you'd be suspended for the year.

Thereafter, you attended your lectures, and, in company with other freshmen, you gathered *in the twilight's glow / In front of old Pardee,* and you roamed the woods and the fields and sometimes came down off the Hill to gad about the town. But it was all a drifting through a dream, where, without purpose of your own, you were borne on the flow of the moment, and you couldn't know where you were going or even where you'd been. Unaware, you passed Colton Chapel, the dorms (Blair? McKeen?), the trees in the Quad, the Marquis's statue white against their green; you'd pass all these in your wandering, and at an upper classman's shout (*On the double, frosh!* or *Squat!*), you'd run or hunker down till your better was out of sight. Still, what you did and saw seemed done and seen unknowing: you were somewhere else.

But you *were* there once, and the memory stayed, deep down and in suspension, a grain of salt in the sea of your brain. For your course in English, the mid-term assignment had been a theme to be called *A Personal Experience,* and with only one more day in which to complete it, you had nothing committed to paper: you'd found nothing suitable to say. One of your classmates had shown you his composition, a work that ran to magical transformations of the usual round, to sudden acquisitions of godlike might — the power of levitation and flight, the power to move or pass through solids, to make masses carry out one man's will. You too could've set down such conceits, the whimwhams of a drowsy afternoon, but you knew that they'd've been only the

captive balloons. They weren't experience, they were aerobatic notions—
experience lay below them, on the ground.

You thought back to a lecture hall in South, and as though they were being
said again, the words of your instructor (Gregory, was it?) seemed again to
sound—*a personal experience*—and a memory from a winter's night of walking broke the surface of your mind. It had begun to snow late in the day,
and by evening the fall lay white in the lamplight and blue where it ended.
Drawn out of doors, you'd headed down Third toward the Circle, pausing
now and then to glance back at the wavering track that dogged you along
the street. You'd felt as if you were being followed—

and that was how your essay may have opened.

You felt as if you were being followed.

Sixty years gone, the snows of that night, sixty years a part of the Bushkill
and the Lehigh, and gone too, turned to water, what you wrote of where
you went. Almost nothing remains of your paper, only a squall of flakes,
a single sentence, nor can you recall the route you may have taken with your
footprints at your heels, the voices you may have heard, the faces seen, the
colors—except for the color red. Red, you think, and dimly you can see it
rim the blinds on certain windows, and faintly you remember the want to
see what lay inside. A doorbell rings in your head (who rang it?), and a door
comes open with a wedge of red—

and you wrote of those things—

wrote not of imaginings, but of what you knew and still know to be true:
there were no powers over the pull of g, and there was no dominant will.
Sixty years forgot, those scenes, and their title too (*The Red Light,* it might've
been), but you must've written of what you saw, for as in a mutoscope, they
flip past yet, they seem to move—

. . . a parlor where three half-naked women sit before a man in his
suspenders, one of which is hanging down . . . he watches while you make
a choice (by what criteria—youth, beauty, the color of an aureole?) . . . and
you climb a flight of stairs to a room perfumed with carbolic, like a urinal. . . .

and you wrote of such things—

. . . and you stand beside a bed, looking down at someone looking up,
not at you but the ceiling, as if the plaster were the sky . . . and she waits
(for what—the sun to rise, a bird to fall, or one more commotion between
her thighs?) . . . and then, sensing what you have in mind, she hands you
a sheaf of papers, all from the same prescription-pad, and save for different
dates, they read *I have this day examined* . . . but you never reached the
name. . . .

and you wrote of such things—

. . . of shaking your head and saying nothing, of paying and going away, of walking home through the streets of Easton, of the snow, blue where the light-circles ended, of sitting down to write what you were trying to remember now.

The next day, soon after turning the paper in, you were notified that you were to meet your instructor at the Van Wickle library during the noon-hour. You found him on the circular stairway leading to the stacks (his name *was* Gregory), and you joined him on the iron steps. He had your paper in his hand, and he studied you for a moment, as though trying to match you with what you'd written.

"If it's no good," you said, "I'm sorry."
"It isn't good," he said, "but I'm going to give you an A for it."
"Why?"
"What you've written is what you've read. I don't know where—de Maupassant, maybe. But the experience was yours. That's what I called for, and that's what earns the A." He rose and went down a few steps to the floor, turning there to hand you the paper and say, "By the way, did you really find that sentence in de Maupassant?"
"Which one?"
" 'I felt a clammy hand at my throat.' "
"No," you said. "That was mine."
"Even so, you get the A."

You went out into the snow and the glare, and before you'd gone a dozen yards, you heard *On the double!* from somewhere across the Quad, and you fled the cry till the sound left your head. By then, your mind was adrift again, going where the currents bore it, and no more A's came your way that year.

SCENE 130

TRANSCONTINENTAL: A BUMMING-TRIP (1922)

I take to the open road,

        Walt said

healthy,
free,
the world before me,

        and he said,

the long brown path before me
leading wherever I choose

That summer, you too were on the road, but yours was a blind course only, only motion, and you inhaled no *great draughts of space,* as he did, nor did you see what he saw — the unseen. At eighteen years of age, you read no history in the unmarked places, the nameless streams, the faces unfamiliar, or the walls,

the paths,

        he said,

the irregular hollows

that lined the road — you passed it all, you left it all behind. You did not greet the tree and the hill, the flagstoned street, you did not embrace, as he did,

the ferries,
the arches, the ascending steps,
the transparent shells

called windows — you merely passed them by.

    You bore westward. You crossed the prairie and the plain, you went against the grain of time, and for days there were mountains before you in the distance like a wave about to break. And you crossed those too, in a fall of snow at thirteen thousand feet, and beyond, on the high plateau, the air shook as though the earth below had come to a boil. And there the road wore away to a trail strung through sagebrush and greasewood, a road no more. You took to the rails now, to the box-cars of the Western Pacific, and on track laid down by Chinamen, you were borne as far as the Feather River Gorge — and further then to the Bay.

"I am happy that you are making such wonderful progress," your father wrote, "but I want to warn you that you should be very careful about the company you fall into. . . . "

You'd fallen in with learned vags, Whitmans all, and with jockers and punks, with harvest-stiffs, their balloons slung like bandoliers. Your company had been the beggar and the bum, the fit-thrower and the sniffer of snow, Weary Willie, Happy Hooligan, summer strays with a craze to move — like you. *Be very careful*, your father had written, but you hadn't known enough to be careful, and there they were, that company, there in those high red cars, and only later did you wonder what you'd've done if one had held you down while another went for your fly.

And it'd be later still that you'd write* of things you'd taken in that you hadn't been aware of:

The fluid ash of America moved past his feet in the grand national open drain: the brown sap and syrup, the skim, the scum, and the slag, and with it crumbled counties slowly tumbling the blanketed bones of DeSoto toward the sewer of the Gulf. Snags turned over and came to rest for another year, and on the Milk in Montana a shelf caved in to become submarine sand and mud, along with turds of fish and fowl, flakes of gold, and cigar-butts — all this was part of the river, and rain too, and rust, and a two-masted shingle once launched by a boy on the Cumberland. Engine-oil rode the ripples, and feathers and leaves spun in the eddies among potato-peels tossed from a stern-wheeler, and in the main stream lay odd letters from a press baptized at Alton, a chunk of bark leaned against by La Salle, and the salt of tears shed for dead Ann in the Sangamon. The spew and rubble of cities drifted by, the polished bones of Ojibways, the knees and noses of Nez Perces, a piece of the True Cross and other splinters, solid shot from Donelson, still thinning Shiloh blood, Copperhead gall, Jesuit wafers, and wampum — all this went to make the undrinkable drink — the Mississippi.

---

* in *A Man Without Shoes*, 1951.

THE COLOR OF THE AIR, XII

JOHN WILKES BOOTH — 1865
PLAY WITHIN A PLAY

Ah, you've a bad hand; the lines all cris-cras.
— a fortune-teller

The hand held a single-shot brass derringer firing a .41 caliber
ball. . . .

What was the hand's history? Where had it been, what had it
done, in the twenty-seven years of its age? Had it trifled with the
sun and moon, with lone stars and Charles's Wain, with the beaded
bars of a crib? Had it caught at straws of sound, a bell-tone, a tick
of time, the sharps of a passing bird? Had glass cut or fire burned
it, had it learned the trick of turning pages, had it picked the eyes
from a shag tiger? Had it borne a flag, a toy sword, a toy horn,
had its skin been pricked by a pin, a thorn, or (from within) a broken
bone? Could it take a fly on the wing, cast a stone, wring a neck,
could it make music wave from wire? Was it dry or damp, was it
steady holding cards, deft at pouring wine? Did it slap backs and
pound tables, did it play in public gardens, or was it found in private
parks? Did it make a tight fist, did it write fine, and what oaths
had it sworn, what bargains struck? Was it coked by callus or a soft
touch for children and other things of silk and smoke? Did it sport
rings, hair, scars, was its blood still short of the fourth generation
of those that hated the Lord. . . ?

The derringer weighed half a pound. The ball weighed half an
ounce.

SCENE 131

SECOND SEMESTER AT LAFAYETTE (1922-23)

We'll gather in the twilight's glow

In 65 Blair that fall and winter, the talk was bold and brave. Launched on
pipe-smoke, it could almost be seen to ride the surges — smallcraft words, you'd

211

think, and all would sink beneath the waves. From sprung armchairs, from the banquette and the floor, a frail fleet of opinion would sail, stand out to meet the foe, and with the foe founder. The image, though, would soon give way, and words would become words again, and then, standing at a window and staring at the Quad by day or nothing at night, you'd hear Nat, Charlie, Eddie, Herb, and there'd be phrases on the rise-and-fall-and-sway of smoke, but you'd rarely turn, for you knew how little you had to say.

If you learned almost nothing from the lifted lore of your friends, at least it was the first age at which you learned at all. Instead of being a mere unit, a bead, a ball bearing, a sphere just touched by other spheres, you felt for once a need to expand: it was not enough to be one of many and much the same. And so when you came back from the view, the Chapel black against the sky or the sward outspread below (was the rail fence there in '22?), sometimes you'd speak from *lack* of knowledge, guess at what you couldn't prove, and then you'd be bested by Herb and Nat and Ed and Al (Al what?), and for a while you'd feel diminished, a smaller bead or bearing, but still, when another day came, you'd have another say (Goff! His name was Al Goff!).

In front of old Pardee

" 'My dear Julian,' " your father wrote, " 'I am very much disappointed in your request, as only last year I purchased for you a good coat and you discarded it immediately. . . . A boy ought to be happy that he obtains one without any effort or expense, and to discard same (as you say, it is not stylish) is really a crime. My wish is that you should make the other do for another season.' "

" 'You are buying too many clothes,' " your father wrote. " 'I did not authorize you to get two suits, only one. You did not heed my wishes and purchased two.' "

" 'I want you to tell me,' " your father wrote, " 'whether a boy of your age is justified in spending so much money. From last fall, you purchased two suits ($65), one overcoat ($36.50), one suit ($35), one overcoat ($50), two suits ($101), one suit ($45) – $332.50. I am not adding all the other small items for furnishings, which I do not mind.' "

" 'Now Julian,' " your father wrote, " 'tell me frankly in the face of the above figures, which do not lie, are you justified in ordering more clothes. I frankly and honestly say no . . . Julian, I am willing to do any and every thing in my power for you. My love for you would compel me to, but you must be reasonable and fair and just.' "

" 'I am sure,' " your father wrote, " 'any other parent after receiving your telegram would have telegraphed back a flat refusal, but I did not do that. I waited until I had an opportunity to reply by letter.' "

And he wrote, " 'If you are still of the opinion that you must have the new overcoat because you want to be in style (want to look swell) then you may do so, but much against my wishes, and the thought will remain that you are taking advantage. . . .' "

In all the world no other scene

The Black Diamond Express left Pennsylvania Station at five minutes before midnight, and you were aboard, returning to school from a weekend in New York. A moment earlier, you'd watched a girl and a man embrace in the vestibule of your car, and now she was alone in a seat across the aisle. She wasn't pretty, but you found other things to dwell on, manner, dress, hands, shoes—shoes! you thought, and you realized that for miles your eyes had been fixed on a pair of shoes. All the way through the Hudson tunnel, she'd spelled you with shoes, and somewhere out on The Meadows, they compelled you to sit at her side. When you spoke, you weren't turned away—and it was over seventy miles to Phillipsburg and Easton, a two-hour ride.

"It was the shoes!" you said to Herb in 65 Blair. You hadn't stopped at your boardinghouse near the Karldon down on Third; you'd hurried past and up the Hill to the second floor of Blair. "It was the shoes, Herb!" you said. "She wasn't pretty, but the shoes were, and they made me stop thinking of pretty. All the way to P-burg, I tried to remember what someone said about feet, but I couldn't."

"Solomon," Herb said. "How beautiful are thy feet with shoes. Now for God's sake, go home. It's three in the morning."

"She's Greek, she told me, and she goes to school in Bethlehem—Bishop Thorpe Manor. She's got the most beautiful feet in Lehigh Valley!"

"Who was the guy in the vestibule?"

"Her brother, she said."

"Said she," Herb said, and he moved you toward the door, saying, "Were you ever attracted by feet before?"

"Not that I recall," you said, and you were across the campus and well past South—you were near the pee-tree, you remember—when you heard two words clearly, as though someone had said them aloud: *Aunt Rae.*

So fair, so dear to me

" 'Dear Julian,' " your father wrote, " 'I received your letter this week and have carefully read the same. You certainly are very much agitated about the bill you owe for your suit and overcoat. . . . You mention a few things which you could very well have left unsaid. You mention, more than once, that I am not a poor man. I want to disabuse your mind. I am not even comfortably fixed. . . .' "

And he wrote, " 'You speak as though I owed you a duty and was derelict.
. . . A father is animated by love and affection, and when a father refuses
any request, it does not mean that he has lost the love and affection. It is
based upon his conception of what is good and what is injurious for that
son. . . .' "

And he wrote, " 'I am going to be the only judge in the future of your
needs. I am going to give you everything that a son justly deserves and that
is in my power to give you, both in clothes and education, and I am going
to refuse to give you anything which I consider unnecessary.' "

And he wrote, " 'You know, or should know, that my children are very
dear to me, dearer than anything or anybody else in the world, and I am
going to give them anything and everything in my power, but I must be
the judge, and when I refuse, there is to be no criticism.' "

And he wrote, " 'I am enclosing $60 which you give the tailor on account,
as I am a little short. I have had quite a heavy drain lately and will send the
balance in two weeks.' "

And he wrote, " 'Lovingly' "

O Lafayette, O Lafayette

During Christmas Week, you were invited by the Greek girl to attend
a prom at Bishop Thorpe, and on the day she'd named, you boarded one of
the fast red cars of the Interurban and started for Bethlehem, a twelve-mile
ride up the valley of the Lehigh. Through the windows, you could see the
long low chine of Blue Mountain, a far-off ridge that might've been only
the frayed skirts of the sky. Evening was coming on, and you stared out at
its lavender cast, at the river, at farms and fencing, at the sled of lights the
car dragged over the snow. You stared at the world through those windows,
and in the end, you knew you'd only been trying to see inside: from the car's
reflection, you'd been looking in at you.

And then the car stopped, and you walked a few dark streets to the
school, and there, waiting at the gate, you found girls in furs, one of them
your Greek, and you went with her through the grounds, where night-
black pines made blacker shadow. Off in the grove somewhere, softened by
the trees, the snow, distance, music was being played, and you listened to
a tune reduced to drum-beat and the now-and-then bleat of a reed. You felt
the girl come up against you, and along with her perfume, you drew in the
perfume of the pelts she wore—the smell of what? you wondered, the tan,
the dye, the lime, the seal itself? And while you stood there, savoring the
mix of her coat and her, she put her mouth to yours and forced it with her
tongue—stunned you with its undulations. The music! the snow on the pines

and underfoot! the flavored fur! the Greek girl's taking tongue . . . !

And later, riding the red car back to Easton, again you saw the car outside, but now you knew you were looking in, and someone (you!) spoke the words *Aunt Rae,* and from her you then broke free.

To thee our voices raise

"You want to be taken on as a writer," he said, "but you aren't a writer. You'd like to be one, fine, but you haven't written anything."

He was one of the editors of the Lafayette *Mélange,* and you were in his office—in the Pardee basement, it might've been, or on the ground floor of South. You'd gone there to see him, hoping to become a member of the staff, but it'd taken him only a moment to dispose of you; he hadn't even asked you to sit down.

And, standing, you said, "What should I write about?"

"That's a poor question, Shapro. A writer would be ashamed to ask it." You were opening the door, thinking of the way he mispronounced your name, when he said, "Write about what you see, what you know."

For a few days, you went about looking for something to see and preparing yourself to know, but little by little your awareness deteriorated, and in the end you were merely making your usual round, seeing in the sense that you avoided collisions and knowing only what you'd known before: there was nothing to write about. And then, one afternoon you heard a brass band playing somewhere near the Square. You went toward the sound in step with the air, and stopping at the Monument, you watched a parade come toward you along Northampton. You were attracted to the fact of the march, not the occasion, and you never learned whether it was martial, social, or religious. You could've inquired, but all you did was watch from the curb, no more the aspirant scrivener looking for something to see—but all the same you saw!

Platoons in spangled garb had passed, and a troop of ribboned horse, and there were flags in strange colors and with stranger bearings, and people had gone by you, eyes-front and unrelenting, liegemen all to some unknown lord, and then a fire-engine had come, a street-sweeper, a watering-cart, and automobiles with braying horns. Among these last had been a touring-car with the top down, *a burnished throne* whereon, seated alone, was the fullback of the football team—Doc Elliott. You saw! and home you went to become a writer.

When you handed in your story about the parade, the editor read it then and there, both of you standing. It took him only a moment to say, "Shapro, explain what you mean by this sentence: 'Doc Elliott sat there emanating an Italian politician.' "

"I mean he was trying to look like a candidate in an election. Imitating a politician."

"Why an *Italian* politician?"

"I don't know. I could've said Polish, I guess."

"You couldn't've said either. No one looks like an Italian, not even an Italian. You'd better learn that before you come here again. That and a lot more." And then he handed back your story, saying, "I'm afraid you've only been emanating a writer, Shapro."

While loyal lips and loyal hearts

On the paths leading to Jenks Hall halfway down the Hill from Pardee, flows of students wound toward the main entry. Some moved slowly with open books in hand, trying to master some law, some definition or nomenclature, for the mid-year final in Biology, now only moments off. The Science of Life, you thought, and you moved even more slowly than your stream. *Go not,* you thought, *like the quarry-slave,* but like the quarry-slave you went, scourged, not sustained and soothed, for no pleasant dreams awaited you: you knew you were due to fail.

In your mind, there was a turbulence of data, a churn of classes and orders and adaptations with names infolded like coloring matter, Lyell, Darwin, Linnaeus, with drawings of the amoeba and the paramecium, of cell structure and molecular arrangement, of grades and subgrades, kingdoms and sub-kingdoms, Arthropoda, Mollusca, Protozoa, Vermes, the properties of living matter—ah, God, what were you to do with all those numbers and syllables, which questions would they answer, where did they belong! *Go not,* but going you were—and knowing you'd fail, you entered Jenks, *that mysterious realm.*

Earlier in the morning, there'd been great rejoicing among certain of your classmates. One of them, in a hole-and-corner way, had learned that the exam was to be of the True-and-False variety, and when he confided his findings to the group, there were gleeful grins, back-slaps, heartfelt tenders of cigarettes. How they exulted, for who could fail under the system they'd devised! As imparted to you, it called for watching one A-student in particular for the way in which, after answering a question, he poised his pencil: it would be vertical for True and horizontal for False. Christ, they said, all you had to do was stay awake!

When the bell sounded, the papers were distributed by a monitor, and the exam was under way. You signed your name, rose, and went down the aisle

216

to the lectern, someone tugging at your jacket as you passed. *I'm going for a walk,* you said to the professor (Doc Kunkel, was it?), and you left the classroom.

Why? you wondered at the time, and Why? you wonder yet. You'd cheated before at De Witt, and it was late in the day to save your honor, so why not cheat once more? But there is no one to give you a sign for True or a sign for False, and the question has never been answered.

Given a failing grade in Biology, you were dropped back, as you'd been warned, to the Class of 1926. Rather than endure the loss of standing, you said goodbye to Lafayette.

> *Unite to sing thy praise.*
> *(Chorus)*
> *We'll gather in the twilight's glow*
> *In front of old Pardee, etc.*

SCENE 132

THE TIME OF FIGS WAS NOT YET (1923)

Of the first meeting with your father on returning from Lafayette, nothing has endured, neither where and when it occurred nor a word of what was said. There must've been a day of doom and a Seat of Judgment, and at that time and place, you must've had to face the charge of a wasted year, hear of your lapsed resolves and broken promises, of the weekly letters you'd inflated with *say*—you must've been told that your word was only air. With no memory of an arraignment, though—no *How say you, Julian?* and no plea recalled to mind—you try to believe that your fate was kind. But you know in the end that you're sparing yourself, that *you're* being kind, and refusing your own favor, you conjure that forgotten doomsday and the hard way of judgment.

"Of course it was right not to cheat," your father must've said, "but cheating should never have entered your head. Who sends a boy to college to sneak his answers from someone else? Watching a pencil for a Yes or a No!"

And you must've said, "Half the class was watching that pencil."

"And you expect praise for not doing the same—is that it?"

"Well, at least I didn't cheat."

"I think you did, Julian," he must've said. "You cheated me for one whole year. I sent you to Lafayette to study, and you didn't study hard enough

217

to pass without cheating—which in itself was cheating. . . ."

" 'Julian,' " he'd written early in the term, " 'I am still waiting to hear from you as to the meaning of the letter from the Dean. I refuse to believe that you have broken your word to get down to study. Attendance at a place of learning is not for frivolity and horseplay. Many boys realizing the value of a college education deprive themselves of the very necessities of life in order to work their way through college. You neither have to strive or deprive yourself. As long as I have the means, I shall be only too glad to help you, provided you do not waste your time and my money. . . .' "

And he wrote, " 'Enclosed is a $10 bill. Remember that they cost $120 a dozen. . . .' "

You try to think of what you may have said, the words you used to deflect his aim, but not even now can you frame a defense (you *had* cheated him), and maybe you said nothing at all.

It was almost three years since he'd remarried, and you had yet to set foot inside his home, yet to see your waiting bed and at its head the beaded lampshade the painted woman had made, yet to see your private bath and the color of its tile. You must, therefore, have met your father at his office, sat across the desk from him listening to sound from the outer rooms, bursts of typing, voices reduced to murmurs, and now and then a laugh. And you must've watched your father tilt his chair, swivel to face a window, gaze out at things that weren't there, and back to you through tobacco-smoke, and he must've said

"Well, kid, what next?"

And you must've said, "I'm trying to get into Northwestern."

"And where's Northwestern?"

"Evanston, Illinois."

"What do you expect to find out there?"

"It's a good school. Better than Lafayette."

And he must've turned to you then, saying, "If it's better, it must be harder. You'd have to study, and study doesn't seem to be your long suit."

"That could change."

"What would change it, Julian? All those clothes you bought? Will those New Haven tweeds make you less of a foolish boy?"

"I don't think I'm a fool, pop."

"Maybe not. Maybe I'm the fool. Some of my friends say so."

"Do they? Why?"

"For not bringing you up short."

"What've I done that's wrong?"

And he must've said, "Nothing, really. You haven't held up a bank. But it's not enough to refrain from wrong. What've you done that's right?"

Nothing, really, you must've thought.

The remembrance is exclamatory: he let you go to Northwestern! And on your being accepted, he paid your railroad fare and enrolment-fees! he agreed to a weekly allowance! he blew you to a going-away lunch! and he even saw you off! What did you say at train-side? you wonder. Did you take more vows, did you add to your store of resolutions, and was your father swayed, did he come to feel you were a new-made Julian—or did he simply nod to show that he'd heard? And then you waved goodbye from a window and watched him walk away.

Your stay at Northwestern lasted a week. A few forgotten lectures in a few forgotten courses, a winter's walk along the lake-front, a trip or two to the Loop—it all lay behind you in the span of a week. Because of the Greek girl, you transferred to Lehigh, and soon, the next day, you too would be in Bethlehem and only a mile away. You must've avoided New York, for you have no memory of seeing your father, of hearing from him what you'd surely have heard.

"Julian, Julian" he'd've said, and he'd've raised his hands and let them fall, as though they were too heavy to bear, and "Julian, Julian" would've been all he could say. And you'd've stood there, remembering what he'd written once (" 'You may have already tasted the things of life that make a man oblivious to everything, but that is only transitory, ephemeral, spasmodic, and when it wears off and you are yourself again, you will see that morality is the only road to pursue.' ")

From a letterhead lying before you, you read:

TO WHOM IT MAY CONCERN: This certifies that Julian L. Shapiro was admitted to Lehigh University on February 16th, 1923 and withdrew voluntarily on March 1, 1923. H. Eckfeldt, Acting Secretary of the Faculty.

You turn the sheet, hoping to find notes, figures, explanations, but the reverse is blank, and back you turn to the typewritten lines, the signature of H. Eckfeldt, the heading—Lehigh—at the top of the page. This certifies, you read, that Julian L. Shapiro. . . . This certifies that three colleges have known you in as many weeks. This certifies that you're at large again and ready for another three (Bowdoin, Brown, and Swarthmore?). This certifies that you think nothing of a thousand miles going and a thousand coming back, that you're free to move with your misbegotten tweeds to (Cornell, Oberlin, Washington & Lee?). This certifies that the time of figs is not yet come.

"Lafayette, Northwestern, Lehigh," your father must've said. "Where will all this running end?"

What colored his tone? you must've wondered—anger, despair, shame? Would your endless flight have disgraced him, as though he'd been to blame?

"I thought I understood you, Julian. I thought you were just a headstrong boy, and not wanting to break your spirit, I let you have your way. But I see now that it isn't spirit at all—it's *lack* of spirit, it's disregard. As I think of you now, you care for nothing."

And what must you have said—that he was wrong? Or would he have read you aright, and were you heedless after all?

"You're almost nineteen, and what can you show for it? Enough clothes to stock a store—but where's your high school diploma, where are your credits for a year at college, what've you earned on your own?"

To stock a store, you'd've thought, and you'd've seen your twenty-seven ties of foulard alone—twenty-seven! And you'd've tried to recall why they'd been bought when they made knots too small, when they soiled and frayed—and still there they hung displayed on a rack, green on yellow, black on red, and seldom worn.

To his anger, his despair, would you have said, "When I do things that you don't like, you give me a talking-to, as you're doing now, but that's about all. You look sore, and I guess you really are sore, but it never comes to more than that, I never get punished, and I don't know why."

And would he have said this? "You're my son."

"Does that mean I can get away with anything? Suppose I stole from you. Suppose I forged your name to a check."

Would he have laughed at that? "If you do, kid, don't make it too big. It'll bounce."

"I'm serious, pop. I'm trying to find something out. If you didn't have confidence in me, you wouldn't always be letting me off—isn't that so?"

"I suppose it is."

"You must think I'll change. You must think I'll suit you some day."

Would he have said, "Hope, not think. If I thought, I might lose hope."

And would that have been when you said, "I'm going to try to get into Fordham in the fall."

"That'll be your fourth college in a year."

And watching his face for pleasure, would you then have said, "What I meant was Fordham Law."

As you left your father's office and went toward the outer door, you read names in reverse through the frosted glass. Your father's headed the gold-leaf list, but the one that drew your eye that day was at the foot: *nietsrellE leumaS*. You pronounced it to yourself as it seemed to you, and then *nietsrellE leumaS* became Samuel Ellerstein, a small, spherical, well-filled man who, for a reason you never asked for, always called you Josh—*Josh,* he'd say, and you can hear him still. He and your father had been friends since their days on the lower

East Side, and though both had been admitted to the Bar, his practice had failed to grow. To add to his earnings, your father had told you, he'd turned to stenography, becoming a Court Reporter in the Traffic Division of Special Sessions. Somewhere in your father's suite of offices, a room had always been reserved for his use, and his name, though few came to seek it, had always appeared on the door: *nietsrellE leumaS.*

You'd grown to know him well, and if you'd seen your father that day, you must also have seen Sam Ellerstein, but how your conversation went can only be supposed.

"Josh!" he'd've said when he saw you. "Last I heard, you were at Lehigh."

"I quit, but don't ask me why."

"I do ask you why."

"I wish I knew," you'd've said.

He probably aligned a few pencils, folded a document, made a mark in a law-book, something to fill a moment of time. "Your father talks to me about you. Did you know that?"

"No, but I could've guessed."

"You worry him with all this standing up and sitting down. When will it stop?"

"This fall, maybe," you said. "If I get into Law School."

That time, he may have filled a moment by keeping still. "Go in and tell your father, Josh."

"I just told him."

"It must've made him happy."

"It did," you said, "and I hate to spoil it."

"What do you mean — spoil it?"

"I haven't got the credits," you said. "Fordham won't enroll me without a high school diploma."

"Are you saying you never got a diploma from De Witt?"

"I cheated on the English exam."

"Jesus Christ!"

"I guess my father keeps some things to himself."

"Why am I hearing your confession?"

"I've got to get that diploma!" you said.

"And you want Sam Ellerstein to help you?"

nietsrellE leumaS, you thought, and you said, "Yes."

"And of course you want me to tell your father."

And you said, "No."

A few days later, you and he boarded the Empire State Express at Grand Central Station and rode it as far as Albany. You hadn't been told of your destination, and your questions along the way had evoked no replies. Many sights had been seen, the Palisades on the further shore of the Hudson, the broad called Tappan Zee, the granite of West Point, gray against green, and then the Catskills in the distance, another palisade—but there'd been no answers. At Albany, you walked up State Street to the Education Building, and there, on some upper floor, you knocked on the door of one of the rooms—304 or 516, who can say now? And when it opened, you did as told, you spoke your name, whereupon a hand emerged with a rolled sheet of paper tied with a purple ribbon, and the door then quickly closed.

You started to slip the ribbon off, but Mr. Ellerstein stopped you, saying, "Not here, Josh. On the train."

And on the train, you read: *Diploma of Graduation. This Diploma is awarded to Julian Shapiro who has completed the General Course of 4 years in the De Witt Clinton High School and has satisfactorily passed all examinaitons required for graduation.* You let the paper scroll itself, and you stared through the window at the Catskills, at West Point, Tappan Zee, the Palisades.

The time of figs was not yet.

SCENE 133

THE CAMPUS ON THE 28th FLOOR (1923)

Your new College Hill was neither a glacial deposit nor a volcanic rise; it was a man-made sheer of glazed terra cotta fifty-six stories into the sky. No grass grew on its four faces, no trees threw shadow on the earth at its feet: there was no earth, only gray-black street, trolley-track, and starts and stops of cars and people, a great vale of a thousand smokes. Halfway to the top of the stack were the classrooms of Fordham University Law School, all, in one or another direction, giving on the island of Manhattan. From the windows, you could see Paumonok, a long smear into the gauze of distance, and northward rose and ran the Palisades; in swells and swales, Jersey spread away, and when the day was fine, you could raise sun-dogs on the lower bay. Straight down, though, twenty-eight stories below you, there was only pavement at the base of your Hill.

Within a week, your courses would begin, and with lectures in Civil Practice and cases in Bills and Notes, you'd try to solve the legal maze. You'd read in Coke, and in Coke upon Lyttelton, and in the Commentaries of Kent, and you'd hear for the first and lasting time that *water is a movable and wandering thing,* and it would marvel you to find so bright a stone in the gravel of the Law. *A movable and wandering thing,* you'd think, not yet knowing that the phrase was in your mind to stay. There was no Bushkill to be seen from that Hill, no Delaware, no movable and wandering thing.

SCENE 134

FALSUS IN UNO (1923)

The Clinton diploma has never been framed; for sixty years, it has remained in a scroll and tied with a ribbon. Rarely do you take it from the cupboard where you store it, the file, the shelf, the drawer, and more rarely still do you unfurl it to read its inscription, nor have you need, for it is inked as well on your mind. *This diploma is awarded,* you think. . . .

You remember the day you were enrolled at Law School, and you remember handing the Registrar the diploma (*awarded to Julian Shapiro*) and having it handed back. Beyond him were the Hudson, the Hoboken docks, the toy towns on the Jersey shore, and you were reminded of the view from the Clinton lunchroom, a few miles upstream but much the same, and you felt linked by the vellum (*completed the General Course and satisfactorily passed*) to your Clinton shame. You'd completed nothing, and you'd failed, not passed—but there in your grasp was that spurious certificate, and you went toward the door, thinking *the lawyer-to-be! the champion of justice!*

Two hundred miles away, just across the Charles from the city of Boston, two Italians sat, stood, lay in their cells under sentence of death for a pair of murders, but you were unaware of their place and crime, of even so little as their names. Up there in the white spire of the Woolworth Building twenty-eight stories from the ground, nothing reached you, neither the sound of out-landish voices nor the effluvium of eels. *Braintree, Brockton, Dedham—Where are such places?* you'd've said, and *Who is Webster Thayer?* To you then, the words were only sound, and you were dead to it that day with your ill-gotten diploma twenty-eight flights up from the ground.

SCENE 135

AN INKLING OF SAVANNAH (1923)

It shows only in a single flash, in one bright fast-shutter instant, always of the same place and in the same colors, and always photo-still. In that blink of time, what you see is the corner of a city square, a park, possibly, and that is all, and with it the remembrance ends. You can revive it at will, but it never varies, and it never lasts long, and as the glimmer comes and goes, you read the name Savannah on a postcard in your mind.

But Savannah or not, why were you there, and by what means, and out of what fear, and from whom were you running in the winter of that year? Only days before, you'd been in a classroom four hundred feet above the street, and you'd been listening to case-book trove and text-book lore, to recitations in Real Property, Contracts, Wills, to the arguments of counsel for some dead-and-gone appellant, to the dicta of jurists, the Rule in Shelley's Case, and to how matters stood in Scott vs Sheppard (*If this were not Assize time, I should run you through and through!*). In Savannah, if you were in Savannah, all that lay behind you and four hundred feet in the air, and you were walking, running, riding past the corner of a square. What were you doing in that place at that time, and how had you gotten there — by rail, was it, or had you hit the long brown Whitman trail?

You'd made your father happy, *leumaS* Samuel had said, by deciding on the law, but what when he read your farewell letter — had you mailed it, you wonder, pinned it to your pillow, pasted it on a wall, had you written it at all? What did he say, how did he explain to Sam his friend or his sister Sarah, what did he do to kill the pain? You've never asked, and you were never told, and what you're shown through the years is your act alone, still wayward, still stunning to behold.

Another flight, it must've been, another headlong avoidance of nothing you could name, another blind run from the black hole of your mind — to Savannah! where all you saw was the corner of a square. No faces, flowers, wharves, no signs, no dogs, no monuments, not even the one of Jasper grasping the fallen flag. Nor, later, were you aware of crossing the Ogeechee, or the Altamaha, or where you saw your first of Florida — at Fernandina, could it have been, or only at St. Augustine?

There, though, or thereabouts, images begin to be seen, and they come now not in separate stills but successions of motion. In these, cars and people pass, water falls in courtyard Fountains of Youth, and the fronds of palm trees thrash. And you move too, making fixed things recede, salt marsh, wayside shacks, orchard aisles, saw palmettoes on the dunes—you move, not toward but from, and you've never known from what.

On a map that lies before you, you read the names of towns you must've passed, you see the railway, the swamps and lakes, the many miles of Indian River that for days lay on your left, but through a haze of hunger and estrangement, you recover little that seems actual—someone (you?) eating a handout, someone asleep in a car or a doorway, someone on a bridge or standing beside a road. Who slowed for you, you wonder, and who took you in on the fly, who said *What do you think of the South, boy?* and how did you reply?

—A night on the sand under a stand of pines. A mist that must've passed through orange groves. A rasping sound as from something starched—some clash of collars, you think—and then the sound is around and upon you, and you're in headlong flight from a shoal of crabs!

—You run away under tinselled oaks until you reach a spur of track, and letting yourself be led by the rails, you follow them to a buffer near the platform of a packing-shed. There a black man sits in the stuffing of a broken chair. Fearing the ground, the crabs! you say, "Would you mind if I . . . ?" and he cedes you his place.

Deep in yellow filler, you fall asleep and dream of space, silent, still, and achromatic, and after a moment, an hour, a day and a night, a light shines in your face, and you're shaken awake, and someone says, "You come with me."

On a car nearby is an arc of capitals in gilt—SHERIFF BROWARD COUNTY—and before you're taken away, you glance back at the black watchman (why had he . . . ? you wonder), and again he's seated in his blown-out chair.

—At the Fort Lauderdale lock-up, you're put into a cell with three other prisoners. Two of them are short-pants kids who tell you at once of their crime: beating a man with a jack-handle and stealing his automobile. "But they can't do us nothing," they say; "we're under age." The third is older, somewhere in his twenties, and all he does is lie on his cot and stare at the ceiling.

One of the kids brags him up, saying, "He held up a bank in Pensacola," and he kicks the man's cot-spring. "Ain't that right, Jesse?"

The other kid says, "He don't talk much, but he thinks a lot. About who's screwing his wife, and all like that," and he too kicks the cot. "Ain't that right, Jesse?"

Then they both want to know how you broke the law—the nature of the felony, the degree, the weapon used—and when you say, "Vagrancy," they say, "Vagrancy!" and they seem to be offended.

— The morning meal is something in flour-gravy, which the kids call bull-fuck, and they take half shares of yours when you refuse it. At mid-day, a trusty brings sowbelly and grits, more bull-fuck, and they split that too. In the afternoon, you're taken before a magistrate, who fines you eighteen dollars for having no money, and still having none, you're sentenced to thirty days. You ask for leave to send a telegram.

— "To who?" one of the kids says when you're back in the cell.
"My father."
"Mine wouldn't pay a dime to get Christ out of the cave."
The other kid is on his knees with an eye to a keyhole in an iron door.
"What's he watching?" you say.
"Some guy trying to piss."
"What do you mean — trying?"
"He's got the clap, and it's stuck shut."
The kid at the keyhole lets out a holler and comes away holding a hand to his eye. "Son-of-a-bitch!" he says. "He squirted me with his clap-gun!"
The bank-robber laughs.
"What's he do?" the other kid says.
"Who?"
"Your old man."
"He's a lawyer."

— A letter addressed to you at the County Jail, dated Dec. 18, 1923:

Dear Julian,
Received your telegram. Was shocked to hear of your incarceration for vagrancy. Have written to the Police Chief of the town to let me know details. I asked him whether the fine was in addition to the sentence, or whether it will relieve you of the 30 day sentence. Upon a satisfactory reply from him will forward the money. Let me hear from you on this matter at once. Yours as ever,
Father
(On the back of the letter, two names appear in your handwriting of the time: *Harry Blaisdell* and *Sherwood Kelly*. The kids? you wonder)

— The sheriff brings you a pair of striped pants and takes you downstairs to his apartment on the ground floor. "You're now a trusty, Shapio," he says. "My woman is a slob, and your job is to clean up the dump." And out he goes.
On the kitchen sink and table, leftovers are aswarm with flies: they walk on smears of grease and jelly, they drink at the rims of coffee-cups, and one of them swims and swims in a pitcher of milk. Even so, you go for whatever you think will stay down — fruit, bread, sugar, the white of a hard-boiled egg.
"You're a trusty," the sheriff had said, and after setting his dump to rights,

you go out into the jailhouse yard. The gates are open, and you sit down outside in the shade of the wall. After a while, a train stops on the East Coast track, and when a woman stares at you from one of the windows, you give her a wave. "You're a trusty, Shapio."

— "Well, you been tried in the court," one kid says, "and now we're going to try you in here."

"That's their court out there," the other kid says. "This one's ours. Kangaroo Court, it's called, and we're going to kangaroo you."

"What's that mean?" you say.

"It means you're guilty."

"Of what?"

"Of having money."

"I just told the judge I'm broke."

"You also told him your father wasn't," one of them says.

And the other says, "So we fine you three dollars."

"To be paid when you get out."

"And don't forget, or wherever you are, we'll find you some day and cockalize you."

"You now been kangarooed."

The bank robber laughs.

(Which was Harry Blaisdell? you wonder, and which was Sherwood Kelly?)

— Every morning now, you go down to the sheriff's quarters, and while you're straightening up the kitchen, you feed yourself enough to last you past the bull-fuck of the day, and when you go back upstairs at night, the kids ask you for the bill of fare.

"The usual crap," you say. "They don't leave much, and what's there is covered with flies. I never saw so many flies."

"Fly-shit is kind of tasty," one kid says. "Ain't you never et fly-shit?"

— On being taken from the cell one morning, you're shown into the yard. There, on a trestle-table, you see a pile of dead birds — ducks, they are, mallards and teal.

"Friend of mine brung 'em in from a shoot on Okeechobee," the sheriff says. "What you do today, Sharpio, is pull feathers."

"It's Shapiro," you say.

"You a dago or something? You don't look like a dago."

"I never plucked feathers before."

"Pluck must be the dago word. We say pull."

"Pull or pluck, I still don't know how."

"What do dagoes do — cook 'em with the feathers on? Watch, and I'll show you, Shaprio."

You're all morning long at those birds, and by the time you're finished, the white stripes on your pants are red.

227

"What're you going to do with all these?" you say to the sheriff.

"Eat 'em."

"All forty? How about a few for upstairs?"

"Ducks for jailbirds!"

"They'll only go bad on you."

"Higher they get, the better," the sheriff says. "You dagoes don't know a theng."

Up in the cell that evening, you tell the kids about the birds. "Forty!" you say. "I counted forty birds!"

"And all for a dog-shit sheriff!" a kid says.

"You should've told him you wasn't his nigger," the other kid says. "Get your old lady to do it, you should've said."

"She's too busy picking nits out of her twat," the first one says.

"Speaking of old ladies," the second one says, "what's yours doing, Jesse?"

"Who do you think she's screwing tonight, Jesse?"

"Some sheriff, maybe?"

"There she is up in Pensacola, Jesse, with a big fat sheriff sweating on her belly."

"And he's saying what your old man don't know won't hurt him."

"And she's saying it ain't hurting me none neither."

The kids begin to laugh, and in the middle of a ha-ha, one of them is snatched up from his cot and slammed against a wall. (Blaisdell? was it, or Sherwood Kelly?) His body falls as if he's only clothes.

"You killed him!" the other kid screams at Jesse.

But from the heap on the floor, you hear a voice (Harry's? Sherwood's?), and it says, "He's no killer. He's only got one ball. That's why he's so worried about his gash."

And lying on his cot again, Jesse only laughs.

—A day or two later, when the sheriff comes for you in the morning, he tells you that your father has paid your fine, and you're free to go. You say goodbye to the kids (is that when you wrote the names?), and you say goodbye to Jesse James.

"Don't forget that kangaroo stuff," Harry or Sherwood says.

"Send us those three bucks," Sherwood or Harry says, "or else you get cockalized."

"What if I keep the money when it comes through?" the sheriff says.

"Mister," one or the other says, "you just ain't got enough jism to do that."

—On the way downstairs, you say to the sheriff, "Are they as hard as they sound?"

"What did they tell you they was in for?" he says.

"Beating somebody and taking his car."

"Broken his head open like a goddamn coconut. Killed the sombitch."

Your father had sent enough money to pay your railway fare as well as your fine, but you ride the cars only as far as Jacksonville, where the right-of-way lies along St. John's River. From there, you see the Clyde Line docks and the stacks of ships. One, you learn, will sail for New York in the afternoon — the *Comanche* — and when it does, you're standing near a lifeboat and looking over the rail, and you're thinking *The fine son returns by sea, not to be stoned for stubbornness and rebellion, but as from some voyage of conquest, with smoke and pennants streaming.*

Still, there are no crowds on Pier 36, North River, and what cheering you hear is all in your head, along with a sense of fear.

SCENE 136

A GIRL NAMED B. (1923)

You met her at a family wedding where, thinned by other streams, blood joined with blood for an evening and then took its separate ways. She was your third cousin, you were told, but from whom she had descended, no one thought to say. Her gown was either pale pink or peach, you remember, with a head-band to match that was tied with a bow. Braving rigging for one so plain, and she might've left your mind if you hadn't watched her walk away. Despite the straight-fall lines of the style that year, she made you imagine her cambers and concaves, and later, when you danced with her, you felt through pink or peach the proof of what you'd fancied. Cousin or not, removed or german, you knew you'd see her again and soon.

At the outset, it was supposed by her people that your calls were those of a kinsman, that you were drawn to them by some tribal capillarity. They were all therefore pleasantly present when you appeared out of a clear or rainy evening, and you were invited to join them beneath the diningroom chandelier, there to crack hazel nuts from a cut-glass bowl, or to peel, if you would, a tangerine. And as piles of shells and rinds rose, there was talk of this aunt and that uncle, and there were inquiries into whos and whoms, into deaths, scandals, changes of name. And then tea was made and *Mandelbrot* brought, and cigarette-smoke grayed the air, and at ten or near enough, you were in the street again on that clear or rainy evening.

But as your visits continued, less and less long were you part of a company. You were received by the father, the mother, the sister if unengaged, but the *Klatsches* around the fruit-bowl were over when you arrived, and presences other than the girl named B. betook themselves away. Where in that six-room flat did they repair to, you wondered, and what did they do when there? Did they read, sleep, bathe, sit guessing what you and B. were up to, listen for words, whispers, the sound of sofa-springs? And on hearing nothing, what did they make of the silence, what goings-on did they imagine in their rooms along the hall?

What could they have heard—the dry-leaf slide of silk on silk, textile murmurs, a third cousin's hand on his third cousin's skin? They could hardly have traced its course, known where it paused and pried, followed it over hill and dale to the dove in the cleft of the rock. They could not have heard from the end of the hall. You'd gone exploring and spoken not at all, as though you'd been alone.

SCENE 137

WANDERJAHR (1924)

You'd hardly come back from Florida when your Grandpa Nevins gave up his home. It was no longer needed: poor misfortunate Romie had for years been shut away in an upstate institution, and he'd turn up no more with a *Ta-da tsing!*; your Uncle Dave had become a series of postage stamps cancelled at Moskva, Bucuresti, Firenze, Athinai; and with your sister at boarding school in Tarrytown, only you remained of the former household. At the age of twenty, you were thought to be capable of standing on your own. Why? you'd later wonder—you'd always stood on someone else.

Again your father offered you the room with the beaded lampshade, the bath with the unknown tint of tile, and again you refused, and he shook his head in the end, marveling that golden Julian had turned so soon to lead. Still, he increased your allowance to cover rooming-house rent on West End Avenue, and one day you installed yourself with all your haberdash splendor and the one book that you recall, an india-paper edition of *Vanity Fair* borrowed from a girl named B.

For five dollars a week, you secured the right to sleep in a bed that had not forgotten others, that spoke to you of their condition, the kind and quality of their exudations, even, you thought, their turn of mind. At the edge of your field of memory, a bureau seems to have existed, and out there too squats an ottoman with a bottom that sags to the floor. You shared a bathroom with someone you never saw, a man, a woman, a disincarnation that caused water to flush or pour. In the month or two of your residence, there was never an encounter, a someone seen on the stair. Only your nights were spent in that five-dollar room, and sometimes you'd lie listening to sounds that came through the door—the snap of a lightswitch, impinging objects, the derision of a drain—but you never learned who or what had made them, the man, the woman, the presence at the end of the hall.

The rooming-house was only a halt, a port of call (for coal? repairs? cargo?), and soon you were somewhere else, the Allerton, a hotel on lower Lexington Avenue. Nothing had drawn or driven you there save your need to be in motion—it was as though, being placeless, you could stay at no place long. Nor did the Allerton detain you, nor the homes of Nat and Herb, your friends from Lafayette, nor for more than days did you lie in the bays of other isles. At one such roadstead (a second furnished room? a third or fourth hotel?), you left behind a trunk containing the treasured trash of twenty years—letters from whom? whose photos? keys that would open what? the pressed flowers of which occasion?

And you moved on.

SCENE 138

QUESTION AND ANSWER (1924)

It was the day for the payment of fees at Fordham, and with your father's check in your pocket, you crossed City Hall Park in the long blue shadow of the Woolworth Building. There, among a sheaf of passengers, you rode upward in one of the fast hydraulics to the Law School floor, where you joined a line of students leading to the office of the Bursar.

The advance was slow, barely a pace at a time, and with little to look at in the dim corridor, you looked at nothing until you became aware of a girl just before you in the queue. A blonde, she seemed to be, but when she moved her head, strands of hair ran red and gold. You thought of a current, an arc across a broken circuit, a spark you remember yet.

"Would it make any difference," you'd say, "if I said I was a Jew?"

And she'd stare at you as if you were an intruder, saying, "All the difference in the world!"

In one of the courses you took that year, your chair was in the same aisle as hers, and you could see her face in profile and watch light at work in her hair. After class one evening, you spoke to her for the first time (what did you say, and what did she?), and then the two of you were crossing Broadway to the park, walking with each other in the downtown dark (what were you saying, and what was she?). Bright squares of window still showed here and there, and festoons of light outlined the Bridge, and you too may have glowed in the night when

you said *Would it make any difference . . . ?* and died down when
she said *All the difference in the world!*

At another time, you learned that her middle name was Ursula, for the saint slain by the Huns along with her train of eleven thousand virgins. That was in the Third century. It was in the Twentieth that you said *Would it make any difference . . . ?* You'd be three years together at Law School, three years you'd sit with her through the same courses in the same set of rooms, always within sight of each other and sometimes side by side, but she'd never speak to you again.

For two of those three years, whatever you did in class was a performance for one pair of eyes, one pair of ears. When you rose to recite, you were aware of no other face or form, and it was before her alone that you presented a case, argued a cause, disclosed what you thought an error in the law. On no occasion did she watch your turn, nor when it ended did she show her favor or disapprove—she merely endured you, as if waiting through some intermission where nothing was occurring but time.

But it was not only at school that you were in her company: in fancy, she'd leave on your arm, walk where you chose to walk, see your sights, climb your peaks, swim your seas, and always she'd lie beside you, even when you lay with someone else—she'd be so much there that the other became she. Ursula, you'd think, who died with all her virgins a long way back in the past.

All the difference . . . !

SCENE 139

FORDHAM LAW SCHOOL (1924-25)

Your father gave you a place of your own that year, a one-room flat in Brooklyn on a street called Columbia Heights. It was on the half-sunk ground fffloor of a private brownstone, and its two barred windows, bare of curtains, stared wide-eyed over the sidewalk at fronts across the way. There was no carpet, you remember, and no pictures or paper subdued the walls—a table, a pair of hard-back chairs, and a couch that would hold only you, nothing else graced that one-room place for sleep and clothes, those suits from New Haven, those foulard ties and regimentals.

You were in the evening division at Law School, and when classes ended for the day, you'd take the subway to the Heights and walk back toward the river and the towers of Manhattan that showed above the roofs. And you'd go slowly, for nothing called you to your semi-basement, neither the silken company of your neckware nor your relentless wooden chairs. At times, you'd go past your house, as though you lived somewhere else, or you'd stop beside the door and smoke a cigarette, feeling more at home in the outdoor dark than the night you'd find inside, and always, in that first half-year, you'd be thinking of red-gold hair and a six-word sentence: *All the difference in the world!*

At term's end in January, your grades in the two completed courses were a D in Common Law Pleading and an A+ in Agency, the worst and the best of passing marks, and you were so ashamed of the one that for weeks you suppressed the other. How could you have gotten a D? you wondered, how could you have been so sure of better and done so poorly? The examination had been a fair one, with no baited trap or snare—pleading, you thought, what was there to pleading but the presentation of a grievance in law or equity and a prayer for relief? To spell out a cause of action, you required no help from familiar or unclean spirits, nor would you stand or fall on wizardry with language or Latin sleight-of-hand. Whatever the nature of the case—let it be Wills, Torts, Bills and Notes—if properly stated, it would survive the assault of answer, rejoinder, and demurrer, and prevail. What was there to pleading? you thought one night on the train to Brooklyn—and you found that you were facing your instructor from a seat across the aisle.

He was Joseph Force Crater, in private practice a lawyer who prepared briefs for trial and appellate use, and more than once he'd been engaged by your

233

father's office to abstract the state of the law as it might apply to some pending plea or motion. He was a tall thin man with a head so small that it seemed to have been joined with the wrong body. He was made by this disproportion to look compressed, as though he'd been raised in places too narrow to grow in, in a tube, a crevice. He always wore a high starched collar (could he retract his head? you'd sometimes wonder), and you never saw him smile. Recognizing you, he nodded, and you took a seat at his side.

"What did you think of the exam, Shapiro?" he said.

"It seemed easy enough," you said. "But, sir, I thought my paper was worth more than a D."

"So did I, but a D is the best a repeater ever gets."

"Repeater? I'm no repeater."

"I hope you're not going to say you never took Pleading before. Last year, you sat right in front of my desk."

"For one month," you said. "Then I quit school to go bumming, and I wound up in a Florida jail. I'm a bum, maybe, but not a repeater."

"You didn't take last year's exam?"

"No, sir."

"Then you're right," he said. "If you were marking your own paper, how would you grade it?"

"I'd give me a B."

"B it is, then. Go see the Registrar tomorrow and say I said so."

"Thanks, Mr. Crater."

You were almost at your station, Borough hall, when he said, "What made you throw away a year?"

"That's what my father asked me," you said. "I wish I knew."

And he said, "Give my regards to Phil," just before you left the train.

From Court Square, you walked west along Pierrepont between rows of stern brownstones, unsparing of such as you. Ahead, you could see buildings on the blue-black island and higher than them all the white-gold tip of the Woolworth spire. Tomorrow, you thought, you'd rise to speak (on Jurisprudence? would it be, on Domestic Relations? Crimes? Property?), and she'd sit there taking in your language and leaving you outside. *All the difference,* she'd told you.

SCENE 140

OF THINGS PAST (1925)

Close inshore off Pt. Joe, seven currents of the Pacific cross. There in that collision of forces, three ships have gone down, and their names are in baked enamel on markers among the rocks — the *Cecilia,* the *St. Paul,* and the *George F. Buck.* Gazing out at the boil above their leaving — a propeller blade, a brass lamp, a porthole frame — you think your way back through half a century to another seaboard and the forces that crossed in you. . . .

§

— to afternoons in Jersey when you walk back roads red as rust toward the Monmouth battlefield, and above the trees you see the white belfry of Tennent Church, and through them you hear the guns of Greene,

— or you course the pine plains on a road you make as you go, laying your own trail to an osprey's aerie seventy feet up in a dead chestnut, and over a rim of jackstraws, you're eyed till you walk away,

— or you sit on the sand and watch the surf throw itself at your feet, and you see a girl stand wet and drying in the sun, her suit finding every round and hollow, as if it were your hand, and you know you're thinking of someone else,

— or at Deal, where fishermen seined for mullet, you'd watch them cast their draw-string nets and then bring them in, purses filled with silver change,

— or you'd take the trolley to the Asbury links, and there one day. . . .

You're playing alone, just behind another single, a slow goer, and when he sees that he's holding you up, he waves you ahead. In passing, you recognize him. "Aren't you Nat Weinstein?" you say. "From Harlem?"

"Nathanael," he says.

"I'm Julian Shapiro. I used to see you on Seventh Avenue in front of the De Peyster."

"I lived there. Did you?"

"Around the corner on St. Nick."

"You still in Harlem?"

"Brooklyn," you say.

You pair up there, and for much of the way your talk pertains to the game — mashie, downhill lie, out-of-bounds — but all the while you watch his lunging gait, irregular and blundering, as if he has to remind each foot that its turn has come to stride. And when you see him light a cigarette, you know he's not at home in a world of lifeless matter — he almost lights his face. Later, you'll come to know that all things, all objects having an existence in space, are strange to him, and a danger too, and he'll handle them as if they were paraphernalia of unknown usage that he can only paw at, fumble with, misapply, and thus one day he'll die.

But on that day, somewhere on the second nine, he says, "What've you been doing since Harlem?"

And you say, "Moving around from college to college — Lafayette, Lehigh," and then, a little proud of yourself for once, you say, "Right now, I'm studying law at Fordham."

"I went to Brown," he says. "I'm writing a book."

I went to Brown I'm writing a book — the two parts of his announcement run together in your mind, making a single sentence that withers pride, turns the law itself to *the yellow leaf.* I went to Brown I'm writing a book — and thereafter nothing remains of the day, not the rolling ground, the greens, the flight of a dimpled ball.

Why? you wonder as you tread the grass or wade the rough. What are books to you, who read so little and that little idly? What do you care about the twenty-six signs of the printed language, the stories they tell, the thoughts and pictures they convey? Who is this Nat or Nathanael that his *book* can wither your world?

"What kind of book?" you say.

"A novel, I guess. It's hard to describe."

"What's it about?"

"A lyric poet named Balso Snell," he says. "While wandering in the tall grass outside the ancient city of Troy, he finds the wooden horse of the Greeks. He enters it and has a series of adventures. That's the book. I call it *The Dream Life of Balso Snell.*"

Troy, you think, and your mother's reading comes to mind, of Loki, Jason, Thor, and you remember how real Hector seemed, son of Priam, and how you mourned him, nine times dragged round the city walls. And now you're with one who's been there too, and you watch him stoop over a ball lying in the grass, in long grass far from the walls of Troy. He's ill-jointed, you think, spasmodic, and he moves as if moved by strings.. He'll die of that one day, but the day is still far off. This day (*I'm writing a book*), it's the law that dies. . . .

§

The *Cecilia,* the *St. Paul,* the *George F. Buck* — you read the names and dates on markers among the rocks, and looking out at the clash of currents, you

think of the currents that clashed in you, of Nat, Nathan, Nathanael, dead
in a mangle of metal and wood when his strings were pulled by someone else.

SCENE 141

AARON'S IN TOWN (1860-1938)

He was the eldest of your father's brothers and the family pioneer, forerunning
all the others when he came to America at the age of seventeen. After reading
law for four years, he was admitted to the New York bar and began to practice
from an office in Grand Street, a thoroughfare, it was said by all, that might've
taken its name from him. He was a silk-hat lawyer in a frock coat with satin
facings, and so far from merely construing the law, he laid it down as if he'd
made it. Woe to the client who queried a fee or doubted an opinion; he'd
be handed his papers on the spot and scorned through the door, a diminished
man, if still a man at all. *Go!* Aaron the Lawgiver would say, *go, Dummkopf,
and take your case to some pushcart shyster!* Late or soon, most of his clients
were thus scourged from his presence, none to return save those that loved
the lash—and those that loved him.

One of the latter was a friend named Leon Lait, and on a slack afternoon,
of which there were many, he'd sit facing your Uncle Aaron over a board
with thirty-two pieces and play a game called Chess. Their rivalry was of
long standing, going back to some ancient age in the Old Country, where
it was lost in the emulsion of childhood. Nor was their war on the checkered
field of battle fought wholly with bits of wood; words too were brought
to bear, and blood was let with contumely, with disdain and belittlement,
with calls on imaginary spectators to witness imminent victory or defeat.

"I believe you touched that rook," your uncle would say.

And Mr. Lait's response would be, "I distinctly said *J'adoube*."

"He was adjusting!" your uncle would say. "Always he was only adjusting!"

"Black's move."

"And black moves his castle—thus—to there."

"He moves his castle!" Mr. Lait would say. "Like a foolish man, he moves
his castle!"

"Yes," your uncle would say, "he moves his castle."

"And when I move this man from here—so—what will the foolish man
do next?"

"A clever move, he thinks," your uncle would say.

"A move worthy of the great Tarrasch."

"Tarrasch, he says! Well, here is an answer from Tchigorin!"

On your father's admission to the bar, he and brother Aaron formed a partnership that lasted from the flourishing times of the early century to the blight brought on by the Panic of 1907. Thereafter their practice fell away to the odd jobs of the profession—drawing wills and leases, filing mechanics' liens, defending an insolvent against a notice of dispossess. In the end, your uncle, always one to restore his soul in greener pastures, left the arid field to your father and removed to the city of Chicago, whence, out of a glow like unto the sun, Fortune had seemed to beckon.

The lure was an opportunity to invest in a business devoted to the manufacture of ladies' shirtwaists (*Tomorrow will be too late!*), and into that business, of which he knew nothing, he poured the paltry thousands left from a score of years at the law. Ah, would that he had waited for that morrow!—at the very moment he became the owner of a shirtwaist factory, shirtwaists ceased to be the rage. So swift had been the change and so uncertain the cause that your uncle's investment was gone before he knew of the newer age. The day of the one-piece dress was here, and back came his shipments of dotted swisses, of voiles and marquisettes, back his shining taffetas, his lustrous bombazines. He went bankrupt overnight.

And your Aunt Sarah would call your father and say, "Phil, Aaron's in town."

And your father would laugh and say, "*Meine schöne schwester,* I wonder what he wants."

"Only too well do we know," she'd say.

"How much will it be, Sarah?"

"A thousand from me and Harris, a thousand from you. Can you raise it?"

"I'll raise it," your father would say.

And then you and he would go uptown to Aunt Sarah's, and there you'd find Uncle Aaron in his Prince Albert, in his wing-collar and pinned cravat, and seated in the light and shade of a chandelier, he'd speak of orange groves, of rice-growing in Mississippi, or was it pineapples, or sugar cane? And after a while, you'd be told to leave the room, and when the door had closed behind you, money would pass through the cone of that chandelier, and there'd be more talk then, of cotton-planting, perhaps, of the bonanza in insurance— and your father and his sister would sit thinking of another phone-call on another day.

"Phil," she'd say, "Aaron's in town."
And "How much this time?" he'd say.

In the course of those years, there were many this-times for your Uncle Aaron, many high-hope ventures, many pastures where the grass seemed greener and the waters to stand more still, but always the promise was broken and ever far off the rainbow's end, and one day when

your Aunt Sarah called to say, "Aaron's in town,"
your father said, "This time, Sarah, send him down to see me."

You were not allowed to be present for that meeting, nor would he tell you later what was said. Within a month, though, your uncle had moved his family back to New York, and his name was lettered on the outer doors of the office, and, lo, it led the rest! It was also engraved on the new stationery of a law-firm now called Shapiro Bros., and there too it headed the list of names. Thereafter, and for ten years, your uncle was in command, and once more, when a client balked at the size of a fee, there'd be a thundergust in your uncle's room, and squalls of ridicule would be heard through the transom, and out would slink some flinching cur, some dog of a client, and in his paws he'd clutch his papers.

But quietly your father would lead him away, soothe him, reduce the fee, retrieve the papers, and the dog would become a man again and return as long as he lived. There were ten more years of such uneasy weather before your uncle died.

"Aaron's in town," your Aunt Sarah used to say.

SCENE 142

THE AUTUMN OF 1925

Your Uncle Dave called you one day and told you that his father, Grandpa Nevins, was in the Memorial Hospital on Central Park West. When you arrived, he was waiting for you in the corridor, and he prevented you from entering the room.

"What's the matter with grandpa?" you said.
He answered only after leading you out of the hospital to a bench beside the park wall, and there he said, "Your grandpa is going to die."

You looked up at the red-brick facade across the street from where you sat, and you tried to find a window, a shade, two particular panes of glass (die, you thought, going to die), and you said, "I didn't know he was sick."

"Till a week ago, I didn't either. Then I heard from my mother that he'd been bringing up blood, and I made him see a doctor, and the doctor sent him here. They took a sample of the tissue in his throat, and it turned out to be cancerous."

"Can't they do something?" you said. "Operate?"

"It's too late."

You can't remember whether you said anything then or whether you sat there wondering why you had nothing to say. In one of the rooms above you overlooking the trees, the Reservoir, the pathways of the park, an old man lay knowing all but the day of his going, but you can't recall what you said to his son or whether you spoke at all.

But the son spoke, and this is what he said. "I'm forty years old," he said, "and I never had a kindness from my father. Never, and now he's dying, and in his will he'll call me his Dear David, and that'll be the first and only time he'll use the word—when he's dead."

And he said, "I did whatever he desired of me as a father, but when he showed that he wanted more, when he tried to rule me, we always disagreed. People would reason with him, my mother, my sisters, your own father, but he had a mind as heavy as his hand, and he listened to no one: I was no son if he couldn't run me."

And he said, "I wanted to go to Cornell, but he wouldn't let me. A high school education was enough, he said—he'd had no education at all, and he was rich. And he didn't care for my friends—he called them radicals. A salesman, a teacher, a dermatologist—radicals!"

And he said, "When he told me I ought to get married—settle down, as he put it—I brought home a girl I'd been going with for a year, a girl I really admired, quiet, pretty, bright—and do you know what he did at the dinner-table? He made fun of her, he picked her apart like a piece of meat! I don't know why he did that, but if he was out to break us up, he had his way. I never saw her again after that evening, and he never saw another of my girls. Maybe he'd've liked them better—they were all whores, Hong Kong, Havana, and Cairo whores."

And he said, "He respected only the ability to make money. If you had it, you were worthy; if you didn't, you were not. Your Uncle Harry had the knack, and he got the gold fountain-pen. Your father got the silver."

And he said, "But I didn't even have the desire to make money, so all I ever got was a pencil."

And he said, "Never a smile, a pat on the head, a good-for-you—always the same sour look of disapproval. And when it became too much to bear, I'd run away to the only place where I felt at home—South America. There, ten thousand feet up in the Andes, among fat little Indians with their hats on square, there I felt welcome."

And he said, "Sometimes I'd think of never going back, of taking up with one of the upland Cholos and living out my life in the Sierra. I'd get a job with the copper company and never let my mind leave the boundaries of Peru. To hell with my father! I'd think."

And he said, "But again and again I'd come home, and always I'd find it the same—a home for someone else, but not for me. Still, I couldn't stay away."

And he looked up at the building across the street, and he said, "And now he's up there dying, a hardset old man—and, God damn it! I hate to see him go."

Near your bench, on the tracks of the Eighth Avenue line, a cream-and-green car stopped for a fare, and then its gong rang twice, and it rolled on past. You watched until it was out of sight, but when you turned back to look at your uncle, he didn't know you were there.

SCENE 143

A TRIP TO CALIFORNY (1925)

Your grandpa died for an entire year, but he meant before the end to see the Promised Land, which to him was a place he called Californy. To another Abraham, the Lord had said *Get thee unto a land that I shall shew thee,* and though he knew his stay could not be long, he made the journey. What drew him so? you wonder—was it the marvels he'd heard of, or was it the chance of dying where the sun went down, of watching it go and going himself?

Of the excursion, made in the company of his son-in-law Harry, the only remnant is a picture postcard that he sent you from Los Angeles late in the year. It reads *best Love to you from Grandpa,* and the view displayed is of the Ambassador Hotel and gardens. From the tower, an American flag flies above the red tile roof, the vined colonnade, the beds of pink azaleas. The hues are raw, and the walks and lawns are empty—a chromo Canaan, can that be all he found when he fared so far in those last few days? You search the tiers of windows for a face, a hand, a fluttered signal, but there's nothing behind the glass, no depth dimension deeper than the printer's ink.

Californy, you think—where are its prodigies? Or, despite the deserted pathways, the vacant sward and windows, had he seen what you could not?

THE COLOR OF THE AIR, XIII

UNION PACIFIC — 1869
DESERET*

* *In the Book of Mormon, a coined word meaning* land of the working bee.

The Shoshone on the butte did not call it that, nor did he call it Zion, or Utah, or anything else. He had names for snakes and streams and rain, for other braves and other horses, and for his own and other dogs, and he knew how to summon spirits and tick off certain birds, and he had terms for time and thing and place, and in his tales of the chase and war, the names of the dead would come alive. But this roundabout him was the world, and he could make no sound, no small word, that would take it all in.

Far down, near the great still lake of brine, the diamond stack of *Jupiter* and the straight one of *119* sent black smokes into the sky, and they wrote a sign that he understood who could not read. Die, it told him: take your people and your people's bones, take your no-account ponies and your greasy ginch, take your smell and arraigning eyes, and go away and die—but not too close to the railroad line. That was the sign written in engine smoke.

Under each mile of track, 2,640 ties had been laid, and north and south of the right-of-way, no oak now stood for fifty miles, no cedar, no fir, no ash or cottonwood. Buffalo, shot for their tongues alone, rotted in the sun and starlight and stank both hot and cold. The pronghorns had fled the steel bees and, stung, died on the dead run, and bear were robes now, and gone the four-stripe chipmunk and the porcupine with yellow hair, and in the salt sea, loon and teal were pickled feathers now, killed not for the pot but to kill an afternoon.

A spike-maul spoke in the distance, and small waves broke on the butte: the golden nail was going in.

SCENE 144

NORTH POLE, SOUTH POLE (1925)

One of the friends you'd made during your year at Lafayette was Nat Cohen—Nathan Spiro Cohen. He came from the Bronx, and his father was a travelling salesman who beat up New England with a line of merchandise. You were never told what kind of goods he sold, but he was no great shakes at the game, for all he'd ever gained from it was contained in the five rooms of a walk-up flat near Southern Boulevard. He was a round and pleasant man, beaming out at lifelong failure, and for some reason, unknown now even to you, you always called him Colonel.

His son, a year or so older than you, was angular and unfinished, hewn rather than sawn, a rough stick of wood. He was far from wooden-headed, though, as you soon enough knew, but it took you somewhat longer to admire his diligence. His *purpose* disturbed you, who had no purpose, and it troubled you too that he was so frugal with his time. You'd feel that his presence anywhere was temporary, that he was there only for the spell between two stages, the tick between two tocks, as if he were waiting for a bell. While at college, he received small help from home, if any came at all, but he had ways of making money, and they not only paid for his tuition, but also for his room and board. Studying him, your thoughts were of Alger: on the final pages, you'd think, he'd be rewarded for his constancy and enterprise. Not for him the sample-case, the dry-goods smell of a store.

Part of his campus earnings were derived from the publication of a sports calendar. Each semester, he'd solicit ads from local tradesmen and print them on posters along with the schedules of the college teams. After two terms, his privilege was revoked without explanation (the word *Jew* wafts through the mind), and he was compelled to end his academic days. Transferring to Fordham Law School, he began his professional studies when you did, in the fall of 1924.

Though enrolled in different divisions, he in the morning and you in the night, you saw much of each other that year, talking of many things while walking the streets of the city and the pathways of the park. You'd meet somewhere, in Grand Army Plaza, say, or on a corner of Herald Square, and full of words, you'd sow them as you went, throw them at the air. Not long before, you'd reached the age of twenty-one, and sometimes you'd have a

243

sense of carbonated blood, of holding within you sparkling wine, and for the hour or the afternoon, you'd forget the uncharged years.

The meeting place one day was Windy Corner, the northern end of the Triangle Building, and you reached there first, you remember, and you waited, watching people pass, the women gathering their skirts against a sudden gust or swirl. One of these reminded you of the girl at Fordham (*all the difference in the world*), and you remember too how the effervescent moment died.

You became aware of your friend Nat only when he'd taken you in his arms and made you turn and turn with him as to music for a waltz, and all the while he was saying, "I'm on top of the world, Julie! I'm sitting on top of the world!"

You were still thinking of the stranger borne past you by the wind, still seeing correspondences of figure, coloration, clothing, even, and what you said was, "That's fine. I'm at the bottom."

He let go of you and backed off, diminished to a suitful of trash, and when he could speak again, his voice was that of a punished child. "I was happy all day," he said. "I could've flown. And I did fly till you spoiled things. Why did you have to say that, Julie?"

What could you have told him—that you were heavier than air? Would he have waltzed you again in Madison Square?

"Why did you have to spoil things?" he said, and he walked away, leaving you there on Windy Corner.

SCENE 145

ANOTHER FRIEND FROM LAFAYETTE (1925)

You met him for the first time early in 1922, on the Saturday of Prom Week. You'd reached Easton on the morning train and taken lodgings in a rooming house on North 3rd, and then you'd made your way up the Hill to enroll for the coming semester. At the Registrar's, after paying your fees, you asked for the whereabouts of a student named Herbert Ortman and were told that his room was in the South College dormitory. It had snowed the night before, and as yet there were only a few trails through the glaring Quad; you made a fresh one as you crossed it toward a spire that showed above the trees. On the fourth floor of the building, the mansard story, you found the student seated on the sill of a dormer window and gazing out at the white town below him.

He turned when you entered saying, "My name is Julian Shapiro." His expression made you feel as if you'd bounded in, and your outstretched hand became a paw. "Julian L. Shapiro."

"I'm Herb Ortman, but I guess you know that, or you wouldn't be here. What brings you to 28 South?"

"Your sister came to Camp Wakonda last summer to visit her two boys. One of them was in my bunkhouse, so I got to know her."

"Were you a camper too?"

"A waiter," you said. "She told me about you being at Lafayette. Said to look you up if I got in."

"Did you like it, being a waiter?"

"It wouldn't've been so bad. But the counselor in charge of my table was a prick. He ate like one of those slow-motion movies. Took an hour for breakfast."

"Was his name Clem?" he said.

And you said, "How did you know?"

"You said prick. Who else could it be?"

"Your sister said you were at Camp Paradox, and you were a baseball pitcher."

He began to pat his pockets, and then he glanced around the room. "You got a cigarette on you, Julian L.?"

"You bet!" you said, and you drew out a flat red box of Pall Malls.

"Pretty high living for a waiter," he said.

"Listen. If I can't smoke the best, I won't smoke at all."

He struck a match and looked at you while it flared.

He took you to a tea dance at the Zeta Psi house that afternoon. It was a Christian fraternity, but because of Prom Week, the affair was open to all. There was little intermingling, though, no cutting in for girls from across the invisible line. The Jews, a dozen or more of them, were standing in a group near the staircase when you and Herbert arrived. He introduced you, and you caught a few of the names (Silverman, Charach, Baum, Goff, Frankenstein), and then he asked you for another cigarette. Quickly you produced that flat red box, and, alas! what it held when you opened it was quite as quickly gone. A converge of hands—Charlie's, Al's, Nat's, Frank's—in them now your little oval tubes of weed.

Herbert reached for the empty box as well, saying as he did so, "What does the L. stand for, Julian?"

And you said, "Lawrence."

§

His father, Isaac Ortman, was a dentist with a small neighborhood practice in Bensonhurst. His office had once been the parlor of his home, a two-story frame dwelling on Bay Parkway, one of the many such there, all of them much the same. Each had a porch, a bib of lawn, and shiplap siding, and but for the number on a riser of the stoop, they would've been hard to tell apart. Within, you remember, there was always a medicinal suggestion on the air, of alcohol or phenol, still there under the flavors of anise, lemon, cinnamon.

When you think of Dr. Ortman, the word *grave* seems to volunteer, as if it better than any other could describe his frame of mind. In his company, you tried to suppress the monkeyshine, the rash conclusion — you'd listen when he spoke and do your best to understand.

"Ortman!" his wife would say, "Ortman, your food is getting cold!"

If deep in what he was saying, he'd go on, and you'd find that your food too had gotten cold.

"Ortman!" his wife would say — not Doctor, not Isaac, but "Ortman."

You knew him only toward the end of his life, and you've remembered him best for one particular day. Someone's remark, a reference in a newspaper, a memory that rose of itself — something made him relate a story about his place of origin, a village in Russia.*

— It happened in the Old Country a long time ago, he said. He was only a boy at the time, but he saw it all, and he could see it yet. The people of the village were still in the fields, though it was late in the day, and the sun was going down. There was no wind, and he heard the scythes whispering through the grain — whispering, he said — and it was pleasant to be there, he thought, it was peaceful.

— And then in one heart-beat, the calm was gone. The Soldiers came, a scythe of horsemen that let the grain stand and cut down the people. They tried to run, but they were soon surrounded.

— The Officer ordered all the unmarried women to step forward, and eight girls obeyed him. Then they were told to take off their clothes and climb the trees at the river-bank.

— When they made no move, the Officer cried, "Take off your clothes!"

— Isaac watched his sister loosen her skirt and blouse and drop them to the ground. He saw her bare body, he said, and he could still remember its beauty.

— "Now get up in those trees and sing like birds!" the Officer said.

---

* Ascribed to a fictional character in *The People from Heaven*, 1943.

— The trees shook with the weight of the girls, and from among the leaves a thin little song came floating down. It was sad, and the people on the ground began to cry.

— "No more singing!" the Officer said. "I want you to fly now! Fly like birds!"

— Not knowing what to do, the girls could only flap their arms.

— The Officer said, "That's not flying at all!" and turning to the Soldiers, he gave them a command. "Make those cows fly like birds!"

— The Soldiers fired their rifles at the trees, and eight naked bodies tumbled into the stream.

— "They flew!" the Officer cried. "They flew just like birds!"

— Then he signaled to his men, and they galloped off across the fields, and soon it was quiet once more.

He wept then without a sound; he wept as he may have done that day in the fields.

"Ortman!" his wife said. "Ortman, your food is getting cold!"

He was a grave man. You never made the mistake of calling him Colonel.

SCENE 146

BLUE (June 1925)

Your friend Herb Ortman was about to sail for a summer in France, and you, with a guest of your choosing, were invited to a farewell party at his home in Bensonhurst. Your sister Ruth, then nearly seventeen, had never met Herb or his family, and when you found that she was free for the afternoon named, you asked her to go with you to Brooklyn. You remember what she wore that day — a jacket and skirt of royal blue velvet, with a fillet to match that caught up her hair — and you remember thinking her very pretty.

It was a long subway ride from Washington Heights to Bay Parkway, and when you arrived, the party was well under way. Being detained by someone on the walk outside, you motioned to Ruth to proceed without you. On entering a few moments later, you came upon Herb in the entrance hallway. He was peering through the shuttling crowd, trying to follow a figure in a vivid hue — royal blue velvet.

He gave you only a glance. "Whoever brought her is going to lose her," he said.

"Really?" you said. "To whom?"

"To me—that's the girl I'm going to marry."

"Do you know who she is?"

"I don't give a damn who she is. She's mine."

"You'd better ask my father first," you said. "She's my sister."

He sailed on the following day and returned when the summer ended. But she was not his, then or later.

SCENE 147

THE FALL OF 1926

In your first two years at Fordham, your grades indicated to your father that you'd become a serious student, and he made his approval known by a handsome gift. During the summer, he'd rendered legal services for a client just then completing the construction of the new Fifth Avenue Hotel. Replacing its namesake that once had faced Madison Square, the later building was a twelve-story affair of brick and granite with ball- and banquet-rooms, a restaurant, and a bar that duplicated the Amen Corner of old. On the upper levels were the furnished suites and singles, and one of the latter, in lieu of the fees your father had earned, was assigned to you for the year that remained of your law school career. You never learned the cost of his generosity—the rent per month x twelve—but you did know that there were some who disapproved.

"You don't need their names, kid," he said. "A couple of my associates. A member of the family. Why do you ask?"

"What did they say?" you said.

"That I was being too openhanded with you. That you had yet to learn the value of a dollar."

"And how did you reply, counselor?"

"I said it can have many values."

"A good answer," you said.

"I said some people think it's worth ninety cents, but they're foolish. And some price it at a hundred, which is sensible." He drew a one-dollar bill from his pocket, and putting it before him on his desk, he smoothed it flat. "But save me, I said, from anyone who wants a hundred and four!"

"What bunch am I in?" you said.

And he said, "I don't know yet, kid, but I'll find out some day."

§

One evening early in September of that year, you were in your room abstracting cases assigned for the following day (*Frm a judgt for the Def in an action for gds sld & delivd, Ptf appeals a lower Ct ruling sust a demurrer*). Answering a knock on the door, you found Herb Ortman in the hallway, and with him a tall young man whom you hadn't seen since your Model School days.

"George Brounoff!" you said.

And he said, "Julian!"

"Good God, how long has it been?"

"Must be fifteen years. We met in Kindergarten. Miss Nolen's class."

"Come in, come in," you said, and when you'd made them easy, you looked from one to the other through blue-gray smoke, saying, "Where and how did you two meet?"

"The job your father got for me last summer at Camp Copake," Herb said. "George was a counselor there too. I don't recall how I happened to mention your name to him, but I did, and he said he knew the little man. He remembered the Julian, but not the L."

You said, "Last time I saw you, George, you were with your father, and I was with mine. We were going to a meeting at Wadleigh High School. I don't know what the meeting was about any more, but right in the middle of it, your father stood up and got into an argument with the speaker. Then he clapped on a big black Homburg and dragged you away up the aisle."

"That most certainly was Platon Brounoff," George said.

§

A memory of Platon Brounoff had lain stored away through the years, but brought to light by the sight of his son, it came before you as if it were the original image and not the mind's recall. You saw, stalking toward you along Seventh Avenue, a giant, a giant! — there was that black Homburg, and there too the long black Melton with revers and lining of mink, and you heard people say as he strode the street *Kommt der Professor.* But when he'd passed, you remember, with him went their awe, and from some, as they turned to watch his progress, there'd be less reverential breathings, and one would say *A contentious man,* and another would add *A man with no soft answers.*

(Platon, the Moldavian Plato — but how far apart the Black Sea and the Ionian, how unlike the Slav and the Reasoner of Athens! Platon, so his own son later said, was the bastard of Anton Rubinstein, and if true, from him came

249

his skill on the singing wires—but he couldn't make his tongue stay still, he lacked the frame of mind. He quarreled with—ah, with whom did he quarrel not!—and lost to him thereby the tailed and white-tie evenings at the Hall, gone the Bechstein beside the Maestro, the streams of Brahms and Schumann he might've poured upon the rich. Instead, to earn a living, he taught spiteful snots the keyboard for three dollars an hour.)

§

After reminiscence was over, George began to talk in general, and it soon became plain that of the three in your room that evening, only he had a right to the floor. He held forth on nothing in particular and nothing for long, a notion of his, an article he'd read, a sight or picture seen, but he spoke in color, and his words seemed to move—he put life in the air, enough, you thought, to stir the smoke. You had little to say—what could you say to one so far ahead of you, to one of your age who'd reached another realm? But in speaking, he revealed that place and made you know you'd some day go there.

§

(Platon's wife came from Kherson in the province of that name. They produced two children, the son George and a daughter Olga, but Olia is what she was called.)

SCENE 148

THE WINTER OF 1926

*The Hand-me-down,** you'd call the piece, and it'd describe your meeting with L. G., a girl brought to the hotel by one of your classmates at Fordham. You'd known him little, and what you knew had hardly made a conscript of your mind.

you'd write
—You were something less than friends, and in his company, you often felt a rankle, as though a sore spot were forming for a pimple two days hence. It was strange, that sense of festering, it was hard to ascribe to his use of

---

* *To Feed Their Hopes,* University of Illinois, 1980.

250

certain words: he said *title* when referring to a book. *I bought a title by Nietzsche,* he'd say . . . but how could such a frailty generate pus?

He'd been passing by, he said from a phone at the desk, and he'd wondered whether you were at home to him and a girl he happened to be with — would you think it an intrusion, he said, was he assuming too much? What could you have told him — that a book wasn't a *title,* God damn it! a book, God damn it! was a book? You told him to come up.

you'd write
— The girl was pretty. She wore a dark and simple dress, with little cling or conformation, but it gave you inklings all the same of unobtrusive rounds. Speaking seldom, she listened while her consort talked (of *titles,* was it?), and at times, though watching one of them, you dwelt on the other (*Why did he bring her?* you wondered, and *How could she have come?*), but soon you were watching only her. You liked her hands, you discovered — they were decorations — and she kept them still as she heard tell of *Übermensch,* heard of *Zarathustra.* She was pretty, you thought.

Somehow you gathered that he was showing her off. He hadn't, as he'd said, been passing by, hadn't just dropped from the sky and found you in; he'd come by design, he was there to win your approval, but you couldn't guess why it mattered to him that his girl should catch your eye. At times, he seemed to invite her to speak, almost as though to let you appraise the quality of her voice (hear this chord, this rim of crystal chime), and when she complied, against her will, you thought, indeed she spoke in pleasing tones, and it came to you that you were glad he'd brought her, that you wished. . . .

you'd write
— He sought you out the next day to learn your opinion, and when you conveyed it, he astounded you by saying *She'd be good for you,* and then, giving you a card on which a name and number were written, he walked away. You stared at the card, but what you saw was a dark dress, not quite filled, and hands like ornaments: he'd given you the girl herself, not a name and number. *She'd be good for you,* he'd said.

He'd never been a friend of yours, and you wondered why he'd deprive himself and bestow his goods on you. His goods? you thought — was the girl his goods to be given away? What would she say if she knew she'd been passed from hand to hand? would she be cold or cordial if you called, would she measure you against him and see no difference, would she pass the time of day? For nearly a week, you went about carrying that slip of paper, taking it out often, turning it over, holding it to the light, staring at it as if staring might make it speak. In the end, you rang the number and said the name.

You asked whether she'd see you that evening, and after a pause, she agreed. Later, when you were walking with her through the streets of Murray Hill, you heard yourself say, "I got your number from Superman."

"Do you mean you asked him for it?" she said, and in the cold, you could see her breath against a lamplight's glare. "Or did he make you a present of it?"

"It was a week ago," you said. "I forget how it came about."

She stopped and made you face her, and now your breath folded in with hers, as if both of you were smoking the same cigarette. "You're lying, Julian," she said.

"What difference does it make how I got the number? If I didn't want to see you, I wouldn't be here."

"I think you're here because he suggested it."

"I'm here because you're a damn pretty girl."

"You're nothing to each other. Why are you protecting him?"

"I'd never protect anyone who calls a book a title."

"Don't try to be witty, Julian," she said. "Just tell me the truth about the number."

"He said you'd be good for me."

"What else?"

"That's all."

"And what did you say?"

"Nothing. What could I say to a thing like that?"

"You could've asked him what he meant."

You took her arm, and the walk went on over bright snow below the street-lamps and night-blue in between. "Instead," you said, "I'm going to ask you. What the hell did the son-of-a-bitch mean?"

"He isn't a son-of-a-bitch."

"Why did he bring you up to my room?" you said. "Why did he put you on display for me? Why did he try to give you away? What're you to him, and what's he to you?"

"Stay out of my business," she said.

Thereafter, though his name was rarely mentioned, he was always *understood*, always the omitted word supplied by sense. He was with you in dark rooms and in the open air, he was with you through talk, silence, music, walks in the park—you could never feel quite free of him, nor, as you think, could she. She'd been handed down, and however she might've borne the transfer, she couldn't've endured the *down*. Why, you'd often wonder, had he done what he did? Had an orthodox family forced him to cut and run, had the Jew been made to shun the gentile, or had one simply tired of the other—

tired of those hands! — and passed her on to you? You couldn't know, and he remained a presence that in time put an end to those talks in the open air and to those in darkened rooms.

SCENE 149

THE DEATH OF GRANDPA NEVINS (1926)

He died in a hotel bedroom facing the side of the building next door. He died during the night, and the last sight he saw may have been a lighted window across the court, the movement of figures in a bright area that seemed to be going away. In the morning, a call informed you that he was dead, and when you reached the hotel, you found your Uncle Harry awaiting you near the entrance. He was smoking a cigar, you remember, and as always, the mouth-end was mangled and juicy with spit.

Seizing your arm, he spoke through his saturated cud, saying, "You'll never have to worry about money as long as you live!"

You knew it was wrong to speak or think of money then, but he'd done the one and you in truth the other, and it would not do, would not do, to scorn his greed unless you scorned your own. "What do you mean — never worry?" you said.

"As long as you live!" he said, and still clutching your arm, he drew you through the doorway.

In your mind, you remember, a commotion of numbers arose.

§

Turning a corner, you walked toward a canvas canopy that crossed the sidewalk and overhung the curb. Its scalloped skirt was fretted by the wind, and a flapping legend, *Riverside Memorial Chapel,* misspelled itself in several ways. Sheltered by the awning, a family group waited for the sexton to summon them inside, and among them stood your father, conversing with people he'd neither seen nor served since his remarriage. Once, you thought, some of them had said *He killed your mother, Julian,* but in his presence now, they were the ones with the found-out look, and, discomposed, they bore his lack of spite. You did not know, nor they, that he had never felt it.

With services about to begin, you followed your father as he descended the center aisle. Your Grandma Nevins was in the front row of seats, and at her side sat your Uncle Dave. Stopping before her, your father took her hands in his and kissed them, and then he found a place nearby and gazed at the plain wooden casket, on which a spray of roses lay. He might've been thinking of anything, you thought—of the first time he'd seen your grandpa or the last, of your mother in a white dress, of a wedding at Vienna Hall, of the good days and the bad days of the past—thinking of gold pens and silver pens, of six years spent in another man's home, of unsigned notes that spoke of *your fine son.* . . .

And then began a journey of black-veiled women and black-tied men across a bridge and Brooklyn toward the shore of Jamaica Bay. Twelve years before, you'd gone the same crosstown way, and these were the same buildings that you'd seen then, you thought, the same trees, and even the people in the streets, twelve years older now, walking, watching, stopping to let you pass, even the people might've been the same.

At Bayside Cemetery, the procession drew up near a new mausoleum, a small replica of the Temple of old, built, as was said, without the sound of axe or hammer. Above the iron portal, the name NEVINS had been graven in the gray granite frieze, and after a saying of the Kaddish, the first body was consigned to its vaults, nor when the iron doors closed was the sound of iron heard.

The day was not yet over. Along a gravel path, it was only a short distance to a gate leading to the adjoining cemetery—Acacia—and there again you stood beside your mother's grave. Back through twelve years, you remembered the sham grass on the waiting fill, you remembered the coffin going down, the deep-toned pebbles falling on the lid, and you saw yourself reaching for a shovel and your father holding your arm, and he said . . . what did he say? You watched him now as he took up two little stones and placed them on the lintel of your mother's monument, and though six years married to another woman, he wept for this one.

Then the day was over.

§

As one of your grandpa's legatees, you were notified some days later that his Will would be read at a time and place named, and at that time, along with all the others, you were at that place. Your Uncle Harry's words (*You'll never have to worry*) had never been far from the front of your mind, nor had

254

they retired when you tried to ignore them. They were there or thereabouts for days, and always you thought of numbers! numbers! and always you were ashamed.

Members of the Nevins family filled the room, and as you glanced about, you wondered who among them was nobler than you. Apart from your grandma, who would've come merely to honor a dead peddler from Suwalki *guberniya*? Which of these portioners would be here if his portion were small, which knowing it was nothing at all? Who was recalling some rare endearment, a tear seen on the stone-grim face? Who was pure, who free of numbers, who sat and thought and grieved? But whatever the meanness around you, still you knew you were mean.

"If I may have your attention," a voice said, and eyes converged on your grandpa's lawyer, a man named J. Sidney Bernstein. On the desk before him lay a legal document in a blue cover, and adjusting his pince-nez, he began to read. " 'I, Abraham Nevins, being of sound mind and disposing memory, do hereby make and declare this to be. . . .' "

After a paragraph or two, you found that the words were merging into a single unpunctuated sound. In your mind, you strayed, and for no reason that you knew of, you summoned up the face of your Uncle Romie, still anguished, as on the day he'd been left behind, and then once more you heard your grandpa's language from the grave.

" '. . . to my unfortunate son Jerome, now confined in an institution at Napanoch, N.Y., I give, devise, and bequeath the sum of Ten Thousand ($10,000) Dollars, the said sum nevertheless to be held in trust for him during the course of his lifetime, after which it shall be equally divided among. . . .' "

And then you drifted off again to the number (*You'll never have to worry*) that soon would be your own.

" '. . . to my dear grandchild, Julian Lawrence Shapiro, only son of my beloved daughter, Harriet Esther, I give, devise, and bequeath the sum of Ten Thousand ($10,000) Dollars, the said sum nevertheless to be held in trust for him during the course of his lifetime. . . .' "

Your Uncle Harry poked your back with a finger and leaned forward to whisper, "What did I tell you?" so that all in the room could hear.

" '. . . and to my dear son David, I give, devise, and bequeath the sum of Fifteen Thousand ($15,000) Dollars, the said sum nevertheless to be held in trust for him during the course of his lifetime, after which it shall be divided equally among the several charities and institutions named in Paragraph 12 hereof. . . .' "

You turned to look at your Uncle Dave, but he had turned to look at your Uncle Harry.

" '. . . the Trustees, who may serve without bond, shall be J. Sidney Bernstein, my attorney, Harry W. Perlman, my son-in-law, and Edith Cohen, the younger of my living daughters. They shall invest the trust fund in securities of the United States government, and they shall pay the income derived therefrom to the said David Nevins in equal quarterly instalments. . . .' "

When the reading ended, lawyer J. Sidney Bernstein removed his pince-nez to glance at the heirs of Abraham Nevins, deceased, and then he clamped them back on the bridge of his nose. In that moment, no one spoke but your Uncle Dave.

He said, "God damn it!" and left the room. When you joined him, he said, "We're going downtown to see your father."

During the subway ride from Columbus Circle to City Hall, he sat staring at the ads that curved above the windows, at the numerals and names of the stations, at people across the aisle, at no one or nothing at all. Nor did he speak again except in mouthings that only he could hear, and later, even in your father's presence, his anger almost strangled speech.

"Well," your father said, "you look like a pair of disappointed heirs."
"That no-good crook!" your uncle said. "He's robbed me again!"
"Who has robbed you?"
"Harry Perlman, my son-of-a-bitch of a brother-in-law!"
"Calm down, Dave," your father said. "How has Harry robbed you?"
"He got my father to leave me money I can never touch. All I get is an income from a trust-fund — and, Jesus Christ, Harry's one of the Trustees!"
"It's your father's Will, not Harry's. And if these things are provided for, they're your father's intention."
"Julian is treated in the same way, and so is my poor brother Romie. Only us three, curse it! as if only we were half-wits. That couldn't've been my father's doing. He was worked on by Harry."
"Romie can't look out for himself," your father said, "and it was proper to establish a fund for him. As to Julian, the bequest was put out of his reach to keep it out of *my* reach — as if I'd take my own kid's money."
"All right," your uncle said, "that explains Romie and Julian. How do you explain what was done to me?"
"Your father was a strange man, Dave."
"This was Harry's doing," your uncle said, "and I'm going to *un*do it."
"Bernstein is no fool. He knows how to draw a Will."
"I'll get the Court to throw it out."
"There are only two grounds for overturning a Will in this state," your father said. "Undue influence is one, and a testator's mental incapacity is the other. I don't think you have a chance of proving either."
You spoke for the first time since the conference began. "The day grandpa died," you said, "Uncle Harry said I'd never have to worry about money

256

again. Those were his words: *You'll never have to worry about money again.* At 4%, the income on $10,000 comes to about $8 a week. That's not exactly freedom from worry."

"I got the income from $15,000," your uncle said. "That's $12 a week. A cholera on that Harry! I've despised him from the day Rae first brought him home."

"If you contest the will," your father said, "you'll break up the family, win or lose."

"It was broken up when my father left your office and fell into Harry's hands," your uncle said, and as though it were a playing-card, he snapped down a copy of the Will on your father's desk. "Look at that piece of foolishness! Me and Julian in the same class as Romie!"

Your father laughed, saying, "Unfair to you, maybe, but I'm not so sure of Julian."

"I want you to represent me, Phil," your uncle said. "I'm going to sue."

"I can't do it," your father said. "My son would be involved, and I won't go chasing money for him. I won't let him chase it, either."

"Uncle Harry lied to me," you said. "He told me I'd never. . . ."

But your father was looking at you—examining you, it seemed—and then he rose and quit the room.

§

You parted with your Uncle Dave at the building entrance after agreeing to meet him in the evening at the home of Harry Perlman. Then, crossing Chambers Street to the park, you wandered off alone without direction other than the one you took by chance. It led you into Nassau Street past your father's one-time quarters, the Temple Court. Once you'd gone by, you could not have said whether you'd been aware of breathing its blended breath, of the small dim doorway, of Rocco at the cable of his elevator, of the pads he wore to shield his palms. You knew of nothing but your Uncle Harry's lie: *You'll never have to. . . .*

From the moment he'd mentioned money, money had been in your mind. For twenty-two years, you hadn't thought of it at all—you'd sought it in your pocket or reached out your hand, and there it was, the needful. It came to you almost as though you'd willed it to come, but you'd never known from where. But now the foreign body was in you, the sliver, the piece of shrapnel, and in the course of but a week, a cyst had formed around it, and there it lay in its morbid fluid, there it had come to stay.

You walked the downtown streets until the rush hour was over, and then it was quiet in Trinity Place, in Whitehall, Pearl, and William, and there were few lights in sheer walls of darkness. *You'll never,* you thought, and you remembered the voice, the masticated cigar, the juice-brown mouth. You boarded a Broadway car and rode uptown to the Carlton Terrace, where the Perlman family lived. Your Uncle Dave was waiting for you on the sidewalk.

"Where the hell have you been?" he said.

"Walking around," you said. "Battery Park. Wall Street."

"A stupid place to walk — Wall Street. One of these days, they'll be blowing up Morgan's again."

In the Perlman suite, in addition to your Uncle Harry and your Aunt Rae, you found her sister Edith and J. Sidney Bernstein. Without prelude, your Uncle Dave said, "We think the Will is unfair."

"In what respect, Dave?" the lawyer said.

"You ought to know. You drew it up."

"I did as I was directed to do by your father. The language, of course, is mine, but the dispositions are his, every one of them."

"I don't believe it," your Uncle Dave said.

"What are you suggesting?" the lawyer said.

"That someone poisoned my father's mind against me."

"Someone in this room?"

"Yes," your Uncle Dave said, "and the someone is Harry W. Perlman!"

"That's a terrible thing to say!" your Aunt Rae said. "Your own brother-in-law!"

"My own brother-in-law is a dirty crook," your Uncle Dave said. "He's been a crook all his life, and you know it as well as I do. He stole from our sister Hattie when she was dying, he stole from me when we were in business together, and now he's stealing again with this Will. He's a cheap no-good thief, Rae, and in the Soviet Union, they'd shoot him. Here, he turns up as a Trustee under my father's Will. Trustee! Why, I wouldn't trust him with a hatful of piss! He'd swipe the piss and wear the hat."

"I never took a thing from a living soul, so help me God!" your Uncle Harry said. "You got no right to talk to me like that right in my own home."

"Step out in the hall, then," your Uncle Dave said, "and I'll tell it to you there."

"This must stop!" lawyer Bernstein said. "It's disgraceful!"

"I'm with Uncle Dave in this," you said. "He's being cheated, and so am I."

Your Uncle Harry began to speak, but lawyer Bernstein cut in, saying, "Julian, as a law student, you surely must know the effect of your words. In charging Mr. Perlman with the use of undue influence on your grandfather, you're accusing him of fraud in fact and fraud in law. That's a slanderous impeachment, and it can have serious consequences for you."

Your Uncle Harry could not be stayed any longer, and he said, "If you contest the Will, you little white-headed rat, I'm going to report you to the

Bar Assoshiation. I'll tell them you was in jail in Florida, and you know when they'll let you be a lawyer? Never!"

Your Uncle Dave went to the door, and you followed him. Turning there, he stunned you by taking a small nickel-plated revolver from his pocket and dangling it from its trigger-guard. "Harry, you bastard," he said, "I want Five Thousand dollars in cash by ten o'clock tomorrow morning. If it isn't at Bernstein's office by then, I'll hunt you down and blow your brains out."

Outside in the street again, you said, "Will you really do that?"

And he said, "Yes," and he walked away.

At lawyer Bernstein's office the next day, the money was handed over to him as demanded, and within a week, he'd left the country. It was more than two years before he was heard from. Your grandma telephoned to say that she'd had a postcard from *Dovid*. On it, there was a picture of palm trees and waves; the place was *Hallelujah*, she said.

SCENE 150

IGNORANCE I (1926)

I'm writing a book, Nat Weinstein had said, and ever since, through the course of more than a year, the words had been in suspension near the surface of your mind. As you began the final pair of semesters at Fordham, you were aware of a falling off in interest, of a concern beyond the classroom that drew you away from the law. *I'm writing a book,* he'd said, and in time you knew that the words would never settle, that some day they'd even rise. From then on, you merely coasted at school, and endlessly you and your friend would walk up and down and crisscross the town while he held forth on things of a strange and lustrous dominion.

He knew so much more than you did that you'd wonder why he thought you worth his idle hours. You'd try to believe that he mistook your silence for the tacit *of course* of an equal, but not even in the dark streets could you hide for long from your own darkness. You were vastly uninformed, and you could only marvel at having fallen so far behind: how and when and where had you lost so much ground? You'd think back to the Harlem days, to you at play with marbles, buttons, gyroscopes, to him watching for a while and walking away. To what other world?—but someone would cry *Dubbs! Evries! Knucks down tight!* and he'd be gone from sight.

And now he was back from that world with its tales and names, and it was a glowing place he told of, a luminous people, and you heard the hard histories of gods and giants, and you listened as once before, when your mother read of the tricks of Loki and the thunder made by Thor. Full of the miraculous, he came back from his travels as his own Apollonius of Tyana may have come from Nineveh and India, and up through him welled the fountain you'd known in youth, and when you parted on any evening, you'd take away quotations, movements, jokes, sayings, stories, travails, bits of bitter lives. They filled your head, that store he'd brought from who knows where, and drowned all thought of law.

— Marius the Epicurean and the need to *burn with a hard, gem-like flame*

— the *eaux-fortes* of Meryon, who'd made all Paris in light and shade, built it with his burin, *became* Paris!

— and he said, "I could improve Dostoevsky with a pair of shears"

— Baudelaire (was it Baudelaire?), when a legless beggar pleaded for a coin, said, "I am not poor enough to give alms," and then he kicked the beggar in the face

— and he said, "I read Tolstoy through and through by the time I was nine"

— *Whitely, while benzine/ Rinsings from the moon/ Dissolve all but the windows of the mills*

— names that seemed to run together, streams of *puvisdechavannesjuleslaforgueguillaumeapollinairegeorgegroszmanrayalfredjarrywyndhamezra*

— Jarry used to walk around Paris at night with a carbine on his shoulder, and once, when someone asked him for a light, he pulled the trigger and said, "Voila!"

— *Madama Sosostris, famous clairvoyante,/ Had a bad cold, nevertheless/ Is known to be the wisest woman in Europe,/ With a wicked pack of cards. Here, said she,/ Is your card, the drowned Phoenician Sailor?*

— and he said, "There's a fellow, Hemingway, from out west, Chicago, I think, who writes good stories in lean English"

— Max Beerbohm is deft. He wrote to Theodore Watts-Dunton, Swinburne's lover, and he said, "Theodore, Watts-Dunton?"

— deft, lean — Weinstein words

— the terrible dyings in the arts — de Maupassant's, Modigliani's, and above all Meryon's. He suffered from lypothymia, a profound depression accompanied by hallucinations, in which he supposed himself to be Christ detained by the Pharisees, and therefore he would not eat because the food belonged to the disinherited, and fasting thus, he died in a madhouse at Charenton — and he *Paris!*

— and he said, "A traveller, while visiting Tyana, saw a snake enter the lower part of a man's body. Pardon me, my good man, he said, but a snake has just entered your. . . . Yes, was the rejoinder, he lives there"

SCENE 151

IGNORANCE II (1926)

You treasured that yarn about Baudelaire (or was it Huysmans?) almost as a possession — a medal, a coin, a keepsake — and you'd take it out and toy with it, turn it, toss it, spin it, and at times you'd let it lie and watch it shine. It didn't occur to you that the tale might be an old one and that, when told by your friend, it was well-worn and close to the end of its life, nor being so admiring, did you concern yourself with paradox beyond the clever play on *poor.* You cherished the story, reshaped it, rubbed it up, enriched it, all against the time, the time, the precise and perfect time! And at last it came — at a dinner-party, was it, over a game of cards, in a foyer between the acts? — and you said

"The Boulevard Raspail, did you say?" and you smiled in reminiscence, as if you'd been there with Baudelaire (Mallarmé?). "That puts me in mind of the time Baudelaire was out for a walk. When he reached a certain crossing, he was accosted by a beggar, who held up a cup for a coin. Baudelaire looked down at the man, sitting legless on a little wheeled platform, and he said 'I am not poor enough to give alms!' And with that, he kicked the beggar in the face."

There was a moment of silence, you remember, the silence of savoring, you thought, and then someone spoke quite mildly, saying, "I can understand the remark, Julian, but please explain the kick in the face."

You never told the story again. But was it Rimbaud? Verlaine. . . ?

SCENE 152

IGNORANCE III (1926-27)

Seen from the bay window of Brounoff's parlor, the park seemed to be his private spread of trees and grass. Six flights up from the street, you were on a high verandah looking out across his lawn, a great green rectangle of eight hundred and forty acres: only he could embrace it, you thought; it belonged to this three-faced bay alone. He'd be seated at the piano behind you, gifted with the ability to sight-read a score, and down upon you a dazzle of music would pour, a firework shower, and there you'd stand in the sparks of a scherzo, a polonaise, a sarabande.

To you, notation was a language in cipher. The clefs, the slurs, the swells and ligatures, the enharmonic ties—all were cryptic signs you never learned to read or even understand. What you saw on a page of music was a set of perches for an infinitude of birds, birds with plain or flourished tails, semibreves of birds, minims, crotchets, quavers, and when, as now, someone made them sing, you could only in amazement think they might take wing and fly.

"When I look at those staves," you'd say, "I don't see notes. I see birds on strings of wire."

And he'd play a bar or two of whatever lay before him, and he'd say, "What happens when you hear them?"

"There's no meaning in vibration."

Hardly glancing at the keys, he'd strike several of them simultaneously. "That was a chord," he'd say, "a harmonious blend of tones—an accord, really. What happened when you heard it?"

"I enjoyed the sound—but pleasure isn't thought."

"Suppose I'd kicked a garbage-can cover. Would you still say sound is only sound?"

And you'd say, "Pain has no meaning, either."

He struck a single note, saying, "That's only a sound—a flat, as it happens. It has no power to convey a substantive or even an attribute—red, heavy, soft, norwegian. But as one of many sounds in an arrangement, it can mean a great deal. Not in what it conveys, but in what it evokes. If it evokes nothing, you're dead to music."

Looking past him, you saw a photograph of his father, Platon the Moldavian, his image, as his living self had done, glaring out at his countless enemies. "Not dead," you'd say. "Just deep in sleep."

He traced your gaze to the enlargement on the wall, and he'd say, "Have you read much of Dostoevsky?"

"None," you'd say. "But I know someone who claims he can improve him with a pair of scissors. Said he'd cut out every other page."

"That'd be like improving a stairway by cutting out every other step. Did he impress you with that Davy Crockett bullshit?"

"Everything impresses me these days," you'd say. "He woke me up, this guy did, but I feel like another Rip. Twelve years in Dreamland, and I don't know where to go — the world got away from me. I read and read, and I never catch up."

And he'd say, "What do you read?"

"Whatever I happen to hear of — it's all new. I remember someobdy who told me he was reading the Encyclopedia — entry after entry, just reading what he came to. Christ, here I am, doing the same with books!"

"What books?"

"One day it's *Pierre or The Ambiguities,* and the next it's *Zuleika Dobson.*"

"On whose advice — this guy with the scissors?"

"He doesn't advise," you'd say. "He just talks — sometimes, I think, to an equal, but more often to an empty room."

"What else beside Melville and Beerbohm?"

"He gave me a copy of *Biographia Literaria.* He inscribed it too — something about from one horse's ass to another. And he speaks of somebody who writes for NANA, man name of Hemingway. I haven't got around to him yet, but this guy says his writing is lean. That's a favorite word of his — lean. Another is deft. And there's a poet he likes, Hart Crane, but I can hardly understand him, and e.e. cummings with his punctuation."

"And this friend of yours," he'd say. "He just lets you stab away?"

"I'm twelve years back," you'd say. "He can only holler over his shoulder."

"But, damn it, why does he holler Samuel Taylor Coleridge? What the hell are you going to get out of Coleridge?"

"He hollers other things — Walter Pater, Rainer Maria Rilke, Ford Madox Ford. And as they go by, I grab what I can."

He'd turn back to the piano, and after making two tones tremble, he'd sweep a glissando from the keyboard into space. "Read Dostoevsky," he'd say, and he went on, and because you were looking again at his father's face, you thought for a moment that the words applied to him. "He belonged to a discussion group. It was harmless enough, but they were all arrested and condemned to death. When their time came, they were taken out to be shot in Semyonovsky Square. There they were tied three to a stake, and just as they were saying farewell to each other, the soldiers drew off, and the prisoners were told that their lives had been spared by the Czar. One man went mad on the spot. The rest were sent to Siberia, among them Dostoevsky. . . ."

§

Years later, you'd write a passage for the character Julie Pollard:*

—Love everybody, this Russian man says, but he can't tell me nothing about love. I'm black, and I know what loving is because I know what hating is. When a black loves you, he does it with his whole body, but when a white loves you, he does it with talk, sweet-sweet. We've had talk for three hundred years, sweet-sweet, but your people are still on the toilets, and mine're still swabbing 'em out. That ain't going to last for another three hundred years, but when it's changed, it won't be changed by Jesus or this Russian saying sweet-sweet. . . .

§

"Read Dostoevsky," the son of Platon said.

THE COLOR OF THE AIR, XIV

CRAZY HORSE—1876
HOKA HEY!

This is a good day to die!
—Crazy Horse

There were soldiers along the ridge, and there were soldiers in the wood and on the bluff and backed against the stream, and we killed them in all those places, though they fought bravely and lived till Death came to take the dead away, late in the afternoon. Beside the Little Big Horn, much fine killing was done that day, wherefore truly had Curly spoken when he called it a good day for dying: when whites died, it was always a good day. But what we did not know then, savoring their blood and wearing their hair, was that we too were now dead, not some of us only but all, those of us still under horses in the high grass and those singing in stolen hats and the tops we cut from the soldiers' boots—all. It was a good day to die, Curly said, and thereafter we never lived again. It was the end of living for us, that victory in the hills where the Tongue River rose, and the Rosebud ran.

---

* In *A Man Without Shoes,* Plantin Press, 1951.

SCENE 153

WALKS IN THE DARK (1926-27)

She lived in a converted brownstone residence on Murray Hill, and you were never nearer to her room than the entry hall at ground-level. It was a white area that held a small marble-topped table on which rows of letters lay, and a flight of stairs ascending to landings out of sight. There were no chairs, or none you remember using, and you'd stand waiting at the newel for the sound of descending feet, and she'd always step precisely, as if being graded for poise and grace. And when she joined you, you'd go into a lamp-lit street that led, since you were going nowhere, only to other lamp-lit streets, and you'd walk, talking and not talking, toward Grand Central or Gramercy Square.

Seldom were you free of the notion that someone else was there—and that he went not to either side of the pair you made, but rather in between. His presence was so real at times that he'd seem to block your view, and you'd think that you and he were alone, that she had gone away.

And just then she'd say, "All right, he gave you my number. What I want to know is why you called it. What did you have in mind?"

"That's a hard one to answer," you'd say.

"Try. Words come easy to you. You pitied me, you could say."

"It wouldn't be true."

"You were curious, then. You wanted to see what kind of girl could be given away."

"I liked you when he brought you to my room. I didn't expect to see you again, but I wanted to—and then, hell, I had your number in my hand."

"You could've been above such things. You could've said you didn't want any discards."

"Are you a discard?"

"You have no right to ask questions."

"Why not?" you'd say. "If you can ask why I called, I can ask why you answered. You want to know why *I'm* here. Why are *you*?"

"Why did you make yourself a party to a disaster? Why didn't you just stand around and watch? Or, better still, why didn't you walk away?"

"I couldn't." He was there again, you'd think, El Superhombre, a bulk so huge that he'd try to shrink it—he'd bow, he'd defer, he'd cringe, but always he'd know he stood too high. "I hate to talk when he's around," you'd say.

"When who's around?"

"This eight-foot lout we bring along. How did he get so broad in the beam—at the pianoforte?"

"He does play," she'd say.

"I knew it—and I'll bet he improvises too. Sits in the glow of a fringed lamp, bites his lower lip to hide his anguish, milks dem mournful ivories—and, bango, down comes baby, and also baby's drawers."

"He plays," she'd say, "and he plays well."

"I'm sick of him. I wish I'd never met him."

"But, Julian dear, he brought us together."

"And then never went away!" you'd say. "He's here right now!"

"Only in your mind."

"Not in yours?"

"You're the one who brings him up."

"It bothers me that you don't. It's unnatural. A few weeks ago, you were his girl. Now you're mine. And, God damn it, if I gave you to someone else, I think you'd just go walking with him instead of me! Doesn't it mean anything that you were a gift?"

"What would change if I screamed?" she'd say.

SCENE 154

SUNSETS, DOORYARDS, SPRINKLED STREETS (1926-27)

Seen from this future, that past belongs to someone else—it isn't yours, you tell yourself, it isn't yours at all. How can that be you there on the sprayed pavement, talking rant as you stalk along Fourth Avenue. The emphases, the signs of hand and arm, the words you cannot hear—they're those of some other in that other age, a stranger's rage in Madison Square. But he stops, that not-you he (where? near the obelisk to General Worth, the Farragut bronze, the statue of Seward, Arthur, Roscoe Conkling?), he stops, and you draw near. Ah, God, you think, the frenzy's mine, the raver I!

You're with that pretty girl you'd been given, you were facing her on some corner, some pathway, some worn patch of grass, and you're filling the night air with a gas of grammar that tells her—what? what? What're you trying to say, what attitude are you maintaining, what mood or view would you convey? Or will your harangue, if parsed, fall to pieces, become what you fear from far in the future, from here—mere noise in a bygone winter evening?

—What you could not have been telling her, because you did not know it, was that a pair of Boston ginnies were only eight months away from the Chair. They were still unfamiliar to you (student of the law! aspirant to the Bar!), you'd still not seen their dago faces, still not read of their six years within sight of Bunker Hill, nor had your mentor friends (so knowing of *Pointillisme,* of plain song, of the deft and the lean and Apeneck Sweeney) ever made mention of their names. You were still asleep, but, come a distant day, you'd wake *After the sunsets and the dooryards and the sprinkled streets/ After the novels, after the teacups, after the skirts that trail along the floor*—wake and write of their last night living.

SCENE 155

FINAL YEAR ON THE 28th FLOOR (1926-27)

You took ten courses in those last two terms, from Conflict of Laws through Equity and Trusts to Quasi-Contracts. In both the fall and spring semesters, classes were held for twelve hours a week, and on each of five evenings, you'd present yourself to this or that instructor, two of them Jesuit priests, and there among several dozen students, you'd display the state of your erudition. When called on now, though still aware of one particular presence, you no longer thought of her as the only ear you cared to reach. Two years of alienation had weakened ardor, and it was weakened further by another girl.

Between classes, you'd go out for a smoke, and sometimes in the corridor, you'd encounter the man of *titles,* and you'd hear of one by Anatole France and another by Santayana. And then there'd be a silence, and he'd end it by saying *Is she not what I said she'd be?* but you'd let the question drift, ravel with the smoke: there was no answer. Were there questions of your own, though, that you very nearly asked?

—Were you—how shall I put it?—*intimate,* and if so, for how long a period? how often? and where?
—Was she, well, *pure,* when you first—I'm sure you take my meaning.
—Was the union meant to endure, or might either state secede at will?
—If the former, why did you break away?
—If the former, was it the Jew-and-gentile story again, did papa put his foot down and mama tear her hair?
—If the former, did they call in the Rabbi to menace you with prayer?
—If the former, were they ready to mourn you as dead?

—If the former, did they break you in the end, make you give your schicksa screw the gate?

—And lastly, do you still fuck her on the q.t., giving me no place to go?

The bell rang, and another class began.

SCENE 156

OF THINGS PAST (1926-27)

—Say not that you had a little sister named L. G., and she had no breasts. Say, rather, that they were small, say enough to fill your hands, though not enough to spill—no twin roes, say, but hardly no rounds at all.

—And say that you recall with surprise (why surprise?) that she wore no perfume. Say there came with her no bouquet of lavender, patchouli, bergamot, but only such flavor as she gave the air.

—And say that she'd listen, *listen!* as if it were some rite to be performed in silence while you were spouting words. Say how rarely you could make her speak, take the lead, agree or disagree, and when she did, how little she seemed to care.

—Say how unimpressed she was by achievement, how unmoved by the aim, the deed, the acclaim. Say, as she might've said, that one couldn't *become,* one could only *be.* But say all the same that you kept on striking poses and endlessly shot the bull.

—Say that she was tall, almost eye-to-eye with you, that she could walk miles without tiring, that she liked the night-hours, that at five in the morning you might buy milk off a Borden wagon and sit swigging on a stoop.

—Say that sometimes then, in sudden warmth, she'd lean against you, and you'd think she meant to speak.

—Say her legs were long, say her hands were made for a display of hands, say her breasts were small . . . but you've said those things.

SCENE 157

AN HOUR WITH SILVER PHIL (1927)

Your father's offices were on the Worth Street side of the Emigrant Bank Building. Facing the north, they drew sunlight only at meridian and almost none through the winter season. It was winter now, and sitting near him at his desk, you watched a snowfall through the windows, a slow sedimentation, and though you couldn't see the pavement below, you thought of it as a deep where wheeled creatures crawled through silt. And you thought of classes (Mortgages? Suretyship?), and you thought beyond them to the later evening, when you'd go uptown and find her waiting in your hotel room. Her key would be lying on a table, as if good for one use only without renewal. And you'd say. . . .

Your father took a card from the corner pocket of his blotter and tossed it across the desk. It landed wrong-way-to, but being a back-reader by habit, you read it as it lay: it was the law-school report on your mid-year examinations.

"What happened to you, kid?" your father said, "An A in Constitutional Law. An A+ in Partnership. My associates are laudatory. So am I."

"I picked up a lot in the office," you said. "After all, I've been hanging around for fifteen years."

"I don't throw praise about. When you've earned it, take it."

"The proud shall stumble. Jeremiah."

"An A-student and a reader of the Bible," he said. "You used to be a jailbird and a cheat. You must've seen the error of your ways."

"Some of the error of some of the ways," you said. "For instance, I'm seeing a Christian girl."

"What does seeing mean?"

"Spending time with her."

"Since when?"

"Last fall."

He indicated the card on the desk. "She must be good medicine," he said. "You don't object to her being Christian, then?"

"I do, but it isn't life or death. How serious is the attachment?"

"I don't know," you said, "but it *is* an attachment."

"If she didn't mean something to you, you'd not have mentioned her."

"That's true, but you said serious."

"If a girl is on your mind, it's serious."

"Well," you said, "she's on my mind."

"There are people in our family who'd say *Kaddish* if a son brought home a gentile. He'd be dead."

"Would you feel that way?"

"To me, kid," he said, "you'll only be dead when you die."

"Still, the objection is there."

"Gentiles always have a feeling against Jews."

"Always?" you said. "All gentiles?"

"Nearly always," he said, "and nearly all."

When you let yourself into your room later in the evening, there was your key on the table, and there was she, reading a book in a chair. You thought of asking her how she felt about Jews, but you changed your mind and confined yourself to other things.

SCENE 158

ON A BENCH IN WASHINGTON SQUARE (1927)

At another time, though, you said, "How *do* you feel about the Jews?"

She glanced at you, saying, "That's a peculiar emphasis."

"Where?"

"On the word *do*. As if you'd asked the question before."

"I did—in my mind." It was an early-spring evening, and on leaving the hotel, you'd walked down the Avenue to Waverly Place and found yourselves a seat near the Arch. "This used to be a burialground—Potter's Field. We're sitting on the bones of paupers, lunatics, criminals, unknowns."

"Why do you want to know how I feel about the Jews?" she said.

"My father thinks all gentiles are biased. Nearly all."

"Did the subject come up recently?"

"I told him I was knocking around with a Christian girl."

"And he disapproved."

"Moderately," you said. "He doesn't like me to go where I'm not wanted."

"And you expect me to tell you you're wanted?" she said. "After telling me I'm *not*?"

Looking off across the park at lighted windows that seemed to be hung in the bare dark trees, you said, "My father and I took a motor-trip once, and toward the end of a day, we found we were nearing Richfield Springs, a town on the far side of the Catskills. The gentile side, my father called it, and he said we were going to have trouble finding a room for the night — they were rough on Jews at the Springs. He made me drive around till we came to the shop of a ladies' tailor — Blum, the man's name was. My father sent me in, and, sure enough, he steered us to a place that took us in. Jews help Jews."

"You didn't have to announce what you were," she said. "You could've gone where you pleased and kept it to yourselves."

"Not if you looked Jewish."

"You don't look Jewish."

"My father does," you said. In one of the houses you were facing, a window went black — had someone retired, left the room, blown out the gas? "You had the opposite experience. You were on the Jewish side of the Catskills, and they wouldn't rent you a room."

"You're prying again, Julian!" she said. "I told you to stay out of my affairs!"

"Do you have many?"

She rose and started for a bus parked near the south side of the Square. "Stay where you are," she said. "I've got a dime in my garter."

You overtook her, saying, "How *do* you feel about the Jews?"

"I know how I feel about this one — furious!"

"How about that other one — your friend out of Ring Lardner? Garnett Whaledriver."

"Julian," she said, "you've got to stop this!"

"He got rid of you, and you're sore at me because I know why. Be sore at *him*."

"You simply don't know what you're talking about. You're a fool."

"His family wouldn't have you, and being a dutiful son, he stepped on your face. If you don't believe it, ask him. He's right here between us, the lumbering bastard!"

She climbed aboard the bus, and you followed. A block beyond the hotel, you pulled the cord and said, "Come back to the room," but she shook her head, and you watched her ride away.

An hour later, though, there was a knock on your door, and when you opened it, there she was, and she said, "Do you still want to know how I feel about the Jews?"

SCENE 159

THE FINE ARTS (1927)

Seen from a distance, the year loses definition, merges with other years, and you can't say now where it begins and ends, that single cycle around the sun. What you recall may have befallen earlier, later, or then; it all comes up from time entwined, and you catch it only in segments, in parts of faces, in places that emerge and disappear, and sound too seems always to be going, always growing weaker, like the whistle of a passing train. You try to detain melodies, colors, rhythms, to fix names, moods, hours of the day or night, but they can't be held, they will not stay . . . the Pastoral, the Jupiter, the Ring, rather the ice, the sepia prints of Atget, o day of dappled seaborne clouds, the birds bleed yet in Courbet, and let the liquid siftings fall, *les Cinq, les Six, les Fauves,* to stain the stiff dishonoured shroud. . . .

You remember a concert or recital at the Hall, but not who played or what you heard, and you remember her hands lying in her black lap, almost never moving and never tapping time, and you remember the crowd coming out and someone calling *We'll be at Child's,* and across to Fifth the two of you went—and you remember that at the door of the white restaurant, she balked and began to walk away.

"I just can't," she said.

"No harm done," you said. "But why?"

"I don't like them. I don't like those people."

At Fifty-sixth, she made you bear toward Madison, as though Fifth were too bright for her, too full of sound and motion, and for a way you went without speaking, respectful of the stiller streets. And then you said, "Some of them are my good friends. One in particular—George."

"You've got too much regard for him. When you talk, you're sometimes wild and often childish, but I'd sooner listen to you. I don't want what someone taught him."

You passed the Rectory at the rear of St. Patrick's, and after a block or two of silence, you reached the entry of the Ritz, where a few cabs dozed near the lighted overhang.

"Wild and childish," you said.

And when you were crossing Forty-second, she said, "I'm thinking of going back to New England."

SCENE 160

ROOM 1021 (1927)

You were sitting in the dark.

"I'm sure you'll miss me," she said. "After all, we've been—how did you put it? Knocking about for six months."

Your chairs were turned to face the open window, and against the low illumination in the court, you watched smoke draw away on a slow drift of air. "I'll miss you," you said.

"Of course. Without me, the room won't seem the same. When you come in, you'll stop in the entry, as if you'd opened the wrong door. By the way, here's your key."

"The other night, you didn't like my friends. Tonight, you don't like me."

"Oh, I like you, Jule—I like you very much. I always have regard for the man I knock around with."

"It was just a phrase," you said. "Don't tell me you're leaving New York on account of a phrase."

Through the air-shaft came sounds made in other rooms—escapes of laughter, as from a valve; music sung and music played; encounters of metal, china, glass.

"That's not the reason," she said.

"What is—our mutual friend, our guest? There are three of us in this room, you know."

"Well, when I leave, there'll only be two."

"Take him along. I can't stand the sight of him."

"You want to know why I'm leaving New York?" she said. "You! You're the reason! You can't forget the way we met."

"Can you?"

"Yes."

"I don't believe you," you said. "You're running from him."

"How asinine! If that's what I'm doing, why didn't I do it long ago?"

"You were hoping. Hoping he'd find out you were good for *him*."

In a room deep down the well, someone sang *Sing Hallelujah!* for the sixth or seventh time. "Where in New England?" you said.

"Boston, and then home to Concord."

"What'll you do there?"

"The same as here—work, knock around with the boys." And then, her tone changing, she said, "I'll miss you, Jule. I'm the one who'll be in the wrong room. Will you write? Will you ever come to see me?"

You said, "Yes."

And again you heard *Sing Hallelujah!*

SCENE 161

JEALOUSY IS CRUEL AS THE GRAVE (1927)

You were to see her after school hours on another evening, but when you returned to your room to change, you found a message under your door. *L. G. called at 7.35 p.m.*, it said. *Unable to keep appmnt. with you. Will call tomorr.* You stood there, looking in at the matched furniture, the lamp on the table and the lamp on the floor, the print of waves forever breaking on an unknown shore; you saw the meaningless pattern of the carpet, the standard color of the paint on the walls (bisque, was it called?); you saw the hotel's gray and gold stationery stacked in the escritoire, the *War and Peace* above it, the thirty-seven volumes of your mother's Shakespeare, or was it thirty-nine? What did *unable* mean? you wondered. Did it imply a lack of power, a weakness in herself, or had she encountered prevention of a kind, had force been used against her, or, God damn it! had she simply changed her mind?

You concluded (piss on it!) that there was no disability, that she was under no restraint, that she hadn't fallen down the stairs: she was seeing someone else. In that moment, Room 1021 seemed to lose in size, and you felt oppressed, as if dressed in clothes too small. You left the hotel and wandered away through the mews, the alleys, the one-block lanes of the Village. *Unable,* you thought on Grove and Greenwich and crooked 4th, *unable to keep appmnt.,* you thought on Minetta, McDougal, Washington Place—and then you walked with an aim, to the east and the north until you came to Murray Hill.

The house you wanted to watch was on 37th Street between Fourth and Lexington, and choosing a nearby entrance, you seated yourself on the doorstep in the shadows cast by the corner lamps. Few cars passed, and fewer people, and there were intermissions of stillness, of run-down sound and slow motion—and then, crossing one of the avenues, a low-slung two-seater appeared, a fast-looking machine stripped to its gun-metal self, a shell on wheels. It went by you and stopped before the house you'd been observing, and for a long time the driver and his passenger sat talking in the dark, but all you could hear was occasional laughter. At length, they kissed and parted, and the car snarled away, the driver waving to the girl and she waving back. Then she turned away from the curb and came straight up the street to you.

She stopped a step below you. "Did you think you were invisible?" she said.
"I guess I did."

274

"I will not be spied on! I will not bear it!"

You held up a slip of paper that you'd taken from your pocket. "*L. G. unable to keep appmnt.*, it says. but L. G. was lying to Jewboy Julian, wasn't she?"

"Oh, stop that Mr. Nobody stuff," she said. "I simply had to see that boy tonight, and you should've taken me at my word."

You shook the paper. "*Will call tomorr.*, it says. Would you have called tomorr.?"

"He's a boy I know from Concord. I've known him for a long time. He went to St. Paul's."

"Protestant Episcopal, no doubt."

"Where was he supposed to go, Jewboy Jule? To Hebrew school?"

"Why did you simply have to see this uncircumsized dog tonight?"

"Forget him," she said. "You've been hanging around here because you thought I was out with someone else."

"You're sharp, L. G."

"Suppose I had been. What would you have done?"

"Nothing," you said. "But I'd've known where I stood."

"You'll never know where you stand, Jule. There's something that stops you."

You lit a cigarette, and for a moment you made it glow and fade in the dark. "I wish someone would tell me what it is," you said.

"I don't know you well enough—but after six months, maybe that's revealing. We never seem to be looking at the same thing."

"We are. What you mean is that you see it as it is, and I as it ain't."

"We don't even think alike," she said. "When you think at all." She dwelt on the last, saying, "When you think at all."

"I'm trying to improve myself," you said. "I read good books, I listen to deep talk, and only last week, I stood through four hours of Tristan at the Met. Any day now, I'll be speaking of *titles*."

She walked off toward her house, and halfway there she turned to say across the distance, "Do you know what you've been doing all along?"

"No."

"You've been asking yourself whether I *am* good for you."

"Have I?" you said. "And how did I answer?"

"You didn't answer. You still don't know."

As she entered her doorway, you said, "Will you call me tomorr.," but she was gone.

SCENE 162

A WALK WITH THE ADVERSARY (1927)

Late in May, after one of your last few evenings at law school, you were heading for a street-car stop when he overtook you near the Park Place corner.

"If you're going uptown," he said, "we might walk for a way."

Nodding, you waited for him to fall in with you, and when he shortened stride to match your own, the two of you went in silence for several blocks, as though nothing safe could be found to say. At the Chambers Street crossing, you passed the premises of the New York *Sun* (*A. T. Stewart's used to be here,* your father had told you. *It was where Mrs. Lincoln bought her six hundred pairs of gloves*), and at Franklin, you reached the fourteen-story building of the one-time Central Bank.

"My father had offices here before I was born," you said. "Two letters to my mother were written from this address (*hattiedarlingIhaveonlyonethoughtandthatisofyou*). There's no telephone number on the letterheads. It simply says Telephone Connection."

"How do you happen to have the letters?" he said.

"I came across them in his desk."

"Why not your mother's desk?"

"She's dead," you said. "Died a dozen years ago."

"Then *he* must've saved them," he said. "That's a rare thing."

(*Harryhasjusthandedmeapieceofcandyandhesaysitwillsweetenthetoneofthisnotenothingbutmybeingwithyouwithyouinmyarms*) "Why do you call it rare?"

"Those letters must be twenty-five years old. People don't usually care that long."

From there, you thought, how far was it to the heart of the matter—how much was he still cared for? Side by side, you walked with him through the bright and dim spaces of Broadway, traversing the adjacent worlds of leather goods, textiles, notions, sweat-shop lofts. Ahead, you could see the Grace Church spire, and as you went toward it, you turned over questions that would never be answered because they'd never be asked. What you longed to know you'd never learn: you'd penetrate no privacy, decode no whispers, light no darkling ways. Did they meet still, you wondered, and, if so, what subjects did they treat and dispose of, where did they repair to, what did they do when there? Was all as before—and *what* was before?—or did they begin again, pretend each that the other was new, did she flee and he pursue, and how did things go when he caught her? Did she lie down to be undressed, did he feel for a breast and kiss it when found, did her thighs part of themselves or only for his hand? You tried to become a presence for *him,* as he'd been for you, but you'd never know whether he knew you were there.

When you reached the church, you paused to gaze at its white limestone base and its white marble spire — graceful Grace — and then you parted with your companion and went westward along Tenth.

He let you go a few steps before saying, "Good luck on the Finals." And you glanced back and said, "The same."

SCENE 163

THE BED IN ROOM 1021 (1927)

She came to the hotel one night when you and your classmate Herbert were reading for your examinations, then but a week away. You had six courses in review, two of them full-year studies, and on the desk, the tables, and part of the floor, there were stacks of place-marked casebooks and sheaves of classroom notes. Jackets off and shoes unlaced, the two of you had been all day at work when she fitted her key and opened the door.

Half-opened, you thought, for, having stopped short, she still stood half in the hall. She removed her hand from the giveaway key, not yet withdrawn from the slot, and then she quickly turned to leave. For some reason (what reason — to show Herb your *savoir-vivre?*), you pressed her to stay, and for a reason of her own that she alone knew, she agreed.

"Counsellors," she said on entering, "let justice be done though the heavens fall," and she seated herself in the lap of a chair. "I'll admire from here."

Resuming your cram, you and Herb took turns at putting queries and reciting to each other, at stating rules, doctrines, tendencies, at distinguishing the code from the common law. All the while, though, you were conscious of the girl in that chair behind you and conscious too of the word *admire. Admire,* you thought, and in the end it became so importunate that you had to acknowledge it to be as much a presence as the one in the chair. *Admire,* you thought, and you knew that your legal screeds and sermonets were all a performance for her approval. She was your audience, not your classmate Herb, and it was to her that you made your pleas and spoke your periods: you were trying to expunge from her mind that other, still between you though months had passed.

After several such posturings, your classmate said, "The next case will be tried in the bathroom." There, handing you a tome on Suretyship, he sat you on the downturned lid of the toilet, after which he stretched himself out in the bathtub, saying, "You may cross-examine me, Jules."

You were still aware of a figure in black, quiet hands, blonde hair, but for the better part of an hour, you confined yourself to sureties, guarantors, principal debtors, to privity of contract, to the ability of a feme covert to make a separate undertaking. Then the hands and the hair carried you away to where, in an armchair near the window. . . .

But she was no longer in the chair; she was outflung before it on the floor. Her hair, undone by the fall, made an eddy on the carpet, and her hands, ending in dark cuffs, lay as if detached. If she'd been dead to the world, she was alive to it now, but she said nothing when you carried her to the bed and tried to arrange her dress and hair.

"You'd better get a doctor," your classmate said.

A Dr. Brownson was on call to the hotel, and when he arrived, you could almost watch an inference form as he scanned the room — *two men and a girl and a bed, a bed and a girl and two men.* Barely heeding your account of how things stood, he ordered you and Herb into the corridor. After an interval of several moments, he admitted you again, but he showed no change of assumption. Indeed, he seemed more certain than ever of what two men had done to the girl on the bed.

"The young lady is in a state of extreme agitation," he said. "I've administered something that will make her calmer. When it takes effect, she ought to go home." On his way to the door, he took in the strewn books, the fans of notes. "Students?"

"Law school," you said. "Final exams."

"You'll be a credit to your profession," he said, and he left the room.

SCENE 164

WHEN SHALL WE THREE MEET AGAIN (1927)

At Grand Central Station, you stood with her on a platform near the cars of the Back Bay Express, a string of black Pullmans that would leave soon for Providence and Boston. There at the mouth of the tunnel, the light was dim, rather as if it were night instead of morning.

"When shall we three meet again?" you said.

And she said, "Two. Two, Jule."

People passed, baggage-trucks, trunks on dollies, slight commotions in the gloom, and you said, "Do you know why I've never asked you about him?"

"You knew I wouldn't answer."

"It goes beyond that: I wouldn't've believed what I might be told. Once I'd've believed anything, but before long, there was no such thing as truth. There was only what I imagined."

"Only what you wished for," she said. "That's why you say three when I say two. What're you afraid of, Jule? Why must someone else be here?"

Was she right, you wondered, did you require him, did you want him to be where he was, between you and her? "I'm a romantic," you said.

SCENE 165

A LETTER DATED JUNE 7, 1927

Julian, dear—

I wonder what you did after waving goodbye for the last time. As the train pulled out I buried my face in the flowers and didn't emerge until I heard a thundering and persistent voice repeating "Miss" in my ear and looked up to see the porter reaching for my bags. It was a glad awakening. Boston seemed so clean and quiet.

I immediately went up to my aunt's and after a wonderful dinner I felt I could even be sentimental so I listened to the Roxy Theatre program and thought of you until train time. From Boston to Concord I was too miserable to think at all.

I hope you didn't have a terrible time taking care of my books and I don't know what else. It was stupid of me to leave in such haste.

I was quite ill by the time I reached home but feel much improved since I've been with mother.

I don't know yet what my plans for the summer will be. I have so much to say but feel unable to write more.

Write to me as soon as you can. I am looking forward to your letters more than anything.

With love
L. G.

4 Glen St.
Concord N. H.

SCENE 166

MIDSUMMER NIGHT (1927)

With your friend and classmate Herb, you were on the subway, heading for his home in Bensonhurst. Forgotten now where you were coming from and forgotten too what you'd done there: up to that hour, the day is merely time lived and lost to mind. You spoke little to each other if you spoke at all, and gazing through the windows, you stared at the car's ghastly emanation in the glass, a transparency through which station after station passed—Myrtle, DeKalb, Pacific.

At 36th Street, a man rose and rushed out, realizing only when the doors had closed that he'd left his newspaper behind. As you reached for it, you saw him glare at you from the platform, and you lip-read his one-word comment as the train moved off. The paper was the early edition of the next day's *Tribune,* and idly you took in its banners, headings, and columns of print, all of them diffused by your inattention. You hardly knew why you were turning the pages, gray blurs of letters and numerals, and only now and then did some phrase rise to be seen and read: it was as if you sat too far away. You turned still another page, and there, above a great alphabetical spread of names you saw

BAR EXAMINATION RESULTS

The following have successfully completed their. . . .

and quickly your glance flowed across the sticks of type to the one that was headed by S, and then down it ran to *Shapiro, Julian L.* Below the O, alas, there was no *Ortman, Herbert S.*

You looked out at a station-sign — Fort Hamilton Parkway, you read — and then the blue and white enamel slid away on the black sky. In the car outside the car, you saw your friend riding half-asleep and nodding, and you wondered what you felt about the absence of his name — was it regret, surprise, nothing, a flash of pleasure? You jostled his arm and gave him the paper, but you looked away when he scanned the list that was headed by O.

"It isn't here!" he said. "I flunked!"

"Maybe there's some mistake," you said.

"I flunked!" he said. "Jesus Christ, six months to go before the next one! I'll forget what I know, and even that wasn't enough!" He flung the paper back at you. "God, what'm I going to do?"

As you gathered up the scattered pages, you saw a sub-heading that you'd failed to note before. *Manhattan,* it said, and you realized that there were separate lists for each of the five boroughs. You turned to the proper page, and without examining it, you handed the paper over to Herb, saying, "Pray hard and look under Brooklyn."

This time you watched him, and after a moment he smiled.

SCENE 167

AUGUST 22, 1927

You were in the company of some friends that night — George was one of them, and Pete, and Pep West, and Abe — and a time came, you seem to recall, when somebody began to toy with a box containing tubes that would convert electric waves to speech, and all but you listened, waiting for vibrations to reach the room by air. You sat at a window watching the Hudson fracture rods of light from the Jersey shore, and your mind was there, out beyond the glass, pondering, perhaps, the untranslated French in *Tristram Shandy,* or the edible aquarelles of Demuth, or the surging first line of a story: *None of them knew the color of the sky. . . .*

And then someone (Abe? was it) said, "Well, they burned 'em."

And it was August 23rd, and after seven years of dying, they were dead.

SCENE 168

"Burned who?" you said.

And George said, or Pep or Pete or Abe, "Are you serious, Julian?"

And you said, "Of course I'm serious. Burned who?"

"You're making a bad joke."

"You're the joker," you said. "I want to know who burned."

Abe, Pete, Pep, or George said, "Do these names mean anything to you—Nicola Sacco, Bartolomeo Vanzetti?"

"No," you said.

"You never heard of Sacco and Vanzetti?"

"Never."

"There are lawyers in your family," one of them said. "You yourself just finished law school, and you've taken and passed the bar. But when you hear the names Sacco and Vanzetti, they don't register, they belong to a couple of unknown wops, they signify nothing. Is that right?"

"Yes," you said. "That's right."

And then George (Pete? Pep? Abe?) said, "All I can say, Julian, is you're one ignorant son-of-a-bitch!"

SCENE 169

AUGUST 24, 1927

Dear Julian

I had forgotten today was my birthday until this evening when I received your wire. . . . I don't know whether I should congratulate you on your success in the bar exams—what do you think?

Ever
L.

282

SCENE 170

EVEN AT THIS LATE DAY (1927)

Well, they burned 'em, someone said.

The truth is, they burned 'em twice. It wasn't enough to strap them to a chair (headrest adjustable), to buckle salted electrodes around their calves and skulls, not enough to skewer them on bolts of lightning (2,000 volts), to blister their skin and dilate forever the pupils of their eyes, not enough to give them a fever of 128°, to tetanize their hearts and turn their blood from red to purple.

No, they had to be drawn through the streets of Boston, their hearses so rushed that mourners ran, they had to be sped to some crematorium out on the Worcester pike (or the Providence? was it, the Portland? the Concord?), and there they had to swap their oaken boxes for boxes of pine and then be shoved into an oven burning gas or coke and reduced to smoke and eight pounds of ash.

Aye, they were cooked a second time, after which they no longer had desquamated skin, livid blood, hearts in spasm — they were lime dust, and they had no staring eyes. They were simplified, and in some out-of-the-way cemetery far from Old Granary Ground, far from the bones of Hancock, of Poor Richard's parents, of the Massacre dead, far from Thayer, Katzmann, Fuller, far from clubs, the Common, all the Cabots, and Sergei at the Hall, there where John Eliot had preached to savages, they were spilled into holes in the earth, whence, when filled, blue wisps were seen by some to rise and drift away.

Though they may not have known it, those who were there, they were watching what no fire could consume, no *nerroved mind little tyrent* burn: words. *If I was a poet,* one of the two wops had said, *I could discribe the red rays of the loving sun,* and the other, the seller of eels, had said, *I could sing to you in terza rima!* We burned 'em, all right, but not those words.

For you, though, even at this late day, it was *Burned who?*

THE COLOR OF THE AIR, XV

THE HAYMARKET – 1886
A JUROR: *I'D HANG ALL THE DAMN BUGGERS*

Not the ones who sold the Army defective guns
And worm-eaten hulls that wouldn't hold a nail,
Nor those who made paper shoes and blue shoddy
That faded to gray and fell apart in the rain,
Nor the peddlers of tainted beef, death in cans,
Nor the ghouls who cashed in on gullible grief,
Shipping mule-bones north as the Union's slain,
Nor the dry witches walking on watered stock,
Nor their one-star shills, the brazen brigadiers,
Nor the trained animals in their act on the Bench,
Nor the pastors and the pastor-masters, the rich.
I'd hang all the damn buggers, the juror said,
And he meant the eight framed in the Haymarket.

The ritual of the law consumed a Chicago summer
Habitually reserved for croquet at Lake Forest,
A bit of garter at one of the better beaches,
And muskellunge on light tackle off Charlevoix,
But Judge Gary (Joseph) made the best of it.
He entertained ladies of fashion behind the Bar,
Executing sleights of hand for their amusement,
Feeding them bonbons, and telling droll fictions
To beguile their minds from the luminous passion
Of eight dirty radicals on trial for their lives.
In general, the fillies and mares were charmed,
And the prosecutor's wife whiled away the time
Covering sheets of paper with knots and nooses.

I'd hang all the damn buggers, the juror said,
But he was given only five — only four, really,
Because Louis Lingg smoked a stick of dynamite
That a policeman concealed in a nickel cigar,
And you couldn't snap a spine that you couldn't find.

SCENE 171

S.S. *CARONIA* (1927)

> built: Glasgow, 1905
> length: 650.0 ft.
> breadth: 72.2 ft.
> depth: 40.2 ft.
> gross tonnage: 19,687
> speed: 19 knots
> propulsion: twin screws
> h.p.: 21,000
> material: steel

One day late in August of that year, you left your father's office and walked down Broadway among the noontime crowds. You moved southward on a flow of straw hats, dingy from a summer's wear and soon to be scaled from a window, a ferry deck, the platform of a train. At Battery Park, you rounded the Custom House corner into State Street and stopped before a plate-glass front on which, in letters of black rimmed with gold, a pair of words appeared: CUNARD LINE. A boulder in a stream of passersby, you stood there for a moment, and then you went inside.

Within, again you paused, this time to take in the oak counters, the folder racks, the ship model in a showcase, and the tilted pictures on the walls. All about you were photographs and paintings of Cunarders early and late, from the *Britannia* (14d. 8hrs. Liverpool to Boston) to the *Mauretania* (4d. 10hrs. Queenstown to Ambrose Light). You thought of the little steamers you knew so well, the *Sandy Hook,* the *Monmouth,* and you remembered the way they'd roll when they reached the swells in the lower bay: they were your liners then, and you were on the main!

Approaching a wicket, you said to a clerk, "I'd like to pick up a reservation."
"Very good, sir," he said. "What ship?"
"The *Caronia.*"
"And your name, sir?"
"Shapiro. Julian Shapiro."
He turned some pages in a great ledger lying before him, and then coursing with his finger, he found your entry. "Shapiro," he said. "Julian L. Cabin B-104."
"I made a deposit of $20," you said. "I owe you $130."
"Correct, sir."

285

You produced a fold of bills, and counting off to thirteen, you passed the money under the grille. The clerk counted it again and placed it in a till. "Your ticket will be ready in a moment, sir," he said.

And soon, even as promised, the ticket was in your pocket, and you were passing through the revolving door. Outside, you stood gazing across the park at the Aquarium — Castle Garden once, you thought; and where Jenny Lind had sung, fish-tanks ringed a pool where seals and sea-lions barked. Pedestrians sheered to avoid you, a stone again in a stream, and all the while you wondered how you'd come to be there. What had brought you to that point or place? you thought, though you knew what would take you away. Through your jacket, you could feel the sailing and landing brochure and your ticket to B-104.

You crossed the streetcar-tracks to a path that wound away over the grass. In the shade of trees and shrubbery, you found a great *déjeuner sur l'herbe,* and traversing a litter of people and food, you made your way to the walk that rimmed the Hudson, and there you leaned against a railing and watched the river swirl and pass.

It was bottle-green and clouded here with the silt and outfall of three hundred miles of running from a lake so small that the Indians had called it Tear. You looked down-bay past Bedloe's Island, asking yourself how you could've lived all your life so near the Statue and never gone to see what she saw with her copper-lidded eyes. Soon now, you'd be going far, you'd be crossing vaster waters than those of the bay, but you knew, as you peered at the haze that hid the Narrows, that you could not have said what you'd be seeking — what did you hope to find there? what did you wish to leave behind. . . ?

§

A few weeks earlier, after a two-piano recital at Steinway Hall, you and three or four others had gone to Child's for the usual hour or so of discussion, or, more properly, for a lecture session led by everyone's docent, George. *He teaches,* L. G. had said, but at his feet, as beneath a tree, what fell to you was the offcast and the outgrown, the leaves and layers of other years, the straw of greater knowledge, brought on the wind and caught on the fly.

There at those glass-topped tables, what was passed through the coffee-steam and the smoke of the weed? Was it not there that Truth was pondered, Reality, the meaning of Meaning? there that mournful mention was made of Wilfred Owen (*Death never gives his squad a Stand-at-ease*)? there, through those vapors, that you heard of the Doppler effect, the FitzGerald contraction, the First Cause, the Third Coming? and what of *il miglior fabbro* — was Tom doffing his hat or knocking the hat off Ezra. . . ?

Midway into some illumination (of Willard Gibbs? of Charles Peirce? of the dice of drowned men's bones?), George suddenly glanced at a clock on the wall and said, "Christ, I'll be late! I promised to call for my sister!"

For no reason that you could've given then or later, you said, "I'll go."

Relieved, George sat back, saying, "She's at the Ziegfeld, over on 54th." As you headed for the door, he made an addition. "The stage entrance is on Sixth."

By the time you reached the theatre, the performance was over and the foyer dark, but the alley adjoining was dimly lit, and you waited there against a wall. Why, you wondered, had you offered to call for someone you hardly knew, and you wondered too whether you'd find her as pretty as you'd found her before. Would she be tall, as you seemed to remember, would she fill the eye still, and when she spoke, would she speak as she sang, in the mezzo range? You tried to think of her name—Olia, was it, or was Olia an affectionate for one you'd never heard?—and when she came through the alley, what would you say to her and she to you?

"You're Julian, aren't you?" she said.

"And you're—Olia, is it?"

"To those who know me well. To others, Olga."

As you walked her along Sixth, you said, "George told me you were a singer, but I thought he meant the concert kind."

"He did," she said. "I sing in shows for a living."

"He was supposed to pick you up, he said, but he's over at Child's, holding forth for spellbound multitudes."

"How did you get away?"

"I volunteered," you said.

"You did? Why?"

"I don't know."

Reaching 57th Street, neither of you paused for a turn toward Child's. Instead, you made for Central Park, a dark mass that ended the Avenue two blocks ahead.

"George tells me you and he were in kindergarten together."

"In 1909," you said. "We had Miss Nolen. I've known George longer than anyone outside of my family."

"Why didn't you become friends sooner?"

"I remember liking him as a kid," you said. "But things happen, and you lose track of people."

"What kind of things?"

Following the park wall and an arc of the Circle, you went northward past the Sheepfold and The Green. It was near midnight now, and few people were in sight under the trees that lined the walk. For some reason (what reason?), you'd taken her by the arm, and as you walked, sometimes out of step, your hand met a round of her body—her hip, her breast—but instead of drawing away, she pressed the hand against her, and you left it where it was.

"What things?" she said.

"Someone told me about an English poet named Wilfred Owen. He was killed in the last few days of the War. He didn't write much, but one of his lines was *Death never gives his squad a Stand-at-ease.*"

"George has a book of Owen's," she said. "It must've been George who told you."

"Maybe it was," you said. "That book was all that Owen wrote—sixty pages, and he was dead. Things happen."

"What stops you from saying what they were?"

"My mother died when I was ten. And for the next ten years, I stayed where I was. It was as if I'd been driven into the ground. Looking back, I see something stock-still. George moved on; I didn't."

"And now that you've met again?" she said.

"Met," you said. "We haven't really met. He has a ten-year lead."

§

"In a few more weeks," you said, "I'll be leaving for England."

She was silent for a step or two, and then she said, "George didn't mention it."

"George doesn't know."

"What will you do in England?"

"Several months ago," you said, "I applied for admission to Oxford."

"To study what?"

"International Law."

Her eyes were on the pavement ahead. The street-lamps seemed to be suspended from the trees, and they threw light and shade on the walk below. "International Law," she said. "That's impressive."

"I think it is," you said. "The law of nations instead of the law of landlord and tenant."

"Aren't they the same thing on a different scale?"

"How can they be?" you said. "One has to do with the customs and usages of civilized states. The other with a couple of sharpies trying to cheat each other."

"Nations can be sharpies too," she said. "At which college will you learn about their customs and usages?"

"You don't think much of the idea, do you?"

"Well, I'm not very high-flown, and that's what the idea is."

"Why high-flown?"

"It makes people seem small."

"They *are* small."

"Where did you get your low opinion of them?" she said. "Not from George, I'm sure."

"The latter-day Mishkin!" you said. "He's man's best friend!"

"From whom, then?"

"If I have any opinions about people, high or low, I get them from people."

"Have they treated you badly?"

"The fact is, I've been treated well."

"I think you ought to learn about man before you go off to learn about nations."

"They may not let me," you said.

"They?"

"I told you I'd applied for admission. I didn't say I'd been accepted."

She studied you before saying "You're just taking a trip, Julian."

§

You watched a ferry leave a nearby slip, churning up a jade emulsion as it moved off toward Staten Island. It went without visible effort, like a water-fowl, and it soon merged with the haze on the bay's skyline. In an hour's time, it would be seen again, free of the harbor's crepe de Chine and returning to its place of beginning. Were you about to do the same? you wondered. Were you a mere voyager, seeing only what you saw in a finder (*You're just taking a trip, Julian*), a writer of postcards on lonely evenings, a taker of notes on rum and alien ways? Was your purpose high or simply *high-flown*?

You'd been in correspondence with the Overseas Adviser at Oxford for several months, and nothing he'd written had been encouraging — indeed, all had been the reverse. In your behalf, he'd shown your credentials to Balliol, Christ Church, Oriel, Brasenose, and Magdalen, and all had declared themselves full. At other colleges, Lincoln, Jesus, Exeter, and New, your Fordham degree had been deemed insufficient to entitle you to Senior standing. And the finisher had been delivered by the Non-Collegiate Delegacy: *Dear Sir, With reference to your letter, the regulation concerning Latin is laid down by the University and is not (as you appear to suppose) a private rule of Colleges. I cannot therefore admit you. Faithfully yours, J. Bernard Baker.* Alas, you had no Latin.

A self-important tug chugged past, an ugly duckling that thought itself a swan.

I cannot therefore admit you, you thought, and still you were going, though you knew there was no knowing why.

§

"Tell me about yourself," you said (that night? the following night? the next after that?). "Tell me about your singing. I hear you have a voice."

"I sing Lieder," she said. "In English, they're called Art Songs."

"I don't know what they are."

"Poetry set to music — music written especially to express its meaning. The better the poetry, the better the songs. Assuming the composer to be a Schubert, a Brahms."

"What happens if he's not?"

"You get trash. The essence of the form is the nobility of its elements."

You said, "Wouldn't you say that's high-flown too?"

It was late now, and in buildings across the way, a few lighted windows were scattered among the black spaces, rather like pieces left on a game-board. It had been a mean-spirited question, you thought.

In low tones, almost to herself, she sang *Wenn ich in dein Augen seh'/ So schwindet all mein Leid und Weh/ Doch wenn ich küsse deinen Mund/ So werd' ich ganz und gar gesund/ So muss ich weinen bitterlich.*

Not knowing what to say, you said, "One of the Lieder?"

"It's called Dichterliebe," she said. "A Poet's Love."

"I caught only a few of the words. I'm not up in German."

" 'When I look into your eyes/ Gone are pain and sorrow/ And when I kiss your mouth/ Life becomes worth the living/ Still, I weep bitterly.' "

You paused to light a cigarette, and a pace or two beyond, she stopped too. Shaking out the match, you spoke in smoke and said, "Is that what you meant by noble?"

"Don't judge Schumann by my translation."

"By any translation, how can that be poetry, and this too? — 'Age cannot wither her, nor custom stale/ Her infinite variety.' "

She came back a pace or two, saying, *Wenn ich in dein Augen seh',* and then she kissed you, and through the taste of smoke, you thought you tasted milk.

"I'm sorry you didn't care for the song," she said.

"I once walked out on Claudia Muzio."

She indicated a lighted entry in one of the houses across the street, and you made for it over the car-tracks and the torn-up roadway. She looked down at you from a two-step stoop, saying, "I stole your thunder, didn't I?"

"How so?" you said.

"By kissing you."

"I've been wondering about that."

"I did it because I wanted to."

"Why?"

"I like you."

"We've only met twice, three times."

"How long does it take?"

"I've got a girl."

"I know that," she said. "George told me." Opening the door, she glanced back to say, "Did you really walk out on Muzio?"

"I was thirteen years old."

"You're still thirteen," she said, and then she went inside.

§

You walked away from the river and through the always strange streets at the lower end of the island—Whitehall, Water, Front, and Pearl. Here were the city's beginnings, you thought, the Blockhouse, the Bowling Green, the cedar palisade, all now buried under stories of stone. Only these paved ways showed where they had been, but the city had moved on, and few recalled other days while they trod on history, few cared that Manhattan was Lenni-Lenape for *those that dwell upon an island.*

§

The evening was a warm one, and on the open deck of a bus, you'd ridden down to the Square, and then, staying aboard, you'd ridden it back uptown. It was on the Drive now, and across the river you could see the electric jewelry of Jersey, the earrings, the lavalières of light, and you watched a band of brilliants spell out words and tell the time: *It is now 12:04.*

There were few other passengers, none near enough to hear you say, "Your mouth tasted of milk."

"I drink it," she said. "I don't like it, but I have to."

"Why?"

"My surgeon says so."

"Surgeon?" you said.

"After an operation a couple of years ago, I developed adhesions."

"What're adhesions?"

"Sometimes tissues grow together when they ought to stay separate—in the lungs, in the intestines, other places too."

"And when that happens. . . ?"

"They take a piece of you out," she said. "It's happened to me four times."

The bus had passed the Claremont and Grant's Tomb before either of you spoke again. You were on the Viaduct above Manhattanville when you said, "Why the milk?"

"You're not thinking of milk," she said. "You're thinking of four operations, and you're wondering where." She took your hand and placed it on her belly, and through the sheer material of her dress, you could feel a crosshatch of welted scars. "They aren't pretty," she said, looking away at the spangled river. "Hardly the subject for lyric poetry."

"You haven't told me about the milk," you said. "What's milk supposed to do?"

She laughed, saying, "Prevent adhesions," and then, putting her hand over yours, she kept it where it was. "Why did you tell me about your girl?"

"It was only fair, I thought."

"Are you going to tell her about me?"

"There's nothing to tell."

"But there is," she said.

§

You drifted past named and numbered docks (7 Erie RR, 13 N Y — Cuba SS, 20 Standard Fruit), past warehouses with iron awnings, past markets and ferry-slips, all the while moving through the acrid savor of roasting coffee. Where did it come from, you wondered as you went, from which of these one-time tenements, these red-brick lofts?

"But there is," she'd said.

§

"You give me the advantage," you said.

"Use it," she said, "when you tell your girl."

The bus had turned away from the river and into Broadway, and it was running north again, now between the two dark divisions of Trinity Cemetery. "She was a gift," you said. "Did you know that people can be given away?"

"How do you mean — given away?"

"Someone brought her around to my place one night to show her off. Next day, he made me a present of her. Here, he as much as said, take her off my hands."

"And you took her?"

"She was pretty, she was a tall blonde Christian, with small breasts and narrow size-6 shoes."

"How could a man do a thing like that?"

"I've never been able to ask him."

"I mean you," she said. "How could you accept?"

At 168th Street, the bus completed its final run of the night, and walking back along Broadway, you passed the area where the Tabernacle once had stood. It was boarded off now, and behind the fence a great rise of half-finished buildings stood against the sky. "When I'm with her," you said, "sometimes I feel like an intruder."

"What about her? How does she feel?"

"Again, I've never asked."

"My God!" she said. "You lead an odd life."

You gestured at the arched portal of Trinity Church, saying, "The day my mother died, my uncle sat me down there to tell me about it. I was ten at the time. I've been odd ever since."

§

Coenties Slip, Maiden Lane, Burling Slip, Peck Slip, and, high overhead, the huge stringed instrument of the Bridge. Before you, the lower East Side spread away, the same brownstone scarps that your father had known fifty years before, the same laden fire-escapes, the same elevated lines, the same signs painted on sweat-shop walls. Had he ever returned, you wondered, had he roamed his past some empty afternoon, sought certain windows, doorways, corners, searched among the living for the faces of the dead. You thought of the *Caronia* and what he'd say (*Julian, Julian!*) when told you were going away.

§

One night, after you'd called for her at the theatre, it began to rain while you were walking, and she asked to be taken home. Finding the flat dark, you supposed that George and her mother were asleep.

But she said, "He took her to Jersey to visit a cousin. They'll be gone for a couple of days."

Leaving the lights off, you turned a pair of chairs to face the windows and sat there staring at the glisten below, the patent-leather roadways, the light-struck car-tracks, the refracting rain.

"Have you told your girl about Oxford?" she said.

"Not yet."

"Don't you think she ought to know?"

"She lives in Boston," you said.

"Is that your excuse?"

"I could write, I guess. I could telephone."

"What would you say? How would you put it?"

"Are there several ways?" you said.

"You call her your girl," she said. "What does she call you?"

"Dearest Jule."

"I don't think you know how you feel about each other. Otherwise you'd be in Boston, or she'd be in New York."

"How can you know about our feelings?"

"I know about mine," she said.

You looked down at gleams on the pavement, at glinting leaves, and you said, "Why do you keep so little back?"

"Am I lowering myself?" she said, and then she left the room.

Had she truly diminished herself? you wondered, and watching rain writhe on a windowpane, you tried to reply in your mind, but all you could do was ask another question: what was she to you?

She was not as slight as your Boston girl. Where you could see her, she was fuller, and where you could not, you sensed what you'd find, you perceived the taper of her thighs, the shape and size of her breasts. She was less immediately pretty, you thought, but she had more command, more presence, and when you scanned her, she disclosed no little beauty. She had brown eyes to go with bronze-brown hair, and you were aware of liking to watch her mouth—was it for the coves at the corners, or were you remembering milk?

The rain, you thought, the empty rooms, the piano stacked with piano-literature, and you thought of far Boston and further Oxford, of the *Caronia*, of Platon glaring down at you in the dark, and at what lay still beyond a still portière.

§

These walk-ups and workshops framed by the Bridge were a part of the city ever ready for the new poor of the Old World: fleeing want there, they'd find it here in these firetrap factories and cold-water flats. You tried to think into sight your father as a boy, to put him among the crowds and the carts, to watch him for signs of you, but raising nothing, you felt a need to see him now. Turning from the river-front, you made your way through Frankfort Street to Park Row. Once there, you were soon beyond the abutment of the Bridge and the Surrogate's Court, soon in your father's chambers four stories up from the street. Caught in an idle hour, he was enjoying a Havana cigar.

"Hello, kid," he said. "Where have you been?"

"Wandering arond," you said. "From the Battery to the Bridge."

"Something on your mind?"

"Nothing in particular."

He studied you through smoke, saying, "By which you mean yes."

"I don't seem to hide much."

"You're like your mother, *selig*. When anything upset her, it showed on her face."

"I never asked you this, but before you met her, did you have many girls?"

"Why do you ask?"

"I told you once that I had a girl," you said. "Now I have two."

"What do you mean by *have*?"

"They both like me."

"And do you like them?"

"Yes."

"Equally?"

"I don't know," you said. "I like them in different ways."

His cigar had gone out, and after looking at it particularly, he dropped it into an ash-receiver, saying, "Are you asking for advice?"

"I'm a fool, but I know better than that."

"Why do you say fool, kid? You're no fool."

"With two girls?" you said.

Again he studied you, and this time he said, "But you're not here to talk about girls, are you?"

"A good question," you said, and reaching for his hand, you kissed it.

"You're a Nevins, kid," he said.

"Only half."

§

Of far Boston, you thought, and further England, of piano scores and Czerny *études,* of the room beyond a still portière. You'd glimpsed it once (when?), and you recalled sparse furnishings and walls almost bare. You could hear tire-treads tear at the pavement below, a fire-engine, a street-car bell, but in the room next door, there was only quiet. Was she awake? you wondered, or had she turned her back on *Dearest Jule* and given you up for sleep? What would you do if she called? Would you let yourself be summoned, stand beside her bed, sit when taken by the sleeve? And then what would you say in the rain-bound darkness of that room?

Would you speak of the grained glare of auto-lamps, the laundered smell of the air? Would you find those scars again, this time not through silk but bare, would you remind your mouth of the taste of milk?

"Julian. . . ," she said from the other room.

§

"Did you?" you said. "Did you have many girls?"

"Aren't you taking a liberty?" your father said.

"If you think so."

He glanced away through a window, but you knew he was looking at nothing outside. "Never two at a time," he said.

"They're both good girls. I could bring them home."

"I know that. What son would tell his father he liked a pair of bums?"

"This son is loony enough for worse."

"You've been leading up to that ever since you got here."

§

"Julian," she said.

For a moment, you stayed where you were, and your mind had time to run the scene to come. You'd sit alongside her on the bed, and she'd say, "Is it still raining?"

And you'd say so clearly that you could hear your voice, "It looks good for the rest of the night."

And she'd say, "You don't have to go."

"What would George do if he knew we'd been here alone?"

"We're alone in other places—walking in the park, standing in a hallway, sitting on the roof. . . . But it isn't being alone, is it? It's being alone *here*."

"This is his home. I'd hate to have him think. . . ."

"Think what?"

Your answer would sound as actual as the question. "That his sister and I . . . ," you'd say.

"That your hand was on his sister's breast—is that what you'd hate for him to think? He has girls, you know. What do you suppose he does with them?"

You'd think of words you'd always tried to censor and always been able to read: *How to know and check the spread of*: and reading them now, you'd know you were concerned with *you* and not with brother George. Your fix would be on the pamphlet sent by your Uncle Dave, on the warnings in print and the pictures now posted in your mind. But where once you'd stared at nameless others, now all of them would be you, as in a glass: that would be you with the eaten nose and the sloughing lip, you the blind gonorrheic, you with those cankered balls.

Still where you were when she'd called you, still there before the window staring at the rain, you'd wonder what it would take to put down fear. A medical certificate, test returns, exhibits, a minute-by-minute report on her life? Would affidavits satisfy, would witnesses as to character and repute, would the subject's sworn and solemn word? Or, no matter what, would those photos with your faces feaze you, would you be safe only if you stayed in this chair. . . ?

"Julian . . . ," she said again.

She was beautiful, you thought, and you went to join her in the other room.

§

You took the Cunard Line ticket from your pocket and placed it on the desk, and then, as your father watched, you moved it slowly toward him across a sward of blotter. You felt that even without touching the envelope, he was prepared for what it contained. What had informed him, you wondered, what was there about you that always gave you away? Was it that, having found you incapable of ordered thought, he'd taught himself to deal with impulse, with *disorder*? There came to mind one of the few lines you knew of legal poetry — *For water is a movable and wandering thing* — and with it came this, that it must've been known to a father whose son was water too.

"I'm going to England," you said. "I sail in two weeks."

For some reason, your gaze was on his hands. They were small but strong, and even then, nearing fifty, he could numb you with their clasp. The wrestler was still there, as you'd now and again find when you so far forgot yourself as to try your grip on him.

"What do you propose to do there?" he said.

"Go to Oxford," you said. "If I can get in."

"Are you saying that you haven't been accepted?"

"I've been trying by mail. I might do better in person."

"Why have they refused you?"

"They don't recognize my Fordham degree," you said. "Also, I have no credits in Latin."

"And you think they'll waive their requirements because of your winning ways?" he said. "Or are you relying on the cut of your clothes?"

"I don't suppose I'll have much chance over there," you said. "But if I stay here, I'll have none."

"What do you mean to study at Oxford?"

"International Law," you said, hating to say it.

"International Law," he said, but he gave the words no emphasis, as if merely hefting them in his mind. "International Law."

"You make me sound ridiculous."

"International Law," he said, "and you don't even know the law of your own jurisdiction. If that isn't ridiculous, what is it?"

"A high aim," you said. "Is it ridiculous to aim high?"

"Always aim high," he said. "But if you're serious about becoming an international lawyer, why not start here? You can find courses in any law school in America. Why go three thousand miles for them?"

"I haven't asked you for money," you said. "This is being paid for by Grandpa Nevins."

"You talk about money; I talk about time. You'll be wasting your time, Julian, and you've wasted enough already."

"All living is wasting time."

"*Der Philosoph,*" he said. "Time is all you've got, kid, and when it runs out, there's no more to be had. Your tendency is to throw it away. There's no constancy in you. You finish almost nothing—you light for a while, and you're soon gone. Now you have this high aim, as you call it, but I'm afraid it's only another flight to somewhere else. What in the world is the matter with you, Julian?"

"I don't know," you said. "I must take after my Uncle Dave."

"He was always trying to get away from his father. Is that what you've been doing?"

It was one of his good questions, and it surprised you into saying, "I never asked myself that, but it can't be true. You're the best man in this world. I've always thought so, and I always will."

"I'm happy to hear that," he said. "But how come I have so little influence on you? I can't even persuade you to live under my roof."

You touched the Cunard envelope. "At a word from you, I'd turn this in."

"I won't always be here to give you the word. You'd better learn it for yourself. You're willful, Julian. You were that way as a child, and you're that way yet."

You glanced away through the window at windows across the street, at a silent screen of people in motion, typing, walking, moving their arms and mouths, at nothing relevant, really, and what you said may have been taken by your father as irrelevant too. "I guess I was always going off to England."

§

Seated beside her on the bed, you looked down through the dark, saying, "I wish I could tell you what I think when you come toward me on the street, when you enter or leave a room. I wish I could describe colors and curves and the way you sway, but there are no parts of speech for such parts of you. . . ."

"Don't describe them," she said. "Enjoy them."

You heard her even after she'd spoken, and you thought of times to come when you'd hear her again, and she'd not be there. "I can't," you said.

"Because of the one in Boston?"

How to know and check, you thought, but you said, "Because of me."

§

A few days before your departure, you'd asked L. G. to pay you a farewell visit: you had to see her, you'd said, and she'd agreed to come to New York. Now, on one of the train platforms in Grand Central Station, you were watching for her in a current of passengers and baggage-trucks, and when you saw her, she was still a car-length away. At that moment, all motion seemed to slacken speed, and in a slow and listless dream, you wondered back through the year just gone. You thought of the broker who'd brought you together, of twosome days and nights with him as go-between — your ineluctable arranger of others' lives — and you looked for him here, intervening still.

To what hotel did you go, and what did you do when there? Did you watch her unpack, take this and that and shake them out, hang them up to air? And what then? Did you sit and talk, speak the small change of strangers, or, having found your way to the bed, what happened there among the three of you in the fading afternoon?

That evening, several of your friends gave you a leave-taking party at a White Russian café called the Kav Kaz, and there the two girls met for the first and only time. L. G. had never had much to say when others were present, especially these, and on this occasion she was so withdrawn in manner that they left you to yourselves at one end of a long table, almost as though they were at a different revel.

You'd been talking for a while (of what? of whom?) when, having glanced away, you saw George's sister at the far side of the room, where a musician in a Cossack costume was playing the vamp of a song, and when he nodded, she began to sing. You understood nothing of the language she sent through the smoke, and yet in any language the words would've spoken in lament for other times, other conditions — for youth, it might've been, or for love lost or strayed. Under the low ceiling, her voice, augmented by its own resonance, seemed to be accompanied by itself, and it came to you with a dimension of depth that almost made it visible.

"Is she in love with you?" L. G. said, and when you turned to her, she was pressing four parallel lines into the tablecloth with the tines of a fork.
"What makes you ask?" you said.
"She's singing to you."
"Is she? I don't know Russian."
"I don't, either," she said, "but we both understand it."
"I've been seeing something of her. She's a good-looking girl, don't you think?"
She drew four more lines with the fork. "She's a beauty," she said. "It would be hard to blame you."
"Are you in love with me?"
"At times."
"What times?" you said, and you stopped her work with the fork. "What times?"

When she looked at you without speaking, you knew the times she meant —
the ones when he wasn't there.

§

The *Caronia* was due to sail at midnight, but you were hours early at the
pier, and after seeing your luggage aboard, you walked the main deck until
your father found you near the stern, staring at the dark mass of Castle Point.

"I didn't think you'd be here," you said.

"I oughtn't to be, I suppose," he said. "I don't approve of what you're
doing, and it might've been wiser to stay away." He lit a cigar, and you breathed
a fragrance you'd known all your life. "But you're my son, and I couldn't
do that."

"I hope you won't always have to apologize for me."

"Apologize?" he said. "To whom?"

"Your friends. Your advisers."

"I'm not exactly proud of all you've done, but I apologize for you to no
one." He shrugged off the arm you tried to put around him, saying, "That
doesn't mean I endorse the ill-considered things you've done. You're headstrong,
Julian, and you never listen." He shrugged again, this time in resignation.
"But you're what I've got, and what can I do? So go, kid — and good luck."

At the gangplank, you kissed each other goodbye, and then you watched
him move away until he was lost to sight in the crowd.

L. G. had returned to Boston the day before, but awaiting you in your
cabin were all your friends of the Kav Kaz party, among them Olia.

She drew you away to a sheltered place on deck, and there, with her face
against yours, she said, "I don't want you to go, Julian."

"Why didn't you say so before?"

"I did. I said it more than once."

A sign affixed to a davit read: Boat 6 — Capacity 24.

"Please don't go," she said. "There's still time to change your mind."

Boat 6, you thought, Capacity 24.

"It won't be the same when you come back. Something will be lost that
we'll never find. Please, Julian."

But all you could do was shake your head.

Soon after midnight, the *Caronia* was under way. A pair of tugs harassed
her from the pier and turned her bow downstream, and then, on her own
steam, she began to slide past the notched skyline of Manhattan and on toward
the upper bay. It was a known sight, even in the nighttime dimness. You
knew all the light-clusters along the shore, Red Hook, Bayonne, St. George,

you knew the black square of Ft. Wadsworth, and your mind could read the words on its stone: *Cable Crossing—Do Not Anchor.* You'd been there before.

But below the Narrows, the bearing was easterly, to Ambrose Channel and so to the sea. Jersey fell away, and then Long Island, burning to the water's edge, went out, and the ship began to roll. Fifty years earlier, you thought, your father had passed above these sands and between these shoals, and here where he'd come, you were now going away.

Printed August 1985 in Santa Barbara & Ann Arbor
for the Black Sparrow Press by Graham Mackintosh &
Edwards Brothers Inc. Design by Barbara Martin.
This edition is published in paper wrappers; there
are 300 cloth trade copies; 150 hardcover copies have
been numbered and signed by the author; & 26 copies
handbound in boards by Earle Gray have been lettered &
signed by the author.

JOHN SANFORD is the name of the principal character in *The Water Wheel,* a first novel by Julian Shapiro published in 1933. Adopting it as a pseudonym, the writer has used it ever since. Born in the Harlem section of New York on 31 May 1904, he attended the public schools of that city, Lafayette College, and finally Fordham University, where he earned a degree in Law. He was admitted to the Bar in 1929, and at about the same time, influenced by his friend Nathanael West, he too began to write. Published at the outset in vanguard magazines of the period — *The New Review, Tambour, Pagany, Contact* — he soon abandoned the legal profession and produced through the years a series of eight novels. Concerned always with the course of American history, he interspersed his fiction with critical commentaries on the national life from the Left-Liberal point-of-view. As a result of such dissent, he was summoned before the House Committee on Un-American Activities, and for refusing to cooperate with it, he was blacklisted. In spite of difficulty in obtaining publication, he continued to write in his chosen vein, ultimately stripping his work down to its historical content only. During the several years last past, he has written four books of creative interpretations of the Land of the Free: *A More Goodly Country, View from This Wilderness, To Feed Their Hopes,* and *The Winters of That Country.* All four titles derive from a single passage in William Bradford's *History of Plymouth Plantation.* John Sanford has been married to the writer Marguerite Roberts since 1938; they are long-time residents of Santa Barbara, California.